# DIVORCING THE DOW

## Using Revolutionary Market Indicators to Profit from the Stealth Boom Ahead

**JIM TROUP and SHARON MICHALSKY**

WILEY

JOHN WILEY & SONS, INC.

# To Sandy Lapham and Moses Dillard

# CONTENTS

# CONTENTS

# ACKNOWLEDGMENTS

When a book project takes as long as it does for an eighth grader to finish high school and most of college, its authors find themselves needing as much support and encouragement as any determined but anxious young adult. Merely thanking those who provided it falls far short of what we owe them, but we hope they recognize the deeply felt sincerity with which it is offered.

We are grateful to the sisters, brothers, nieces, and nephews of our large family who we never had time to see very much but who we always knew would be there if we needed them. We especially thank our children and grandchildren, Debbie and Glen and Josh and Brittany, who offered their insights and tolerated skipping family festivities and holidays so that we could complete this effort.

This project would never have blossomed without the vision of Jane Wesman and Lori Ames, who believed in its ideas and helped us to convey them in ways people could understand. Without their help we would not have met our friend and agent, the sage and insightful Helen Rees. Without Helen we would not have known our editor, Jeanne Glasser, who understood the magnitude of the financial sea change around us and took charge of making this book a success. We remain deeply indebted to these four people.

Special appreciation goes out to the chief executive officers of the vibrant companies discussed in this book: Les Muma, David Halbert, Richard Haddrill, Jim Sinegal, Ed Labry, Jim Madden, and Jack London. They generously lent their time and expertise in helping us understand the new business culture. We hope that this book reflects some of the extraordinary vision and know-how that characterize each one of these leaders.

For doing the tough job of getting it all down on paper—first one way and then over and over again—we thank Barbara Mosley. She was always there when we needed her, day or night, weekend or holiday.

The endless task of organizing, reorganizing, and assembling data and information could not have been accomplished without our loyal associate Barbara Kaiser and the help of Michelle Todora. Their hard work and positive attitude sustained us throughout this project. Beth Morse's sharp eye and keen suggestions helped to ensure the accuracy of the material.

To our colleagues, Mike Marciniak and Bill James, we are indebted for their insights and expertise and for their belief in us.

Thanks go out to all of our friends who amiably tolerated broken engagements and our generally being out of touch. Your being there meant more than you can know.

Finally, this book would not exist if not for our clients. While we cannot acknowledge you by name, we are grateful for your forbearance in tough times and your balance during the great times. Your inquiries and perceptions have helped to form this book.

# INTRODUCTION

The future can be annoying.

In 1997, when we actually started putting words on paper that would become this book, there was really no reason why anyone should ever want to read them. Investors had dodged a bullet.

In 1994 nearly every investment guru who was being quoted in the media said that the U.S. stock market was over. It was supposed to be going into at least a decade-long decline. Gold, international stocks, and treasury bills were supposed to have been the only places any sane person would put his or her money. What actually transpired made those dire prognostications look cartoonishly foolish.

A new era of prosperity for the American economy began in 1995, and every sector of the stock market posted stellar returns. By 1997 there was universal confidence in U.S. equities, and the advance was in full swing. But although this turn of events delighted us as investors, it troubled us deeply as investment consultants. For the investment community to have been so wrong about the direction of the financial markets in 1994 meant that the traditional methods used to assess them must be fundamentally flawed. Our concern was that if this flaw were not uncovered, we would not be prepared for other significant inevitabilities affecting our clients and our own personal wealth. So we started the research project that grew into this book. We were astounded by what we found.

We knew from the beginning that we would have to do more than revisit the customary lines of reasoning if we were to spot weaknesses in the existing order. It would be necessary to amass copious amounts of cultural, economic, and social information, as well as financial data, and then organize it in a kind of "mapping the investment genome" fashion. We picked the prosperous twelfth century as a starting point. This was when the great cathedrals of Canterbury (1175) and Chartres (1194) were built and the Universities of Paris, Oxford, and

Bologna were founded. How the thriving economy fueled European expansion is an exciting story unto itself.

We moved forward century by century and picked up a thread in the 1800s that appeared to be tied to the present. Cultural parallels materialized, and then economic ones. The action of the financial markets felt uncannily familiar. The more facts we pulled out, the more the conventional explanations for today's market behavior unraveled. When the facts reassembled themselves, they had carved out a pattern that leaves the investment culture ahead of us looking very different from the one we just left behind.

That is why the future can be so annoying. Investors had become absorbed in a process that had worked for a long time. There were reliable formulations, sacrosanct arrangements, and taboos that defined the investment system. Now everything is forced to mean something different.

But even though moving into a new investment culture is annoying, it is annoying like moving into a newly constructed home—a lot of trouble and a lot of new things to figure out, but well worth the effort. The new investment culture is more efficient, is user-friendly, and, yes, has more wealth-creating potential than anything that has come before it. With the help of our clients and a combined 40 years in the investment industry, we have attempted to explain its evolution in a way that everyone can understand.

Compacting all of the information we had accumulated into something readable was a fairly arduous and time-consuming process. As a result, the first chapters, set down in 2000 and 2001, have more age on them than do the last chapters. We decided to update them only slightly prior to submitting the final manuscript at the end of July 2002. We retained sentences such as the following from Chapter 2, written in August 2001, which discusses potential difficulties arising out of the weakening of the old investment culture: "This economic contraction will further stress an already deteriorating old dominant investment system, making it likely that we will see a major disruption of at least one or two companies—like what occurred with U.S. Steel a century earlier."

That was written prior to the bankruptcy of K-Mart, the Enron scandal, and the collapse of Worldcom; it is not meant to show that the authors have any powers of prediction, but rather to illustrate that in studying the process by which another investment culture deteriorated, we can be guided through our own transition process today.

This project was not about organizing the future. That is, of course, impossible and unnecessary. The important work is of a more significant nature. It is to create an understanding of, and an appreciation for, the new investment culture. The mission is to open everyone's eyes to what many have felt but few have seen and to create a language for what is often sensed but not defined. This is a very real and important thing that is happening. We hope we have done it some small justice.

*The attitude . . . beginning in the high places, among men and women of prestige and authority, trickles down, trickles down, with its formulations, to the masses. Now this, now that individual is deflected in their direction. Soon a group has formed definable by the attitude. Then the attitude generates habits. The habits . . . integrate into a common way of life which is now the custom of the group. A tradition grows up centering on the custom and accounting for it. Both become sacrosanct and are hedged about with reverence and taboos; opposition becomes criminal and variation blasphemous. It is the established order now. . . . Yet with alternatives pressing always on the verge.*

—Horace M. Kallen, *The Philosophy of William James*

# Part One

# HOW THE TIMES THAT WERE A-CHANGIN' . . . FINALLY CHANGED

# 1

# BREAKING UP IS HARD TO DO

## How the Stock Market Outgrew the Dow and Will Change Your Future

*Transformation is a marvelous thing. . . . I am thinking especially of butter-
flies. Though wonderful to watch . . . it is not a particularly pleasant process.*
—Vladimir Nabokov

At a New Year's Eve party in 1998, an attorney friend of ours asked if we would meet with a client of his who was on his way to Florida to spend the high social season. The man was the owner of eight private corporations. He was also a sophisticated investor who had practiced classic stock analysis for over 40 years. We were told he was nervous about the stock market. This intrigued us because unlike most people at the end of 1998, we were, too.

This was not a time when many people outside of the financial services industry had qualms about their investments. The Dow had averaged over 27% per year for the last four years. Money was pouring into stocks and mutual funds as everyone became an investor. The only fear most people had was that they would miss out by not getting in fast enough. So we were eager to hear why one nonprofessional, like our prospective new client, apparently saw things differently.

Two weeks later we were standing on the terrace of Mr. R.Q.'s winter residence watching the sun set over the Gulf of Mexico. What would have normally been a serene moment was disrupted by Mr. R.Q.'s hand shaking so badly that we could hear the ice cubes tinkling in his glass. "I've lost millions of dollars over the last few months because I bought blue-chip stocks," he said. "How can that have happened when the environment for investing has been so perfect? I'm 70 years old, and I've been doing this for over half my life. Now suddenly it's not the same anymore. I have no idea what to do." The market *had* changed, and saying things weren't the same anymore was an understatement.

As the market was considered to be soaring in 1998, 488 stocks of the Standard & Poor's (S&P) 500 averaged a return of less than 5%. Mr. R.Q. was stunned by his losses in Coca-Cola and Dupont as these companies, along with a third of the stocks of the Dow Jones Industrial Average, were losing half of their value. These were big losses for what was pitched as the hottest bull market ever. Dow stocks like Merck were falling apart while companies that few recognized, like Pharmaceutical Product Development Inc. (PPDI), were making the bull market happen. This contradiction was sending those inside the financial industry into a tailspin.

With the exception of a handful of investors like Mr. R.Q., most people outside the financial industry did not realize then—nor do they now—how seriously many stocks of the Dow and that ilk have failed them. The reason is that the machinery that markets investing to the masses was able to manipulate investors into ignoring the obvious signals of change. It was a triumph of mass marketing that the shakeout that was taking place, during what was perceived as a roaring bull market, has still not been acknowledged, much less addressed, by most people who have money in stocks or mutual funds.

The last half of the 1990s provided the most fertile environment for the growth of stocks in decades. Interest rates were low; productivity was higher than it had been for 24 years; the economy was booming; demographics were perfect because baby boomers were investing for retirement; and everyone was putting money into 401(k) plans. It was by selling the idea of averages that the attention of the general public could be steered away from the curious fact that so many Dow stocks, and so many blue-chip companies of the S&P 500, were falling in value when the conditions for stocks were so spectacular.

In 1998 the Dow averaged 18.16%. The S&P 500 averaged 28.58%. Regarding the term *average,* the peculiar way by which these numbers are reached—namely, by giving the largest companies, whose shares have gone up the most, a weighting that is many times out of proportion to the other companies in the indexes—produces a number that is not an average at all. The numbers can, and in 1998 and 1999 effectively did, disguise the deterioration of many stocks. By 1999, even the stocks of the 12 companies of the S&P 500 that had increased in value more than 5% the previous year began to falter. As 1999 ended, the list of S&P 500 stocks participating in the bull market dropped to only seven. Still, the S&P 500 index was promoted as averaging 21.04%. This attracted more and more money into mutual funds that duplicated the indexes. As they poured money in, most investors had no idea what companies their hard earned dollars were helping to shore up.

We learned that Mr. R.Q. had figured all of this out for himself. We learned that Mr. R.Q.'s biggest concern was not that he had already lost money, but that if the old reliable companies that made up the Dow Jones Industrial Average could do so poorly in the best environment for stocks in 30 years, what would they do when conditions were less than perfect?

His question was perceptive and his timing uncanny. What had occurred in 1998 was the death of an old investment culture and the birth of a new one. Beginning on that January evening in 1999 and lasting until he returned to New York two months later, we laid out for Mr. R.Q. the collapse of the infrastructure that had made the Dow Jones Industrial Average and the biggest companies in the United States the best place to invest for dependable growth for most of the twentieth century. We detailed for him how a new kind of stock market, with more growth potential than anything we had witnessed before, came into existence. We explained why this would require new investment techniques and how to use them. We illustrated for him in person what we document for you in this book.

• • •

Over the last two centuries a series of awakenings have rejuvenated productivity and introduced new business cultures. Each of these has raised the bar incrementally higher on the profits that can accrue to investors. Each new *business* culture necessarily brings with it a new *investment* culture. It is our good fortune that the new market that began in 1998 brought us the most investor-friendly investment culture that has ever existed. The steps required to use it hang together like an instrument that can be played to suit an infinite variety of individual tastes.

This is not the message being communicated to the general public. The old investment culture is committed to the old-fashioned idea that the market is a single, omnipotent entity represented by the Dow— and, if you insist, by the S&P 500. This restrictive view works in keeping investors' attention off of the more important concern of what they must do to achieve a personal average return goal that they have set for themselves, which would create a mass marketing nightmare. Instead, the message aimed at investors is that they must be concerned about what the Dow did today and where it will be tomorrow. This monotheistic view of finance sets investors up as powerless pawns. It has caused many people to give "the market" authority over their lives. They allow themselves to be lured into taking unnecessary risks and to be frightened away from reasonable opportunities.

The new market culture puts control into the hands of investors. You can find the zone where your financial life and your personal life meet to create your own market, the only one that is necessary for you to follow. Chapter 3 explains how this is done.

Like all things outdated, the fable that the Dow is the center of the financial universe served a purpose once. There is an interesting story behind our progression from that nostalgic time to the present, where the only market that counts is the one that revolves around you.

•   •   •

His boss came just this close to physically throwing him out of the office. He was a young yet talented analyst, but he was always coming up with crazy ideas that his stressed-out superiors had no time for. Business had been a lot easier a few years earlier when the market was booming. Things were pretty good now, but more confusing. Old business models were being replaced, and new kinds of jobs, products, and services were being created. Companies that had been stable and dependable sources of growth for decades were going bankrupt. This was being attributed variously to mismanagement and a slowing economy.

Those that were firmly rooted in the old investment culture believed, or at least fervently hoped, that the new sorts of businesses that were popping up all over would only be more flashes in the pan. Didn't the market disasters of '01 and '02 prove this? Only fools or speculators would invest in these new corporations. The year before was bad enough, but '01 and '02 proved that (1) things were not "different" this time, (2) fundamental principles did not change, and (3) it is best to stick to the basics.

There is no template with which to measure the dynamics of the new style corporation. How was an investor expected to put blind faith in the hope that a company's profits would materialize out of thin air somewhere down the line? It is fine to talk of new technology, efficiency, and productivity. But there is no good way to measure it, and everybody who had any sense knew it.

So on a busy day in a Wall Street office what was not needed was a young man talking about another new company being a good buy around $40 per share. On top of that he had the arrogance to have concluded that it would soon be worth $130. He demonstrated his calculations. He had figured it out. He quantified the new efficiencies and put a value on the company's future growth. He had to be nuts. He was out of there.

The thing was . . . the kid turned out to be exactly right. His calculations worked. We know this because the stock did what he said it would, as have many others. Check for yourself. Was it Concord EFS, AdvancePCS, CACI ? No, none of those.

The company that our rejected young analyst liked was an odd thing called Calculating, Tabulating, and Recording Company. Never heard of it? They wisely changed their name to IBM. The young analyst was Benjamin Graham. The big market drops of '00 and '01 were *19*00 and *19*01 and *19*02—*not* 2000, 2001, and 2002.[1]

We have made a connection for you. The markets at the beginning of the twenty-first century are similar to those at the beginning of the twentieth. An epic change had occurred that would fundamentally alter how companies would work and how investing would work for the next century. In each case the investment establishment ignored the evidence of the transformation and clung so desperately to the past that it got rope burns.

You would have thought that the investment establishment would have immediately embraced Benjamin Graham. He was on to something worth a fortune, and in a capitalistic system you would think that any view that positively impacts the bottom line—whether it be old, new, or from another planet—would immediately be accepted. This is not the case. That the investment world is hopelessly stodgy is the reason why, three years into the twenty-first century, investing is still done the way it was 100 years ago.

After spending two decades in the investment community we have concluded that the resistance to change is one of its most destructive characteristics. We will use IBM again as just one example. After being misunderstood and overlooked for years by most everyone but Benjamin Graham, it eventually became the stock that everyone had to own. By the end of the 1970s, IBM symbolized American technology. Investment dogma practically mandated ownership of the blue-chip stock in any and all mutual funds and stock portfolios.

During the mid 1980s, IBM's earnings fell into decline.[2] This fact was disregarded because it had become almost un-American not to own IBM stock. In 1983 the stock traded at $25. The buying continued even as the company was losing money. Incredibly, by 1987 investors were paying $44 per share for it. Clients would react indignantly if we suggested that $44 was a ridiculously high price for a company with declining earnings.[3] Finally, the stock began to fall, and still you could find very few analysts who would say anything negative about it. Once it became part of the canon of the financial system, logic went out the window. Conformity may be useful in some occupations but it is counterproductive in the investment business. IBM gradually fell from its

1987 high into a trough in which it remained for 10 years. Millions were lost as it went as low as $11 a share, not returning to its 1987 level until 1997 (see Figure 1.1).

What dynamic is at work that makes the investment establishment prefer to stay in a rut? An understanding of where the resistance felt by Benjamin Graham—and by his insightful successors of today—comes from will enable you to empathize with, and then confidently deflect, admonitions from those mired in the past.

The financial markets have some stiff competition for investment dollars. Real estate, art, antiques, jewelry, and collectibles can also deliver profits, and with a huge advantage: You can *see* them. Their ownership offers satisfactions beyond the commercial. Your painting can be admired even as it grows in value, but you cannot invite your friends over to see your new financial assets. There is no inherent emotional connection. Your money appears to have been deposited into thin air, and all you have to show for it is a piece of paper.

Capitalism is a wealth-creating machine, but its concepts are in-

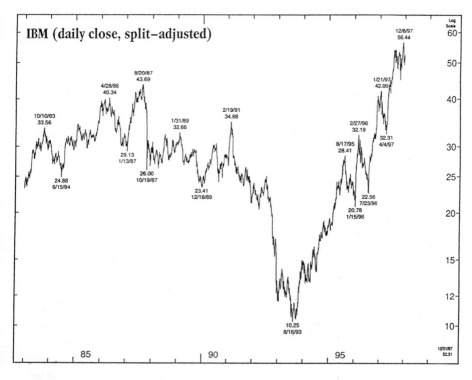

**Figure 1.1** IBM Stock Price, 1983–1997

tangible and to some can even appear vaguely fishy. Governments and political parties share the same problem. Unless their abstract concepts can be made real, they will not attract loyal supporters. The solution is to establish a strong belief system that makes sense to the people one wants to attract and then create symbols and principals that represent the belief system so that people can identify with it. This is exactly the process developed, quite unintentionally, by the financial community.

The general public has always had the wisdom to invest their most important dollars with the businesses that were doing the best job of growing the U.S. economy. With no need to be addled by economic numbers, they have always been able to smoke out the source of their improving lifestyles. Whether by noticing where new jobs were coming from or by which products were changing their lives, these perceptions led to a concentration of investment dollars into what we call the *dominant investment*. Out of the stew of innumerable choices the dominant investment rises to the top because it is the pipeline to the main sources of wealth creation and a way to participate directly in America's economic growth. This is why investors in the dominant investment have always had these experiences:

- They never lost money holding the dominant investment over the long term.
- The dominant investment generally outperformed all others.
- They were reassured to see that all methods of analysis were built around the dominant investment. Peripheral investments were held against that standard.
- They had plenty of company. The "smart money" and "old money" and the wisest investors had the bulk of their wealth in the securities of the dominant investment.

The path from perceptions to experiences finally led to a belief system that would sustain the dominant investment: Patient investors would never lose money, could expect superior performance, and were investing alongside the most seasoned investors when making their blue-chip purchases. Here were the principles that properly elevated the markets above the level of a crapshoot and legitimized investing.

With this arsenal of ideas a dominant investment becomes as audacious as a new nation. People are attracted by its logic and rewarded with results. All that is needed to complete the package is a flag to wave so it can be easily identified. One dominant investment was lucky to have the journalist Charles Dow to put this last piece in place.

Late in the nineteenth century, Dow was perceptive enough to see that new methods of taking natural resources and mass-producing enormous quantities of goods were revolutionizing how business was done. Eventually this would be called the *take it, make it, break it* business model. Dow created the Dow Jones Industrial Average in 1896 to be the barometer of the new types of companies that had taken over the driver's seat of the American economy. The tag, Dow Jones Industrial Average, identified the dominant investment of the twentieth century.

Once named, the dominant investment becomes an institution. A web of interests forms a symbiotic relationship with it. A bureaucracy is created—the web of the *dominant investment system* (see Figure 1.2).

The tricky thing about dominant investment systems is that they are like driving a container ship. It takes a while to overcome inertia to get the momentum going, and it takes an equally long time to stop it. It takes investors a while to warm up to a new dominant investment—and once they do, they don't want to let it go. The investment community takes this stodginess to an even higher level for fear of offending the multitude of interests, outside of the markets themselves, that have become vested in maintaining the status quo.

The *Wall Street Journal,* for example, can be expected to be polite, but hardly enthusiastic, about this book—because that paper as well as *Barron's* is owned by Dow Jones and Company—and this is only one powerful piece of the bureaucracy vested in keeping an old culture alive.

Benjamin Graham's ideas hit this same sort of brick wall nearly a century ago. At another epic turning point in financial history, when an investment culture that had operated for decades was dying on the vine, the securities of the new one that was to replace it, namely Dow stocks, were collectively derided as a fad appealing to a lowbrow and uncultured sort of investor. The more sophisticated, schooled, and discriminating preferred to keep most of their money where they always had—in the securities that never lost money if you kept them for the long term, that eventually always outperformed all others, and that provided the template for how investments should be analyzed. That these securities were *bonds,* more specifically *railroad bonds,* stands as a monument to how dramatically an accepted system of perceived facts can be turned upside down.

During the 1800s, bonds had provided the same set of blue-chip characteristics on which we had come to rely from Dow-type stocks in the 1900s.

Bull bond markets brought impressive capital gains to investors in

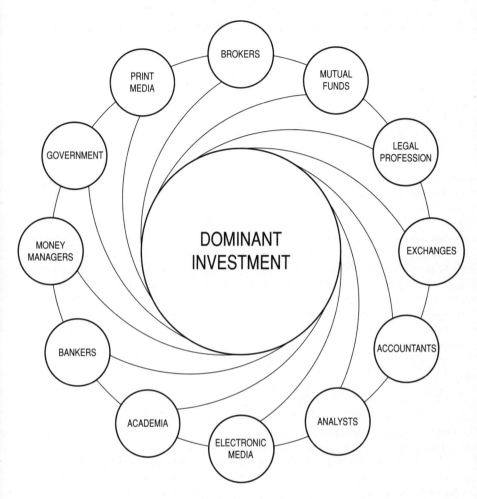

**Figure 1.2**    The Web of a Dominant Investment System

the nineteenth century. Annual returns of 30% and even higher were not uncommon.[4] Although every year was not so lucrative, the average annual returns succeeded in making bonds the dominant investment of the nineteenth century. Figures 1.3 and 1.4 show how similar the growth rate of bonds in the nineteenth century was to Dow stocks in the twentieth.

This version of market history differs from what can only be called the Adam and Eve school of investing. This school of thought holds that stocks like those of the Dow Jones Industrial Average materialized out of nowhere, begat the S&P 500, and together will for-

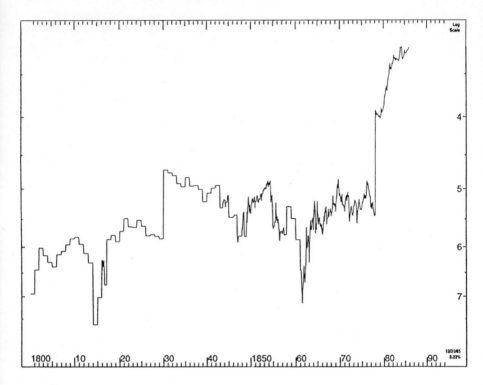

**Figure 1.3**   The Bond Market, 1800–1890

ever dominate the earth. This conveniently avoids the pesky fact that the same evolutionary process that allowed the Dow to supplant bonds as the dominant investment can create a replacement for the Dow itself. The chemistry behind these transitions is refreshingly straightforward.

## PRODUCTIVITY: THE HEARTBEAT OF A DOMINANT INVESTMENT

*Without the long history of productivity growth, incomes would not have risen, life would not have improved, immigrants would not have flocked to these shores, and people could not have moved off the land and into cities. In short, our whole history would have been radically different.*
—Jeremy Atack and Peter Passell, *A New Economic View of History*[5]

Wealth is created by generating more output with lesser input. This is productivity. Not only will a method of doing business that increases productivity enhance profits for the companies that use it, but

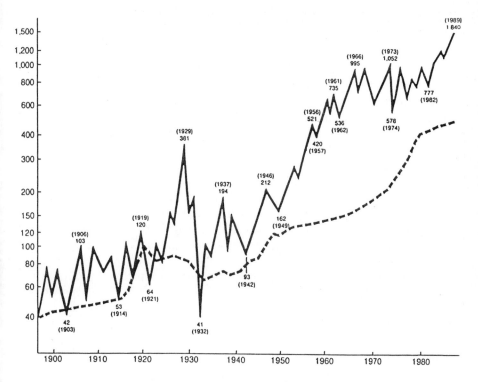

**Figure 1.4**   The Stock Market, 1900–1990

*Note:* The dominant investment of the 1900s follows a pattern that is similar to that of the dominant investment of the 1800s.

the surrounding economy will benefit due to what economists refer to as the *multiplier effect.*[6]

Combine agriculture with a brand new railroad system, for example, and you will have what we call the *pick it and ship it* business model that succeeded in raising American productivity to an annual growth rate of 2.6% for much of the 1800s.

Divergent opinions exist as to the rate of economic growth prior to the 1830s. But Robert Martin (who conducted research in the 1930s); Nobel laureate Simon Kuznets; and agricultural historians Marvin Towne, Wayne Rasmussen, and George Rogers Taylor all agree on one point: A major acceleration of self-sustaining growth occurred in the 1820s and 1830s and is attributable to the railroad.[7] Throughout the nineteenth century railroad bonds were the best way for investors to capitalize on the wealth that this business model generated for the economy and for companies themselves. By the time the energy started to come out of the pick it and ship it business model in the 1870s and productivity fell below 2%, the belief that rail bonds would always be the best place to invest for long-term growth was deeply ingrained in the collective consciousness. This belief sustained rail bonds as the dominant investment for many more years, despite the ominous drop in productivity.

Late in the nineteenth century a new and more productive method of doing business had evolved: the take it, make it, break it model mentioned earlier. In the book *Surfing the Edge of Chaos,*[8] the authors explain that productivity was rejuvenated by *taking* vast quantities of natural sources, *making* products to be mass marketed, and then replacing—*breaking*—them, so that the process can be repeated. This fundamentally altered how business was done in the United States and ushered in productivity growth rates as high as 3% for much of the twentieth century.[9]

While Charles Dow was probably not monitoring productivity numbers, he was enthusiastic enough about the new business methods to discontinue publishing the list of railroad stock prices he had been using since 1887. He wanted his index to represent the new style of company. On May 26, 1896, he published his first average, which excluded railroad companies and contained only take it, make it, break it companies. Three years later stocks outperformed bonds for the first time in history (see Figure 1.5).

Almost exactly 100 years after the take it, make it, break it business model rejuvenated the U.S. economy by improving productivity, it has been replaced with an even more productive model that we call *realize, capitalize, customize.* The juice behind this transformation is the science of semiconductors, which turns information into an energy that is more powerful and efficient than anything that can be pumped from a pipeline.

The importance of semiconductors to U.S. business in the twenty-first century is one of the main courses of study at the best business schools in this country. The reading list in Appendix G contains must-read titles on the subject. In one of the best, *Unleashing the Killer App,* the authors have this to say about the new power that the delivery of information has on business: "Executives in industries as varied as education, advertising, government, pharmaceuticals, consumer products, retail, and wholesale tell us their basic assumptions about products, channels, and customers will be completely changed."[10]

In the book *The Next Economy,* marketing guru Elliott Ettenberg said the following of companies clinging to take it, make it, break it: "Existing corporate structures and measurements of success are incapable of guiding enterprise through the coming changes. To survive

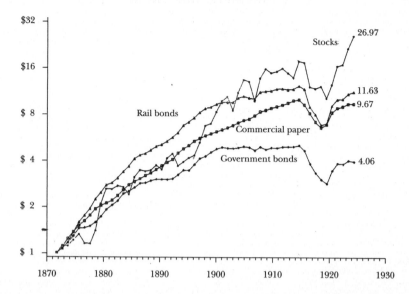

**Figure 1.5**   Cumulative Inflation-Adjusted Total Return on Different Investments Assuming an Initial Investment of $1 in 1871 and the Reinvestment of All Proceeds

*Note:* As the twentieth century began, stocks outperformed bonds for the first time.

*Source:* "Historical Returns and Security Market Development 1872–1925" by Kenneth Snowden in *Explorations in Economic History,* vol. 27 393, 1986. Elsevier Science (USA), Reproduced with permission of the publisher.

and prosper in the Next Economy will require a rethinking of corporate priorities."[11]

Growth in the old industrial business model came from building ever larger corporate bureaucracies, exploiting ever more natural resources, organizing hierarchies of management and regulating competition. Realize, capitalize, customize is the polar opposite.

A new product or service is created and tested in a virtual setting. Creativity and experimentation can be encouraged because trial and error are nearly cost-free. The new project does not have to be overseen by a raft of bean counters. Once the new product is *realized,* it can be *capitalized* via partnerships with suppliers, manufacturers, and venture capitalists or by issuing stock through the capital markets. *Customization* via the ability to gather and rearrange data adds value for the consumer at no added expense to the company. Elliott Ettenberg says that one of the main differences between the twentieth century and the twenty-first century consumer is that the fulfillment of *needs* described the twentieth-century business. People *needed* cars. The twenty-first century companies will profit by fulfilling *wants.* Today's consumers *want* an off-road vehicle, a sports car, and a family car. Consumers used to *need* clothes; today they *want* one set of clothing for the office, another for the golf course, and still another for social events. The profitable company in the twenty-first century uses information management to keep up with key consumers and customize products to fulfill these wants.

Nike is an example of a take it, make it, break it company that has adopted the realize, capitalize, customize model. In the old days they would have expanded by building more shoe factories and buying more trucks and railroad cars in order to mass market a new line of shoes. They would hope to make a profit by prevailing in adversarial negotiations with suppliers, merchants, and customers. Instead, today Nike outsources its manufacturing and distribution to partners connected to Nike by digital information systems. By getting out of the shoe factory business, Nike is free to leverage its brand identity as an athletic company by using high-bandwidth communication channels to promote and manage sporting events. Nike can customize its product line by targeting the wants of the basketball fan differently from the wants of the tennis buff.

The adoption of the new business model by many corporations caused annual productivity growth to soar from 1.25% during 1970–1994 to an annual average rate of 3.75% at the turn of the twenty-first century.[12] That this is a permanent structural shift is confirmed by leading economists: In 2000, chairman of the Federal Reserve Board, Alan Greenspan, stated, "When historians look back at the latter half of the 1990s, a decade or two hence, I suspect that they will conclude we are now living through a pivotal period in economic history." Likewise, David Wheeler, vice president of the Federal Reserve Board, remarked in 2001 that the "increase in productivity growth during the past five years is due to permanent forces, mainly the diffusion of information."

The effect of the new source of productivity on corporate America is no less than that of the asteroid that caused the extinction of the dinosaurs. Smaller companies can now be more profitable than larger ones; costly exploitation of natural resources is unnecessary; teams of employees are more efficient than management bureaucracies; and networks of companies in partnerships are more efficient than turf battles.

The economic slowdown of 2001–2002 shows the power of productivity. Figures 1.6 and 1.7 indicate the loss of jobs in the manufacturing and industrial sectors. It is clear that these less productive, largely twentieth-century businesses, had to get rid of employees way before the "recession" set in late in 2001. It is equally clear that these types of companies—curiously perceived as safe or as the backbone of our economy—offered no place to hide when times got rocky.

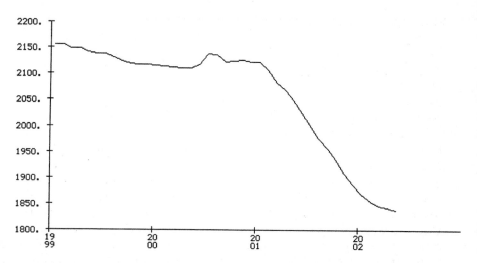

**Figure 1.6**    Total Employment (thousands) in Industrial Machinery and Equipment, 1999–2002

*Note:* During the economic slowdown of 2000–2002, the take it, make it, break it economic sectors suffered significant job losses.

*Source:* Printed with permission of Economagic, LLC and http://www.economagic.com.

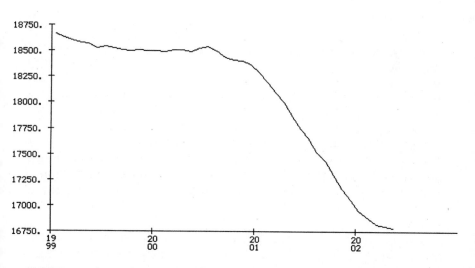

**Figure 1.7**    Total Employment (thousands) in Manufacturing, 1999–June 2002

*Source:* Printed with permission of Economagic, LLC and http://www.economagic.com.

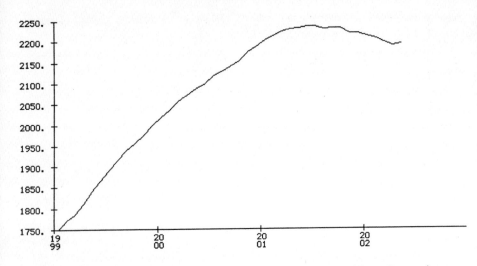

**Figure 1.8** Total Employment (thousands) in Computer and Data Processing Services, 1999–June 2002

*Note:* During the economic slowdown of 2000–2002, the realize, capitalize, customize economic sector had relatively few layoffs.

*Source:* Printed with permission of Economagic, LLC and http://www.economagic.com.

Figure 1.8 lays out a different picture. In 1999, a peak year for the economy, manufacturing and industrial companies were getting rid of employees. Yet data processing and computer services industries could not hire people fast enough. Even more revealing, as the recession set in, the number of job losses in this sector were far lower than were those in the industrial and manufacturing sectors. The more productive companies barreled on through the slower economy.

Suppose we took the labels off of these figures. In a blind test we tell you that each graph represents a different set of companies. Which set would you pick to invest in? Would you not choose the companies represented in Figure 1.8? Obviously, they are more robust and are less affected by crises like economic fluctuations or the attack on the World Trade Center. By and large these are the companies of the new dominant investment system. Most of these companies are found on the NASDAQ stock market.

Independent consultants have polled focus groups of nonprofessional investors in an effort to determine what kinds of securities they thought would represent the financial markets of the twenty-first century.[13] That the overwhelming choice was the kinds of companies that trade on NASDAQ proves again that the general public is perfectly capable of recognizing progress and opportunity when they see it. For now, the NASDAQ composite index[14] will serve as our barometer of the new dominant investment system.

|  | 1800s | 1900s | 2000s |
|---|---|---|---|
| *Business model:* | Pick it and ship it | Take it, make it, break it | Realize, capitalize, customize |
| *Dominant investment system:* | Railroad bonds | Dow Jones Industrial Average | NASDAQ |

At this point we reach a chasm between fantasy and reality so wide that it defies logic: Notwithstanding the fact that the country's foremost economists, business executives, marketing and management experts, and even the general public all recognize that science has brought us innovations that have structurally altered how productivity and profits are achieved, we still look at the Dow Jones Industrial Average, and the investment principles that accompany it, as the essence of finance and the last word in wealth creation. It boggles the mind that we give any weight at all to the importance of 30 industrial stocks.

The disconnect between the new facts of business and the old fancies about investing is brought to us by those vested in the old dominant investment system. They put forth the bursting of the dot-com bubble in 2000 as evidence that investing in technology is risky and futile. Never mind that dot-com stocks have nothing to do with the new dominant investment system. What that was about was mass marketers simply using the Internet to enhance mass marketing. Money was thrown into computers and networks by many executives who had no idea about, or intention of, changing their basic business model. As Larry Downes and Chunka Mui concluded in *Unleashing the Killer App,* technology is not merely a tool to implement an existing strategy—it increases productivity only when it is allowed to eliminate current operating models and underlying assumptions.

Many of us within the investment industry have understood for years that those underlying assumptions have changed and must in turn change the nature of investing. When it is argued that sound investment principles do not change, we point out that for over half of the twentieth century Dow stocks and other blue chips were analyzed within the same framework as were bonds. Those old commandments of analysis were destroyed in the middle of the twentieth century, and the markets survived just fine. Here are some facts:

- Even after Dow stocks and those like them became dominant, they were expected to fit into the old analytical structure of bonds. Stocks had to pay high and regular cash flow to investors in the form of dividends.

- Paying a high dividend was more important than putting that cash into the future growth of the company. Only after 60 years into the Dow's term as the dominant investment did the investment establishment get over this obsession with dividends. Even then it was changes in tax laws that instigated the new view, not the importance of investing for growth.[15]

- Not until 1958 was it acceptable for the yields of stock dividends to fall below the yields of interest payments from bonds.[16]

- We have not heard an analyst recommend a stock solely because it paid a high dividend since 1988.

Markets evolve, the investment establishment eventually adapts to the new environment, and the rules change. How high NASDAQ will be and how many opportunities will be lost by the time that happens in this century are anyone's guess.

Sometimes when we look at things one way long enough, it becomes difficult to see the misguided impressions, the fudged facts, and the beliefs we hold only because we have always held them. An artist friend tells us that she will turn her work upside down to get a fresh perspective. She says that this short-circuits the mind's anticipated connections and that the gaps in logic jump out at her.

Upending the ideology of the stock market is equally enlightening. Here are two examples.

## "THEMARKET"

A couple approaches us at a party and asks us to help resolve a disagreement: "What did 'themarket' do in 1998?"

We replied, "Large-cap value stocks rose about 11%; large-cap growth stocks rose about 42%; small-cap growth stocks fell about 3%; and a small-cap value stocks fell about 5%."[17]

With some irritation they said, "That's nice, but what did themarket do?"

They probably thought we were being difficult, but the fact is that there has not been a "themarket" for over 20 years. There are thousands of companies of different sizes and growth rates that cause them to react differently to economic conditions and perform differently at any given point in time. They can be segregated into style sets. The major ones are defined in the following box. The data are from July 2002.

# MAJOR 2002 MARKET STYLES

| Style Category | Example | Characteristics |
|---|---|---|
| Large-Cap Value | Exxon-Mobil (XOM) | Size: $247.7 billion<br>Growth Rate: 8%<br>Dividend Yield: 2.5%<br>P/E: 20.2<br>Enormous tangible assets. Mature industry |
| Large-Cap Growth | AMGEN (AMGN) | Size: $35.6 billion<br>Growth Rate: 18%<br>Dividend Yield: 0%<br>P/E: 32<br>Leading biotech company created in the late twentieth century. Few tangible assets compared to Exxon-Mobil. Its wealth is in its patents, revenues from product sales, and research and development. |
| Small-Cap Growth | Concord EFS (CE) | Size: $13.8 billion<br>Growth Rate: 30%<br>Dividend Yield: 0%<br>P/E: 47.6<br>Fastest growing provider of electronic funds processing and transaction authorization. |
| Small-Cap Value | Costco Wholesale (COST) | Size: $16.8 billion<br>Growth Rate: 12%<br>Dividend Yield: 0%<br>P/E: 26.9<br>Market leader in megawarehouse shopping clubs |
| International | UniLever (UN) | Size: $57 billion<br>Growth Rate: 6%<br>Dividend Yield: 1.8%<br>P/E: 33.9<br>Second largest consumer goods company behind Philip Morris. Based in the Netherlands, it markets foods, home, and personal care products. |
| Emerging Markets | China Mobile (CHL) | Size: $54.7 billion<br>Growth Rate: 30%<br>Dividend Yield: 0%<br>P/E: 16<br>Provides cellular communications in China. Had 69 million subscribers in 2001. |

*Note:* "Cap" stands for market capitalization, or the number of shares times their value, which equals the size of the company. "P/E" refers to the price/earnings ratio. "International" refers to the major developed economies outside the United States, such as France, Japan, and Great Britain. "Emerging Markets" refers to the world's developing economies.

Small-cap companies can be worth billions of dollars. All growth rates are 5-year estimates. Notice the difference in growth rates between growth and value stocks.

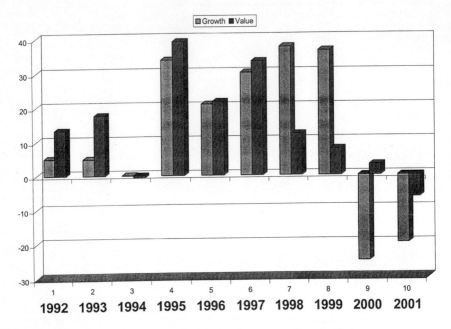

**Figure 1.9**   Performance Comparison: Value versus Growth Style
*Source:* Data Courtesy of Wilshire Associates

That these styles had become distinct by the 1970s coincides with the Dow's passing its peak years as the dominant investment. The course of this event is explored in Part II, which supplies the historical data and context for each investment culture.

The significance of these style sets for an investor today is illustrated in Figures 1.9, 1.10, and 1.11. A style will be the top performer for a while, but inevitably the stocks it represents will fall in value, and stocks of a different style will take their place as the best performers. The data used to construct the graphs were provided courtesy of Wilshire.

## ANALYZE THIS

The magazines of pop finance have been filled with articles such as these:

- 1999: The New Way to Value Stock Prices: Old Rules Are Broken
- 2000: Mystery of Stock Values: Will the New Rules Keep Working?

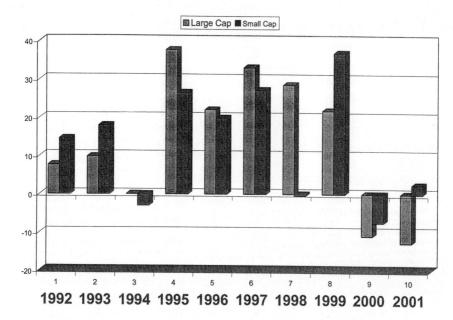

**Figure 1.10**   Performance Comparison: Large versus Small Capitalization
*Source:* Data Courtesy of Wilshire Associates

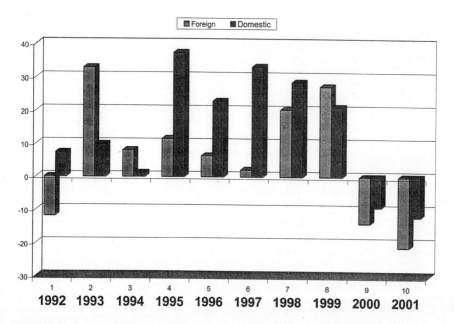

**Figure 1.11**   Performance Comparison: Foreign versus Domestic Stocks
*Source:* Data Courtesy of Wilshire Associates

- 2001–2002: Salvaging Your Portfolio: Back to the Basics, the Old Rules Are Best
- 2003–????: Evaluating Stock Prices: Some New Rules Might Work After All

The truth is that there have been distinctly different ways of analyzing stocks for over 20 years. Because large-cap value, large-cap growth, small-cap value, and small-cap growth stocks have so little in common that they react differently to economic conditions, a financial ratio that is appropriate for evaluating one company may be irrelevant for another.

The distinctions between stock styles are so extreme that a professional money manager is required to specialize in one style or another. If a large-cap value manager should suddenly begin to buy small-cap growth stocks, we would view that in the same way as you would if your gynecologist hung out a shingle professing to be qualified to do brain surgery.

Yet, every day we hear people from within and outside our business reject one NASDAQ stock or another as a poor investment because its characteristics do not fit some misconception of what is "normal." Their conclusions are often a dead giveaway that they filter their facts through a prism of investment clichés built around the stock model of the Dow Jones Industrial Average.

That brings us to that thing about P/E ratios.[18] Because this is one of the simplest financial ratios used to evaluate stocks, it has undergone a number of new applications over the last few years. At dinner parties, for instance, when the conversation turns to "themarket," it can be used like this to impress your friends: "I only buy stocks for my portfolio if the P/E is _____."

The P/E ratio can be an excellent tool when you want to prove to your teenager that in fact you do know something about buying stocks online, as in, "Of course I know how to set up the online trading account. I just don't want to do it right now because the market's P/E is too high" (too low, or whatever).

Best of all (and we have used this one ourselves), the P/E ratio's value as a topic for magazine articles or newsletters cannot be overstated:

- "What to Buy Now? 20 Stocks with the Lowest P/Es"
- "Why the New Economy Stocks Should/Should Not (whatever) Have High P/E Ratios"
- "The Right P/E for the Market"

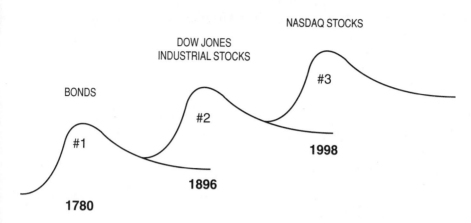

NASDAQ STOCKS

DOW JONES
INDUSTRIAL STOCKS

BONDS

#3

#2

#1

**1998**

**1896**

**1780**

**Figure 1.12** The Three Dominant Investment Systems

Evaluating either the market or an individual stock by its P/E ra-tio is like judging someone's character by his or her shoe size—it can be one thing to consider in concert with other factors, but by itself it doesn't mean a lot.

• • •

We can be left feeling unmoored when a new investment culture ma-terializes and an old one slips away. If blue-chip companies will no longer be the best place to invest for the long term, what does one do? When the Dow has a significant decline, we used to be able to say, "Be patient, it will bounce back, it always does." What happens when we can't say that anymore?

We looked to history for the answer. After two years of searching, bells started ringing when we discovered that dominant investment systems begin and end in similar patterns (see Figure 1.12). The next chapter lays out how closely the path of the NASDAQ—since it came to represent the new dominant investment system in 1998—correlates with the pattern the Dow followed when it became the new investment force of the 1900s. This discovery has helped us to anticipate the direction of stocks and has been a guide in making in-vestment decisions for our clients and ourselves. It raises the mind out of the rut of the day-to-day market gyrations and sends it down the road of fruitful possibilities.

## NOTES

1. Janet Lowe, *Benjamin Graham on Value Investing* (Chicago: Dearborn Financial Publishing, 1994). Benjamin Graham's pioneering work came to be known as the Graham-Dodd theory of analysis, required reading for any financial analyst today.

2. IBM per share earnings: 1984, $2.930; 1985, $2.680; 1986, $1.952.

3. Prices are adjusted for stock splits.

4. Sidney Homer, *A History of Interest Rates* (New Brunswick, NJ: Rutgers University Press, 1963), p. 309.

5. Jeremy Atack and Peter Passell, *A New Economic View of American History* (New York: W.W. Norton, 1994).

6. Initial bursts of spending create secondary and tertiary bursts. For example, a new construction project means that money is spent on materials. Suppliers will engage in additional spending of their own. The annual effect of the multiplier is about two.

7. *A New Economic View of American History,* p. 8.

8. Richard Pascale, Mark Milleman, and Linda Gioja, *Surfing the Edge of Chaos* (New York: Crown, 2000).

9. Bureau of Economic Analysis, National Income and Productivity Tables.

10. Larry Downes and Chunka Mui, *Unleashing the Killer App* (Boston, MA: Harvard Business School Press, 1998), p. 63.

11. Elliott Ettenburg, *The Next Economy* (New York: McGraw Hill, 2002), p. 4.

12. *The Regional Economist,* Federal Reserve Board of St. Louis, July, 2001.

13. Source: U.S. investor surveys conducted by Roper Starch Worldwide.

14. The NASDAQ composite is an index that includes all domestic and non-U.S. stocks listed on the National Association of Securities Dealers Automated Quotation System. It contains over 5000 stocks.

15. Jeremy Siegel, *Stocks for the Long Run* (Chicago: McGraw Hill, 1994), p. 62.

16. Ibid., p. 26.

17. In 1998 these indexes represented the sectors mentioned and performed as follows: Wilshire Target Large Growth +42.21%, Wilshire Target Large Value +11.25%, Wilshire Target Small-Cap Growth (2.46%), Wilshire Target Small-Cap Value (4.87%).

18. P/E stands for the stock price divided by the company's per-share earnings; for example, a stock price of 100 divided by earnings of $20 per share = P/E of 50.

# 2

# THE FINANCIAL FRONTIER
## The Direction of the Markets Under the New Dominant Investment System

*The wilderness masters the colonist.*
—Frederick Jackson Turner

The last time we witnessed somebody pitching their "Great American Companies" fund by using one of those charts that shows the Dow Jones Industrial Average gently rising over the last 70 years, we began to wonder at what point Americans began to cling to the past. We didn't, after all, used to have one. The advantage this gave our economy over more established cultures such as those of Europe was that we were free of the entrenched, self-serving business bureaucracies that, in the name of convention, keep new, more productive businesses from flourishing. Only one thing mattered to the pioneering spirit: moving forward. That gutsy spark created the wealthiest nation on earth in a very short period of time.

We are no longer free of entrenched, self-serving business bureaucracies. Somewhere along the line they have succeeded in making us forget that inspired innovation and brave foresight, which so threatens them today, are what brought them to power in the first place. If market history is worth exploring, it is to those early creative years that we should look—the years when nothing was certain but that visionary Americans would not let anything stand in their way.

In looking out at the financial frontier ahead of us in the twenty-first century, we can get clues to the new market's direction from the time when the Dow itself was as new and energetic as NASDAQ companies are today. It turns out that NASDAQ is coming close to repeating the Dow's performance in its earliest years. It appears that dominant investment systems begin and end in similar patterns. We had been studying this over the last seven years and in 1999 began to use the correlation between the NASDAQ and the Dow, a century apart, to help us anticipate the direction of the markets in the management of our clients and our own money.

Part II puts the performances of the Dow and NASDAQ in their historic contexts. It was the historic cultural, social, and economic similarities between the beginnings of the two dominant investment systems that led us to compare market performance. Without this framework the market patterns themselves would not hold much significance.

The first principle to emerge was that the early years of a dominant investment system can be divided into three distinct phases:

1. Discovery phase

2. Formulation phase

3. Acceleration phase

Figure 2.1 puts the trend of the three phases together.

As you read the definitions of each phase, keep in mind that these descriptions obtain from what occurred a century ago. This puts a singularly stunning perspective on events today because they are echoing the past.

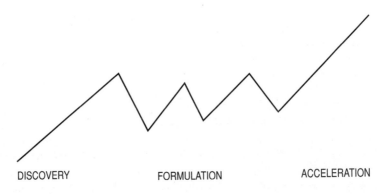

DISCOVERY                    FORMULATION                    ACCELERATION

**Figure 2.1**    The First Three Phases of a New Dominant Investment System

## DISCOVERY PHASE

The securities of what will be the new dominant investment explode out of the gate. Many of the companies they represent had been around 20 years or more, but suddenly they take on a new respectability, enhanced by the fact that they are outperforming everything else by wide margins.

Enthralled with new innovations, efficiencies, products, and services, investors are like kids waiting for Santa. Every wish will be granted. This is hard to argue when the market is soaring.

Nothing less than immediate gratification is tolerated. Returns on investment are expected within days or weeks. There is always a new "next big thing." It is unacceptable for it to take years for the new ideas to transform the world. It must happen overnight.

Babbling speculators and professional investor wanna-bes crawl out of the woodwork. Near the end, the people with neither the wherewithal nor the stomach for investing jump in.

For a while some of the old dominant investments were carried upward with the new (see Figure 2.2 for a comparison of the Dow and NASDAQ). There is confusion about how to analyze price levels. Com-

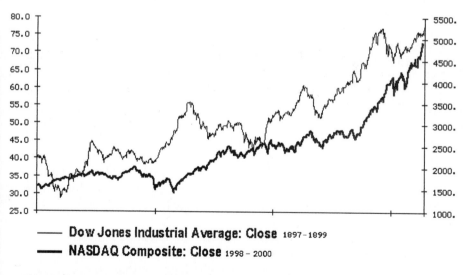

—— Dow Jones Industrial Average: Close 1897–1899
—— NASDAQ Composite: Close 1998–2000

**Figure 2.2**  The Discovery Phases of the Dow Jones Industrial Average (1896–1900) and NASDAQ (1998–2000)

*Note:* During their discovery phases as the new dominant investments, the Dow and NASDAQ followed similar patterns.

*Source:* Printed with permission of Economagic, LLC and http://www.economagic.com.

panies come to market that do not deserve to and reach levels to which
they are not entitled.

Then things *do* change overnight, but not in the way most expected. The market begins a substantial and extended decline. The discovery phase is over.

Discovery Phase of the Second and Third Dominant Investment Systems

| Dominant Investment System | Beginning | | End | | | |
| --- | --- | --- | --- | --- | --- | --- |
| | Date | Price Level | Date | Price Level | Change | Duration |
| Dow Jones | 8/8/1896 | 24.48 | 9/7/1899 | 77.61 | +172.50% | 37 months |
| NASDAQ | 1/9/1998 | 1503 | 3/10/2000 | 5049 | +236% | 27 months |

## FORMULATION PHASE

"If you liked it at $120, you should love it at $60." "Double up." It drops to $20. "Buy more." "Lower your cost basis. It'll turn around any day now." It doesn't. It is the first weeks of the formulation phase. Many are in denial.

Weeks turn into months. Business needed to slow down some to prevent inflation. It has, but still the economy is better than it was seven or eight years ago, and the markets still are not bouncing back. Impatience turns to panic until finally all the air has gone out of the balloon.

What will the markets do now? The consensus of the experts is about as orderly as downtown Manhattan at rush hour with the traffic lights out. Those with vested interests in the old dominant investment system adopt the "I told you so" attitude—Indian chiefs admonishing the tribe for diverging from the old ways. The tribe seems to agree. Money begins to flow back into the securities of the previous dominant investment system. In 2001 this meant that stocks like Philip Morris and Procter and Gamble were looking a lot better than Intel or Microsoft.

But only for a while. . . . The formulation phase is about those companies of the new dominant investment system that survived the abrupt market decline that signaled the start of this phase. During this phase these companies will execute their business plans, establish their brand identity, and educate investors who struggle to understand how they are making so much money.

We like it when we can fit things into the right box. Into which economic sectors will the companies of the new dominant investment system fit? How do we analyze them? Which ones will succeed? These questions jostle against one another, creating the defining characteristics of the formulation phase: market volatility. But we call it the formulation phase because it is during this time that these questions are answered.

There is a lot of money to be made here. Investors who understand what's happening are the ones who will profit; think Benjamin Graham of the Dow Jones Industrial Average's formulation phase. In just one short period, from 1903 to 1906, the Dow more than doubled, going from 42.25 to 103.

Comparing the Formulation Phase of the Second Dominant Investment System (Dow Jones Industrial Average) with the Third (NASDAQ as of June 2002)

| Dominant Investment System | Beginning | | End | | |
| --- | --- | --- | --- | --- | --- |
| | Date | Price Level | Date | Price Level | Duration |
| Dow Jones | 9/7/1899 | 77.61 | 8/24/1921 | 63.90 | 21 years |
| NASDAQ | 3/01/2000 | 5049 | n.a. | n.a. | n.a. |

Figure 2.3 illustrates this surprising rise after over two years of uncertainty. See Figure 2.4 and note the similarities between the NASDAQ and the Dow in the first years of the formulation phase (boxed areas).

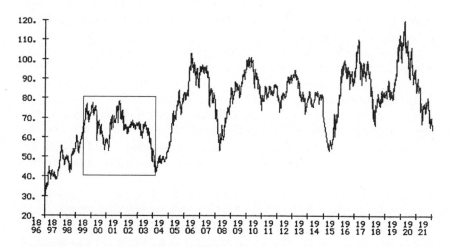

**Figure 2.3** Comparing the Formulation Phase of the Second Dominant Investment System with the Progress So Far of the Third Dominant Investment System.

*Source:* Printed with permission of Economagic, LLC and http://www.economagic.com.

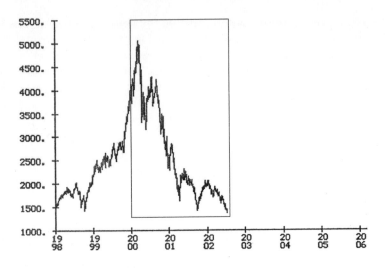

**Figure 2.4**    NASDAQ, 2000–June 2002
*Source:* Printed with permission of Economagic, LLC and http://www.economagic.com.

## ACCELERATION PHASE

The Dow's acceleration phase lasted eight years. During that time the Dow Jones Industrial Average increased 496.5%, an average of 62% per year. These were the Roaring Twenties. New services and technologies that had been created by the time of the discovery phase were refined and developed during the formulation phase and then realized their promise in the acceleration phase.

The financial world enthused over the new companies' possibilities in the discovery phase, learned how to evaluate them in the formulation phase, and finally reached a new level of confidence in their value that helped to propel the acceleration phase.

This was when investors came face to face with what the economy behind this dominant investment system could produce. The Wright

Acceleration Phase of the Second Dominant Investment System

| Dominant Investment System | Beginning | | End | | | |
| | Date | Price Level | Date | Price Level | Change | Duration |
| --- | --- | --- | --- | --- | --- | --- |
| Dow Jones | 8/24/1921 | 63.90 | 9/3/1929 | 381.17 | +496.50% | 96 months |

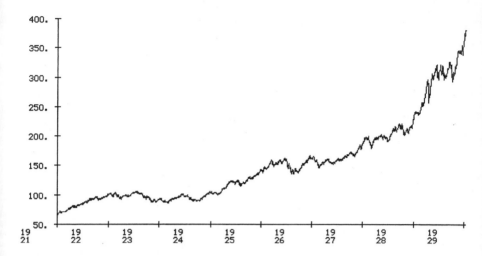

**Figure 2.5**   The Acceleration Phase of the Dow Jones Industrial Average, 1921–1929

*Source:* Printed with permission of Economagic, LLC and http://www.economagic.com.

brothers flew the first plane in 1903 (formulation phase). By the acceleration phase there were coast-to-coast passenger flights and regional airports.[1] In 1903 the 12-minute drama *The Great Train Robbery* flickered away in tiny nickelodeons. By the 1920s people across the country sat in movie theaters that looked like European palaces and watched *The Jazz Singer*[2] (see Figures 2.5 and 2.6).

## WHAT IT MEANS TO US TODAY

We were just as glad to see the NASDAQ's discovery phase end in March 2000. In the last months a person needed a black belt to fight off clients who mistook that stock tip from their dentists (teenagers, plumbers, neighbors, Web sites, etc.) for an investment. When we saw the NASDAQ's gains exceed the percentage increase of the Dow during its own discovery phase, we knew that some significant declines were not far off. We increased the cash and bond allocations in portfolios, where it was appropriate, at the very end of the discovery phase. The methodology that showed us it was time to do this is in Chapter 3.

In considering what to do with that money going forward, we wanted to know two things:

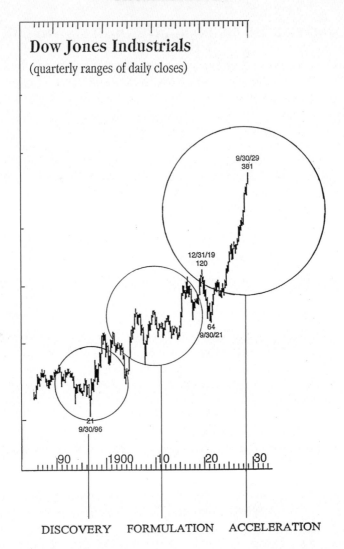

**Figure 2.6** The Discovery, Formulation, and Acceleration Phases of the Dow Jones Industrial Average, 1896–1929

1. What would happen to the old dominant investment, the Dow? If it declined a great deal during the formulation phase, would it become an attractive investment?

2. How long would the NASDAQ's formulation phase last? How well would it do amid the changing business and economic conditions?

We will answer number one first.

## WHERE DO OLD DOMINANT INVESTMENT SYSTEMS GO?

Here is the first thing. The Dow Jones Industrial Average will never go to 26,000 or 36,000 (or anywhere close to the projections that are made whenever times are good and stocks are rising), no matter how long your long term is.

There are two reasons why this is true. The first is the word of experts. According to Warren Buffett, "The Dow Jones Industrial Average should be thought of as a 13% coupon bond."[3] Ron Ryan, president of Ryan Labs, noted that the "S&P 500 is consistently behaving like a 15 year duration corporate bond. All large cap equity indexes behave in a similar risk/reward way."[4]

Warren Buffett is one of the world's most successful Dow system investors and a master at implementing the concepts of Benjamin Graham. Ron Ryan founded Ryan Labs and created the first Lehman Brothers Corporate Bond indexes in 1991. His benchmarks are among the most popular used by today's investment professionals.

Buffett and Ryan are saying that the Dow, the Standard & Poor's 500, and all the big-cap indexes act like enhanced versions of bonds. That is because many of the stocks in these indexes *are* enhanced versions of bonds. Consider the characteristics of the stocks we call blue-chip stocks. The company is of enormous size and is considered stable, and the stock pays a steady dividend—all the characteristics of a good bond.

The farther we have gotten from the days of the dominant bond system, the easier it is to forget that bonds provided the soil from which the Dow system sprung. Remember that before 1958 a stock was not considered a good investment unless its dividend yield exceeded that of a bond. Just as we have come to realize the limits to which bonds will rise before they are pulled back down to earth, we will come to learn that the gravitational pull on Dow stocks may be proportionately less but that in the same way it puts a check on the heights to which they can climb.

The academic view of why we should lower our growth expectations for the big-cap, blue-chip, industrial-age stock is thoroughly explained by Robert J. Arnott, managing partner of First Quadrant, a money management firm, and Ron Ryan. In a landmark paper they coauthored in 2000, the authors concluded that the returns of large-cap industrial companies may average an annual return of .9% *less* than bonds going forward.[5]

Arnott updated his work in the second quarter of 2001 with the Dow at lower levels than in 2000. By then the revival of the big blue chips was in full swing. For the first time in years, so-called experts talked about buying stocks for their dividend yields. Gillette, Coca-Cola, DuPont, and other industrial-age icons offered a safe way to achieve superior returns, and they were at bargain prices. These arguments appealed to investors' need for comfort, not common sense.

Figure 2.7 shows that the performance of the big-cap blue-chip stocks has always moved in direct proportion to the U.S. gross domestic product (GDP).

Today we must add the fact that not all of the GDP growth comes from big-cap blue-chip companies. At least "1% comes from entrepreneurial capitalism,"[6] or what we call the new dominant investment system, the NASDAQ companies where new jobs are being created.

The average dividend yield on Dow-type stocks in 2002 was about 1.5%. With this information, the following simple calculation gives the returns that can be expected from Dow-type stocks.[7] Note that "real return" means adjusted for inflation.

$$\text{Real stock returns} = \text{Dividend yield } (1.5\%) + \text{GDP } (3\%) \\ - \text{ entrepreneurial capitalism } (1\%)$$

$$1.5\% + 3\% - 1\% = 3.5\% \text{ expected real return on Dow Jones} \\ \text{Industrial investment system stocks}$$

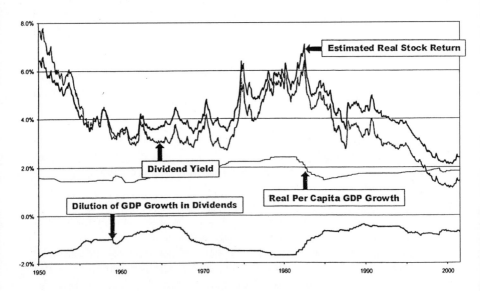

**Figure 2.7**   Estimating Real Stock Returns, 1950–2001

*Note:* Real stock returns equal the dividend yield plus per capital gross domestic product (GDP) growth minus dividend/GDP dilution.

*Source:* "What Risk Premium Is 'Normal'" by Robert D. Arnott, Peter L. Bernstein, 2001. Used by permission Robert D. Arnott.

Smoke, mirrors, and dazzling equations may take investors' expectations for the "real" long-term growth of the twenty-first century big-cap stocks much higher than 3.5% when times are good. But two plus two does not equal 22. Investors who cannot get used to the idea of a new dominant investment system will not find comfort in the old one. When we explore what happened to the first dominant investment, bonds, as it fell from dominance, it reinforces the conclusions just drawn.

## THE CAPITULATION OF THE FIRST DOMINANT INVESTMENT SYSTEM

1896 was the first year of the Dow's dominance and the bond market's last. Still, from 1896 to 1901, bond prices rose astronomically amid universal enthusiasm for investment created by the Dow's discovery phase. A comparison of the events of the period with the twentieth century is outlined below.

### Comparing the Capitulation of the First and Second Dominant Investment Systems

| Bond System | Dow Jones Industrial System |
|---|---|
| **1896**  Depressing economic news: Investors, both professional and amateur, were afraid of the markets. Disastrous declines were predicted for 1897 and the following years. | **1994**  Depressing economic news: Investors, both professional and amateur, were afraid of the markets. Disastrous declines were predicted for 1995 and the following years. |
| **1897**  Every sector of the market rose beyond everyone's expectations. Rail Bonds: +46%[8] U.S. Treasury Bonds: +10.13%[9] Dow Jones Industrial Average: +22.15% | **1995**  Every sector of the market rose beyond everyone's expectations. S&P 500: +37.59% NASDAQ: +39.92% Dow Jones Industrial Average: +36.93% Russell 3000: +36.81% |
| **1898**  All sectors of the U.S. financial markets continued to climb. Rail Bonds: +32.65%[10] U.S. Treasury Bonds: +10.12%[11] Dow Jones Industrial Average: +22.48% | **1996**  All sectors of the U.S. financial markets continued to climb. S&P 500: +22.96% NASDAQ: +22.70% Dow Jones Industrial Average: +28.90% Russell 3000: +21.82% |
| **1899**  Market continues to soar, attracting more and more investors. "Some bond investors would have created capital gains of 100% or more."[12] | **1997**  Market continues to soar, attracting more and more investors. Some Dow stocks rose 50% or more.[13] |

Oblivious to the bitter end, most investors finished off both the Dow's and the bond's dominant periods by enthusiastically bidding up prices. The result is the remarkable similarity in the price trends of the two systems at the end of their periods of dominance, as shown in Figure 2.8.

According to Sydney Homer in his definitive book on the bond market,[14] the first protracted bear market for bonds officially began in 1899, but this did not become noticeable until 1902. Similarly, in 1998 the Dow stocks listed in the following table peaked and, from the perspective of technical analysis, evidenced major structural breakdowns in their previous upward trends.

The shift to a downward bias went unnoticed by most this time as well. It was concealed by the outstanding performance of companies like IBM, who were increasing productivity by replacing old business systems with the new twenty-first century model.[15]

| Company | Date | Price Peaks | Price on 12/29/2000 | Price on 6/30/2002 |
|---|---|---|---|---|
| Texaco | 3/22/1998 | 65 | 62.125 | bought by Chevron |
| J.P. Morgan | 4/13/1998 | 48.82 | 45.43 | 31.36 |
| DuPont | 5/18/1998 | 80.75 | 48.313 | 44.46 |
| Procter & Gamble | 7/6/1998 | 94 | 78.43 | 90.03 |
| Coca-Cola | 7/13/1998 | 86.875 | 60.94 | 56.35 |
| Eastman Kodak | 7/20/1998 | 88.18 | 39.375 | 28.21 |
| Philip Morris | 11/23/1998 | 58.125 | 44.00 | 44.96 |

The decline of the blue chips continued into 1999 and 2000 as two more Dow Jones industrial stocks initiated downward trends.

| Company | Date | Price Peaks | 12/29/2000 | 6/30/2002 |
|---|---|---|---|---|
| Caterpillar | 5/3/1999 | 65.18 | 47.31 | 48.0 |
| Merck | 11/27/2000 | 96.687 | 93.625 | 48.75 |

What can we expect the Dow Jones Industrial Average to do in the future? If it continues to act like the bond market did after relinquishing its own dominance (see Figure 2.9), the answer can be found in Figure 2.10, which shows the course of the bond market from 1899 to 1920. Figure 2.10 shows where the Dow would go if it follows a parallel course.

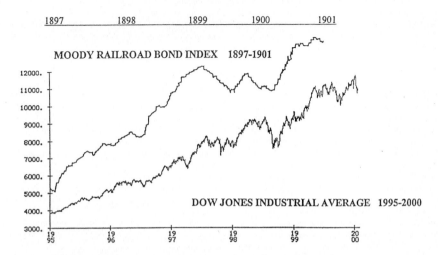

**Figure 2.8** Comparing the End of the First and Second Dominant Investment Systems: Bonds (1897–1900) and the Dow (1995–2000)

*Note:* The first and second investment systems ended their dominance by rising dramatically in value.

*Source:* Printed with permission of Economagic, LLC and http://www.economagic.com.

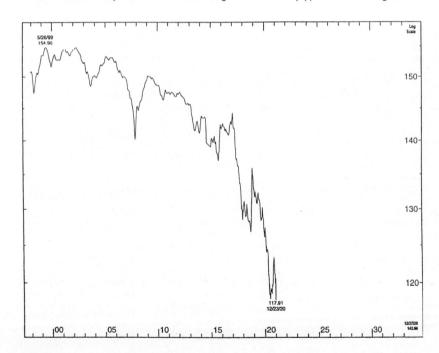

**Figure 2.9** The Capitulation of Two Dominant Investment Systems: Bonds

Note: Moody's Aaa bond prices are shown during the first two decades of the twentieth century.

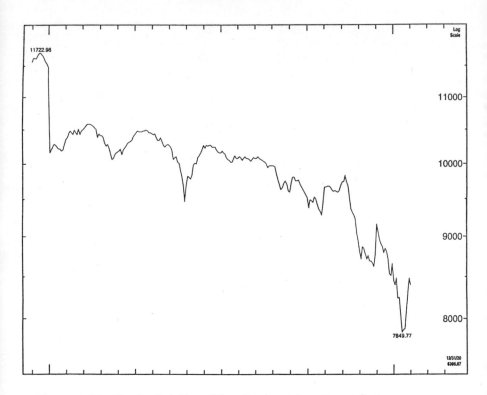

**Figure 2.10**  The Capitulation of Two Dominant Investment Systems:
Dow Jones Industrial Average
*Note:* This is the projected course of the Dow if it repeats the pattern set by bonds after
the culmination of their term as the dominant investment.

By themselves, the graphs may not signify much, but taken together with the observations of Warren Buffett, Ron Ryan, and Rob
Arnott, we can draw these conclusions.

- Expecting better-than-average returns from the Dow even when
  it reaches bargain-basement prices is a mistake.
- Expecting the Dow and stocks of that ilk to outperform all other
  investments over the long term is a mistake.
- The best course is to consider carefully the merits of each stock
  on its own, disregarding the fact that it is a part of the Dow or
  the S&P 500 index.

## CROSSING THE FRIENDLY FRONTIER

The seepage of energy out of the Dow at the end of its dominance bears
no resemblance to the power it had during its formulation phase.

There were healthy rebounds out of each correction. We have not discovered a single economic historian who does not marvel at the general mood of confidence that existed during the first two decades of the twentieth century. It is typically described like this: "marked by a sustained sense of prosperity. A few short downturns did not disrupt the prevailing optimism."[16]

The first of these downturns ended the Dow's discovery phase and marked the beginning of the formulation phase.

The Dow's First Formulation Phase Contraction

|  | 9/7/1899 | 9/24/1900 | % Change |
|---|---|---|---|
| DJIA Price | 77.61 | 52.96 | −31.76 |

The period was followed by a rally of 47.77% over 9 months.

The Dow's First Formulation Phase Rally

|  | 9/24/1900 | 6/17/1901 |  |
|---|---|---|---|
| DJIA Price | 52.96 | 78.26 | +47.77% |

After the NASDAQ declined to 1638.80 at the end of its discovery phase, it had a similar rally of 41.19% (see Figure 2.11).

The NASDAQ's First Formulation Phase Rally

|  | 4/04/01 | 5/22/01 |  |
|---|---|---|---|
| NASDAQ Comp Price | 1638.80 | 2313.85 | +41.19% |

During just one week of this rally the NASDAQ rose 14%, the second highest percentage increase ever,[17] whereas the Dow rose only 3.4% during the same period. This hints at the power that NASDAQ stocks are building during this phase. Most are missing these signals to the prosperity ahead. We have not found one person outside our industry and very few within it who even realized that this historic increase occurred.

## THE SECOND MAJOR FORMULATION PHASE CONTRACTION

In shifting back a century to see what happens next, we find the Dow in another formulation phase correction of −46.01% lasting 28 months. This occurred between June 17, 1901, and November 13, 1903. It was

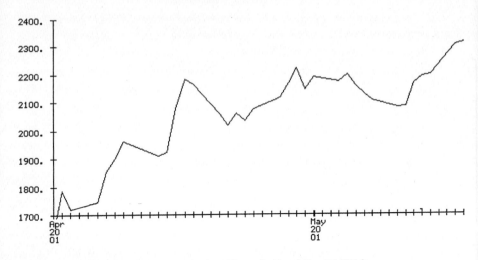

**Figure 2.11**    The First Formulation Phase Rally of the NASDAQ
*Note:* Shown are NASDAQ closing prices from April 4, 2001, to May 22, 2001.

blamed on a 23-month business contraction in 1902.[18] In 1903 U.S. Steel missed a dividend, and a merger in the shipbuilding industry fell through, exacerbating the decline that was called the *Rich Man's Panic*.[19]

We find ourselves today (August 2001) at the beginning of a similar business contraction and a similar market decline. Chapter 5 explains the economic parallels between the 1902 contraction and today's; without this information, however, the coincidence of the timing by itself gets one's attention. The NASDAQ has declined 16% since its historic May 2001 rally, and business has slowed considerably. This economic contraction will further stress an already deteriorating old dominant investment system, making it likely that we will see a major disruption of at least one or two companies—like what occurred with U.S. Steel a century earlier. This, on top of reports of earnings declines from many companies, is likely to send the NASDAQ lower. But there is some very good news ahead. The Dow's 30-month decline that began in 1901 was eventually followed by a 144.4% rally. A similar rally today could put the NASDAQ around 3500. The Dow's second formulation phase rally is illustrated in Figure 2.12.

| The Dow's Second Formulation Phase Rally | | | |
|---|---|---|---|
| | 11/13/1903 | 1/19/1906 | % Increase |
| DJIA Price | 42.15 | 103 | +144.4 |

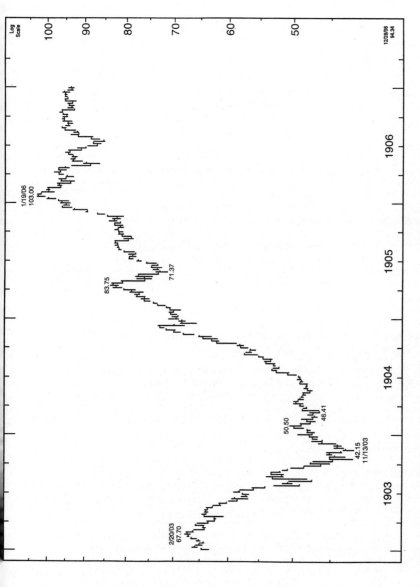

**Figure 2.12** The Second Formulation of the Dow Jones Industrial Average

*Note:* Shown are the Dow Jones 12 Industrials (weekly) from November 13, 1903, to January 19, 1906.

Source: Printed with permission of Economagic, LLC and http://www.economagic.com.

• • •

The next major event in the Dow's Formulation Phase occurred in 1907, when unemployment surged from 2% to 8% in 1908.[20] This setback of panic proportions was caused by deceitful and naive banking practices[21] and sent the Dow falling 48.54% over 22 months from January 19, 1906, to November 15, 1907.

The Dow's formulation phase reversals were viewed as devastating at the time, but in hindsight economists agree they were only potholes in a gently climbing road of prosperity. The stable economic base created by the new productivity of the industrial age is what made it so.

Digital resources give us that same productive boost and economic stability today. Those that overreact to market corrections will find themselves on the sidelines when the NASDAQ stocks surge out of these troughs. Here's how the Dow recovered from the panic of 1907 caused by the banking industry:

The Dow's Third Formulation Phase Rally

|            | 11/15/1907 | 11/19/1909 | % Increase |
|------------|------------|------------|------------|
| DJIA Price | 53         | 100.53     | +89.67     |

Even after the market disruption between 1912 and 1915 caused by World War I, the Dow had a robust gain.

The Dow's World War I Formulation Phase Rally

|            | 2/24/1915 | 11/21/1916 | % Increase |
|------------|-----------|------------|------------|
| DJIA Price | 54.22     | 110.15     | +103.15    |

War drains a country's resources. It is expensive in terms of human energy and financial cost. Productivity is spent on things that will either be destroyed or never used again. For the Dow to have doubled in value by 1916 is only another testament to the underlying prosperity of the early years of the Dow's dominance. This stands in contrast to the Dow's waning resilience years later as it matured.

In 1973 the Dow's high close on January 11 was 1051.70. The Vietnam War ended in 1975. The Dow went nowhere for 10 years, only reaching 1070.55 by December 27, 1982. With its youthful vigor depleted, the recovery from the trauma of war this time took a decade.

## IF IT'S NOT ONE THING . . .

The NASDAQ has its own atmosphere, which will respond in its own way to unforeseen events over the next several years. Everyone will be affected by them whether invested or not. What NASDAQ companies do will impact interest rates, real estate, and jobs.

What we learn from the Dow's formulation phase is that negative events may last a year or two and then be quickly compensated for by a vigorous rise in the performance of the dominant investment. This was true even in the worst-case scenario of World War I. This knowledge will help in making important personal and familial economic decisions unrelated to the stock market. The techniques to make the most of the formulation phase as an investor are explained in Chapter 3.

## HOW LONG WILL THE FORMULATION PHASE LAST?

We know that events occur faster today than they did a century ago, so we have to come up with a way to convert Dow years to NASDAQ years. All we have to base a conversion factor on is how long the NASDAQ's discovery phase lasted compared to the Dow's. The NASDAQ's discovery phase lasted 27 months, 27% less time than the Dow's 37-month discovery phase. Putting this information into the formula $(A \times B)/(A + B)$, we can estimate the duration of the NASDAQ's formulation phase. The result is 8.8 years.[22]

If we do not have a protracted disaster like World War I, today's NASDAQ formulation phase could be shorter. By substituting World War I's 29-month bear market for a 12-month bear market, we shorten NASDAQ's formulation phase to 8.3 years. This means that one NASDAQ year equals about 2.5 Dow years, putting the beginning of the acceleration phase between 2008 and 2009.

Colleagues have said that our estimate is far too long. They argue that we are not giving enough weight to the evolving speed of technology, citing examples such as if transportation (railroads) had evolved at the same speed in the nineteenth century that digital technology has today, we could have put someone on the moon in 1904.

Our response is that having technology is one thing, but creating a successful commercial application is another. Besides, time flies. The formulation phase is happening to us right now, and there are only a few years left to profit from it and get in position for the acceleration phase.

## THE ACCELERATION PHASE: THE ROARING TWENTIES IN THE TWENTY-FIRST CENTURY

Actually, it will be the Roaring Nine, Ten, and Eleven. Using our formula, we calculate it will last about three years, so it should be over around 2011.

There will be high volume and active investor participation in the acceleration phase. Who will those investors be? Many of them will be employees, executives, and directors of NASDAQ companies themselves because they will understand what their stock is really worth. Money managers who have learned how to evaluate the twenty-first century companies, whose clients are the pension funds worth trillions of dollars, will be huge investors in this market. In January 2000 the MIT Sloan School of Management launched a five-year $10 million program to understand the "new rules of the shifting business landscape . . . focusing on the growing importance of intangible assets including brands, relationships, and knowledge."[23] The Wharton School of Finance, the University of Chicago, and the Peter F. Drucker Graduate School of Management are committed to rethinking how a company's management should be evaluated. During the next six years their discoveries will be disseminated to mutual fund managers around the planet, all having access to NASDAQ stocks 24 hours a day (see Figures 2.13 and 2.14).

## DIGITAL DOW² INDEX FOR THE NEW DOMINANT INVESTMENT SYSTEM

A problem arises in using the NASDAQ composite to represent the new market culture. We explained in Chapter 1 how the major market indexes count the performance of the biggest companies a lot more than they do the smaller ones. Because the realize, capitalize, customize business model allows smaller companies to be more productive than large ones, an appropriate index should give them at least equal credit.

To solve this problem, we selected 60 stocks from a variety of sectors that represent the twenty-first century economy. Each company's business model meets our definition of realize, capitalize, customize.

We call the index *Digital Dow²*. *Digital* innovation is driving the twenty-first century economy; *Dow* acknowledges the evolutionary nature of investing; and the superscript explains the new dominant investment's exponential increase in energy over the old investment culture.

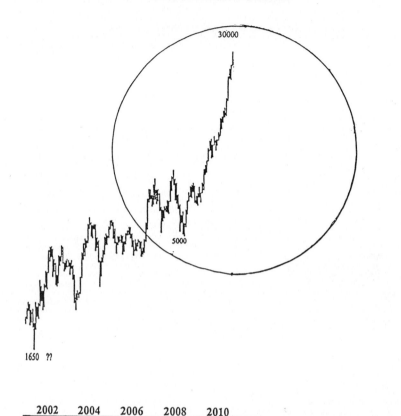

**Figure 2.13** The Great Acceleration of NASDAQ

*Note:* This is the projected path of NASDAQ from 2008 to 2011. Could NASDAQ repeat the pattern of the Dow's acceleration phase?

The intent is for the index to represent important sectors of the modern economy. This is where it differs from other popular indexes. Where the S&P 500, for example, includes industrial, transportation, financial, and utility sectors, the Digital Dow[2] is expanded to include new sectors such as education, merchandising, and healthcare, to name just a few. Although this entire book is devoted to explaining why financial matters should now be viewed differently, Chapters 7 and 8 make it especially clear why any index that holds itself out as being representative of the market must include these new economic sectors.

The index is not meant to be a list of top picks and factors such as current earnings, and stock price are disregarded. The four criteria that companies must meet to be included in the index are as follows:

**Figure 2.14**  The Great Acceleration of the Dow Jones Industrial Average
*Note:* Shown is the Dow's acceleration phase from 1920 to 1929.

1. *Capitalist Toolbox:* Artfully organize and implement the following tools:
   - *Learning interfaces* were coined by computer scientist Alan Kay and refer to the method of collecting data about consumer needs in order to enhance relationships.
   - *Partner interfaces* connect manufacturers, warehouses, suppliers, shippers, haulers, wholesalers, or retailers to organize information more effectively.
   - *Brand-consumer links* touches the consumer at many levels—TV, print, etc.—and links the Internet with bricks-and-mortar businesses.
   - *Transaction links* facilitate frictionless methods of payment or delivery of products.

2. *Expandable Platform:* Can easily evolve from its core competency. A trucking company, for example, must be able to expand into services like consulting, risk management, or logistics services.

3. *Customize Products:* Be able to make changes to products and services after they hit the market and individualize them to consumers or consumer groups.

4. *Relentless Growth:* Can be organic through acquisitions, expansion of market share, or mergers.

A study of the companies of the Digital Dow$^2$ index adds the comfort of specifics to our list of reasons why we can look forward to the formulation phase rallies and eventually the acceleration phase. Many of these stocks have been compartmentalized under the heading of "tech stocks" by those committed to obscuring the facts of the new environment. As you get to know these companies (see Table 2.1), you will learn that they are far from being just tech stocks and are actually important agents of our working economy. Chapter 7 describes the economic sectors in which some of these companies operate.

An example of how a Digital Dow$^2$ company operates differently from its twentieth-century counterpart can be found in Pharmaceutical Product Development Inc. (PPDI). Its visionary chairman and chief executive officer, Fredric Eshelman, realized that PPDI could do more than sell its research services on a contract basis to drug companies. Today, PPDI is an indispensable link in every stage of drug development from initial research to patient consumption. Because it has no sales force or manufacturing facility, it cost-effectively performs functions that the large drug companies cannot. It is small—$1.2 billion compared to Merck at $157 billion or Bristol-Myers at $112 billion— only if you define size in twentieth-century terms. In the new dominant system assets are overhead. PPDI's smaller size is a strength.

- PPD Discovery isolates chemicals, compounds, and genes; discovers their functions; and tells manufacturers what optimal combinations can be used for a particular purpose.
- PPD Development provides clinical and laboratory trials helping drug companies determine how a new drug is best utilized.

For example, when working on a new compound for Eli Lilly, PPDI discovered that its best use was in preventing premature ejaculation. This did not fit into Lilly's product portfolio or marketing plan. The compound was sold to Alza instead in return for a large up-front pay-

**Table 2.1** The Digital Dow[2]

| Symbol | Description | Symbol | Description |
|--------|-------------|--------|-------------|
| ADBE | ADOBE SYSTEMS INC DE | GCOR | GENENCOR INTL INC |
| ADVP | ADVANCEPCS | ROOM | HOTELS.COM |
| AMZN | AMAZON COM INC | ICUI | ICU MEDICAL INC |
| AMSY | AMERICAN MGMT SYSTEMS INC | IDPH | IDEC PHARMACEUTICALS CORP |
| AMGN | AMGEN INC | IMDC | INAMED CORP |
| ANSS | ANSYS INC | INTC | INTEL |
| APOL | APOLLO GROUP INC CLA | KLAC | KLA-TENCOR CORP |
| AMAT | APPLIED MATERIALS INC DE | KROL | KROLL INC |
| APWR | ASTROPOWER INC | LSTR | LANDSTAR SYSTEMS INC |
| BARZ | BARRA INC | MANH | MANHATTAN ASSOCIATES INC |
| BGEN | BIOGEN INC MASS | MSFT | MICROSOFT |
| BBOX | BLACK BOX CORP DE | MUSE | MICROMUSE INC |
| BRCM | BROADCOM CORP CLA | PNRA | PANERA BREAD CO CLA |
| BUCA | BUCA INC | PAYX | PAYCHEX INC |
| CSGS | CSG SYSTEMS INTL INC | PPDI | PHARMACEUTICAL PRODUCT DEV INC |
| CAI | CACI INTL INC CLA | PLCM | POLYCOM INC |
| CECO | CAREER ED CORP | TROW | T ROWE PRICE GROUP INC |
| CEPH | CEPHALON INC | PHCC | PRIORITY HEALTHCARE CORP CL B |
| CKFR | CHECKFREE CORP | QCOM | QUALCOMM INC |
| CMCSK | COMCAST CORP CLA SPL | RETK | RETEK INC |
| CE | CONCORD EFS INC | SCSC | SCANSOURCE INC |
| CNXT | CONEXANT SYSTEMS INC | SEBL | SIEBEL SYSTEMS INC |
| EXBD | CORPORATE EXECUTIVE BRD CO | SPLS | STAPLES INC |
| COST | COSTCO WHOLESALE CORP NEW | SNPS | SYNOPSYS INC |
| DTPI | DIAMONDCLUSTER INTL | TMPW | TMP WORLDWIDE INC |
| EBAY | EBAY INC | WFMI | WHOLE FOODS MKT INC |
| ERTS | ELECTRONIC ARTS | ZRAN | ZORAN CORP |
| EXPE | EXPEDIA INC CLA | CHKP | *** CHECKPOINT SOFTWARE TECH |
| EXLT | EXULT INC | OFIX | *** ORTHOFIX INTERNATIONAL NV |
| FISV | FISERV INC | FLEX | *** FLEXTRONICS INTL LTD USD |

ment and royalties. The Intellectual Property Discovery Group continues to develop this part of the business.

- PPDI partners with its clients to share in the profits from new drugs.
- From communication centers on both coasts, PPDI has a customized process for monitoring patient use.

For example, you have a serious condition, but after two weeks you stop taking the drug because (1) you forget, (2) you experience side effects, or (3) you feel better. PPDI alerts your pharmacist that you have not had a refill. PPDI prepares a communication for your pharmacist and physician, and you will be contacted until the issue is resolved.

By leveraging its resources, PPDI posted a 21% increase in revenue and a 43% increase in earnings during the economic slump of the second quarter of 2001. By year-end 2002, earnings growth was expected to climb another 30%. Its stock performance left the S&P 500 in the dust during the first formulation phase correction, as shown in Figure 2.15.

## 30,000 BY 2011

Most NASDAQ stocks will participate in the acceleration phase. It is likely that smaller companies will do better than the largest. It is likely that stocks that fit the mold of Digital Dow[2] companies will outperform those that do not. It would be beneficial if we could give more mathematical weight to these companies when performance of the commonly used indexes is calculated, instead of giving more weight to the very largest companies as we do today. If we could do that, and if the NASDAQ mirrors the Dow's acceleration phase, it would put the NASDAQ at 30,000 by 2011.

If that sounds like a long climb in just 10 years from a level of 1,600 in 2002, consider this: In January of 1988 the Dow Jones Industrial Average was 2,015. Eleven years later (1999) the Dow reached 11,000. Most people did not see that in the future either.

Those vested in the old dominant investment system have made some major miscalculations lately about this financial frontier we have begun to cross. There is an anxiety that things are spinning away into unfamiliar territory and that this can be controlled with tariffs, embargoes, unions, political action committees, protectionist legislation, regulation, more bureaucrats, corporate welfare, and more over-

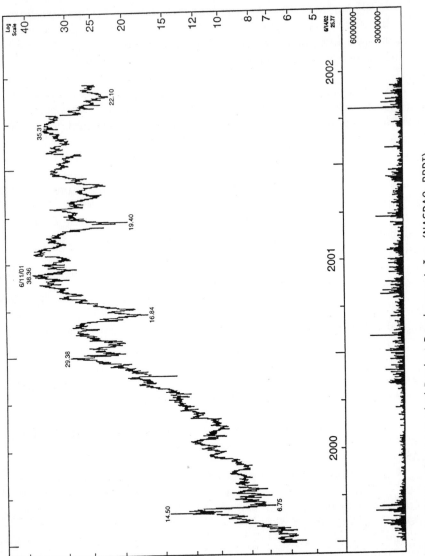

**Figure 2.15** Pharmaceutical Product Development, Inc. (NASDAQ: PPDI)

sight. Fifty years from now, the arrogance of thinking that any of these things will do much more than temporarily slow things down will appear rather silly.

One doesn't control a frontier; the frontier does the controlling. The sage and the visionary adapt to the new environment by welcoming the new idea, watching for openings, and heading for the horizon. That is how we have always done it. Not only are the opportunities intriguing, but it is invigorating to think that the future will change us in ways we do not yet know.

Investing will be as different from the twentieth century as the Internet is from the telegraph. That we know for sure. What is needed is an investment method that can anticipate the future and signal what steps to take. That method is set out for you in the next chapter.

## NOTES

1. Jerry Korn, ed., *This Fabulous Century* (New York: Time-Life Books, 1969), p. 69.

2. Terry Porter, Video Renaissance, personal communication, Sarasota, Florida, June 2001.

3. Mary Greenbaum, "Gauging the Markets Prospects," *Fortune Magazine* 107 (1983): p. 97.

4. Presented at Symposium held at the Plaza Hotel, New York, November 2000.

5. Robert D. Arnott and Ronald J. Ryan, "Death of the Risk Premium," *Journal of Portfolio Management* (2001, summer).

6. Robert D. Arnott, "Partners Message," unpublished paper, May 2001.

7. Robert D. Arnott and Peter Bernstein, "What Risk Premium Is 'Normal'?" unpublished paper, May 2001.

8. Sydney Homer, *A History of Interest Rates* (New Brunswick, NJ: Rutgers University Press, 1963, 1964), pp. 314–316.

9. Ibid.

10. Ibid., pp. 314–316.

11. Ibid.

12. Ibid., p. 239.

13. DuPont is an example.

14. Sydney Homer, *A History of Interest Rates* (New Brunswick, NJ: Rutgers University Press, 1963, 1964), p. 239.

15. IBM stock sold at $85 on December 29, 2000, and at $114.35 on June 30, 2001, for a 34.52% increase.

16. David Hackett Fischer, *The Great Wave* (New York: Oxford University Press, 1996), p. 184.

17. "Business This Week," *The Economist* (2001, April 21): 5.

18. Milton Friedman and Anna Jacobson Schwartz, *A Monetary History*

*of the United States 1867–1960* (Princeton, NJ: National Bureau of Economic Research, 1963).

19. David Hackett Fischer, *The Great Wave* (New York: Oxford University Press, 1996), p. 184.

20. Ibid., p. 184.

21. *A New Economic View of American History: From Colonial Times to 1940* (2nd ed.; New York: W.W. Norton, 1994), p. 510.

22. See Appendix F for calculation.

23. Richard Schmalensee, dean of MIT Sloan School of Management.

# 3

## 911

## Here's the Help You Need to Prosper in the New Investment Culture

*Accumulate all the possible circumstances which shall reinforce the right motives; put yourself assiduously in conditions that encourage the new way.*
—William James, *The Philosophy of William James*

Investing in the era of the new dominant investment system will be easier than in the old one. Like everything else targeted at consumers by the late twentieth century, investing had congealed into a wad of mass-marketing boilerplate. Investors getting skittish about the stock market? Change the name of those growth funds to "growth and income" or "blue-chip growth," and they will keep on selling. Drug stocks in the news because they rose a lot? Cobble together a pharmaceutical fund and shove it down the pipeline. Wall Street as Madison Avenue—pump out product to get even more of investors' dollars jumping on each new bandwagon.

By the very late twentieth century, competition for investment dollars was fierce. It was decided that people would invest more if they felt empowered. They would buy more stocks and mutual funds if they had "control." So, in the 1990s the Internet became to Wall Street what the credit card had become to Madison Avenue a few decades before: the tool that empowered consumers. Investors could check their account values minute by minute, buy and sell stocks, and trade mutual funds 24-7. Just how this would help them create wealth was unclear. (One of the most talented money managers we know still calls us when he wants a stock quote because he is not connected to the Internet.

He does not want his decision making to be clouded by distracting daily, or even weekly, price movements.) Nevertheless, the investing public had its direct link to Wall Street and was supposed to be appreciative.

The bear market of 2000–2002 that ended the discovery phase of the new dominant investment system opened investors' eyes to the flaw in leaving one's personal wealth to the whims of mass marketers. Billions of dollars of unnecessary losses were created because people did not realize that they were concentrated in only one or two sectors of the market. Most still do not understand the characteristics that distinguish the different parts of the market and remain dangerously underdiversified. Nor did the public know that their hard-earned dollars were helping to shore up failing companies like Enron and K-Mart, which were held until the bitter end, in their so-called index and growth funds. The mass-marketing model that brought in hundreds of billions of dollars to banks, insurance companies, trust companies, brokers, and mutual fund companies failed to generate anything close to those kinds of profits for their customers.

## THE ZONE

It is striking how little difference there is between the ad for the battery-powered belt that promises the effortless creation of six-pack abs when strapped to flabby tummies and the ad for the "all-in-one funds" for an "all-in-one strategy" in "just one easy investment." Both are targeted to that part of our nature that wants to believe that life-changing goals can be achieved by taking the path of least resistance.

At some point in the 1990s investment pitchmen took not just a page, but the entire book, from the trillion-dollar vitamin-diet-fitness industry. It is no accident that the words "No Hassle," "Winning Formula," "Superstar," "Smart," "Easy," and "20 Best," which can be found on the cover of *Kiplingers Mutual Funds 2002 Smart Investors Guide,* can also be found on Web sites advertising fad diets and novel muscle-building contraptions. The saying goes that we can never be too rich or too thin, but both of these attributes are very difficult to acquire unless we have inherited either money or perfect genes. So the lure of messages trumpeting the "easy" solution or the "winning formula"— no matter if it is money we want to make or weight we want to lose— is very powerful. But the adult in most of us has learned that life is not so simple.

There is no Santa Claus, and there is no such thing as no-hassle investing. There are no investment superstars or 20 best investments.

What is available is a methodology that is being used right now by fiduciaries responsible for very large pools of money. It will be necessary for individual investors to use this same method in order to navigate the formulation and acceleration phases successfully.

It is sensible that for much of the twentieth century, when the stock market was not as vast and diverse, that the mass marketing business model would have worked as well for investors as it did for customers in all other fields of commerce. But the same realize, capitalize, customize business model that will better serve the twenty-first century consumer of other products and services will also do the best job of sorting through the new complexities of the financial markets.

All of the benefits offered by the realize, capitalize, customize investment methodology can be summarized by saying that it will enable investors to function within their own investment *zones*. We defined this in Chapter 1 as the place where your lifestyle and temperament meet the financial markets. When you are in your zone, you do not have to wonder what the market will do—the system has a built-in mechanism to tell you. The old mass-marketing system told you what to do only *after* market changes had already occurred.

Investment decisions are simpler in your zone. If a stock or fund does not fit into your personalized strategy, you don't need it. You will not have to wonder when to buy or sell; the process will tell you. After a while you may find that your assets are less affected by extreme market conditions.

Getting to your zone requires the application of accepted and proven investment hypotheses. This will take some time and effort to get started, but it will save both in the long run.

### Real Diversification

What will make the realize, capitalize, customize wealth-creation model work is an understanding of the simple concept we call *real diversification*. Most people understand abstractly that they should not put all of their eggs into one basket. In reality, most investors are not aware that they have only a single leaky basket into which they have concentrated their financial future. All of the new clients we have accepted into our practice over the last four years thought that they were diversified, but only 2% actually were. The other 98% were only superficially diversified, if at all. This had led to severe losses during the 2000–2002 market declines. If these people had not taken steps to correct the situation, they would have faced further erosion of their assets during the rest of the formulation phase and would miss out on the acceleration phase altogether.

Superficial diversification is seductively easy—and dangerous. Real diversification is a different matter. There are three reasons why most investors do not do it:

1. Lack of discipline
2. Lack of knowledge
3. Misleading information

Understanding each of these will demystify the investment process (something the old investment culture may not want to see happen) and prove that successful wealth creation is often no more than common sense.

### Lack of Discipline

You know what you have to do to lose weight. Call on your willpower to cut out some of those desserts. Instead, our culture encourages us to delude ourselves into thinking that a pill or a miracle diet will work just as well.

The quirk in our human nature that makes us seek the easy way out has been exploited by the vested interests of the old dominant investment system in a very creative way. We have been convinced that the wee bit of energy required for investing should be spent in front of a computer, digesting diet pills of data, fed to us with the purpose of making everyone feel like an expert. Empowered with all this information, you more readily open your checkbook.

If the dual myths of "everyone can be an expert" and "investing is always easy" are to be maintained, presenting tough choices to those from whom you are trying to extract more investment dollars must be avoided at all costs.

The scheme devised by the mass marketers to solve this problem is to give ratings to funds based on past performance. Those funds that have risen the most get the highest scores. Investors are encouraged to study Web sites and magazines to develop a short list of best funds and then diversify among them. Any diversity arrived at by this process is an illusion.

It fails because the only funds that could have the best performance are the ones that own stocks of the style that has been performing the best. Revisit Figures 1.9 through 1.11 and recall the following: (1) The stock style that performs the best for a few years will peak and then be replaced by another style that will take its turn at being the top performer, and (2) money managers are mandated to specialize in a certain stock style.

We are supposed to feel good about diversifying across our lists of top-rated funds, but this kind of diversity can only be superficial. The names of the funds may differ, but to be the top performers, they must all own stocks of the style that has just risen the most. An analysis of the top-rated funds offered by a variety of financial institutions reveals that they all own pretty much the same stocks. In 1999 the top-ranked funds owned large-cap growth stocks. Their ratings were peddled to the masses, and the money poured in. Push what sells.

In 1999 some of the funds with the worst ratings were those that specialized in large-cap value stocks. Encouraging ownership of large-cap value stocks or the funds that specialized in them was inconsistent with the marketing principle of selling success. According to the rules of the old dominant investment system, only those who were financially dysfunctional would claim ownership of large-cap value investments in 1999. They had averaged only 2% the previous two years, whereas large-cap growth was averaging 39%.[1] Yet, the most constructive decision that investors could have made in 1998 was to move some of their money out of large-cap growth into large-cap value and in 1999 to move even more. The next year large-cap growth lost 17.19%, and large-cap value increased 10.07%.

The discipline required to take profits from a rising investment and put the proceeds into one that seems stagnant is Olympian. Our colleagues will tell you that the toughest part of learning their profession was not taking courses in modern portfolio theory or regression analysis but cultivating the discipline to tune out the witless messages that entice them to follow the herd.

Small-cap value stocks and the fund managers that bought them were another part of the market that has been ignored. They declined 4.87% in 1998 and then fell another 12.32% in 1999. Only the disciplined and the methodical took advantage of this great buying opportunity. In 2000, when the Standard & Poor's (S&P) 500 fell 9.10%, small-cap value funds rose 11.11%. In 2001, when it was hysterically claimed that a crushing bear market had set in, small-cap value stocks rose another 20.15%[2] (see Figure 3.1).

The variety of styles and asset classes that comprise the twenty-first century financial markets are like pistons in an engine. One rises only to fall as another takes its place. Real diversification means that you must have the discipline to add money to, and keep some money in, parts of the market that presently may be lagging in performance. In our business we say, "You aren't diversified unless you hate half of your investments."

### Lack of Knowledge

That the stock market at the beginning of the twenty-first century is a mélange of companies of every size and description, that the most productive of these are not names with which we are most familiar,

| 1991 | 1992 | 1993 | 1994 | 1995 | 1996 | 1997 | 1998 | 1999 | 2000 | 2001 |
|---|---|---|---|---|---|---|---|---|---|---|
| Russell 2000 Growth 51.19% | Russell 2000 Value 29.14% | MSCI EAFE 32.56% | MSCI EAFE 7.78% | Russell 1000 Value 38.36% | S&P 600/BARRA Value 26.10% | S&P 500/BARRA Growth 36.53% | S&P 500/BARRA Growth 42.16% | Russell Mid Cap Growth 51.29% | S&P 400/BARRA Value 27.84% | Russell 2000 Value 14.02% |
| Russell 2000 46.04% | Russell 2000 18.41% | Russell 2000 Value 23.77% | S&P 500/BARRA Growth 3.13% | S&P 500/BARRA Growth 38.13% | S&P 500/BARRA Growth 23.97% | S&P 600/BARRA Growth 36.37% | Russell 1000 Growth 38.71% | Russell 2000 Growth 43.09% | Russell 2000 Value 22.83% | S&P 600/BARRA Value 13.10% |
| Russell 2000 Value 41.70% | S&P 400/BARRA Value 16.02% | Russell 2000 18.88% | Russell 1000 Growth 2.62% | Russell 1000 37.77% | Russell 1000 Growth 23.12% | Russell 1000 Value 35.18% | Russell 3000 Growth 35.02% | Russell 3000 Growth 33.83% | S&P 600/BARRA Value 20.86% | S&P 400/BARRA Value 7.14% |
| Russell 3000 Growth 41.66% | Russell 3000 Value 14.90% | Russell 3000 Value 18.65% | Russell 3000 Growth 2.20% | S&P 500 37.58% | S&P 500 22.96% | Russell 3000 Value 34.83% | S&P 400/BARRA Growth 34.86% | Russell 1000 Growth 33.16% | Russell Mid Cap Value 19.18% | S&P 600 6.54% |
| Russell 1000 Growth 41.27% | Russell 1000 Value 13.58% | S&P 500/BARRA Value 18.60% | S&P 500 1.32% | Russell 1000 Growth 37.18% | Russell 1000 22.45% | Russell Mid Cap Value 34.37% | S&P 500 28.58% | S&P 400/BARRA Growth 28.74% | S&P 400 17.51% | Russell 2000 2.49% |
| S&P 500/BARRA Growth 38.37% | S&P 400 11.91% | Russell 1000 Value 18.07% | Russell 1000 0.39% | Russell 3000 Value 37.03% | S&P 500/BARRA Value 21.99% | S&P 400/BARRA Value 34.32% | Russell 1000 27.02% | S&P 500/BARRA Growth 28.25% | S&P 600 11.80% | Russell Mid Cap Value 2.33% |
| Russell 3000 Value 33.68% | S&P 500/BARRA Value 10.52% | S&P 400/BARRA Value 13.96% | Russell 3000 0.19% | S&P 500/BARRA Value 37.00% | Russell 3000 Growth 21.88% | S&P 500 33.36% | Russell 3000 24.14% | MSCI EAFE 26.96% | S&P 400/BARRA Growth 9.16% | S&P 400 -0.60% |
| Russell 1000 Growth 33.04% | Russell 3000 9.59% | S&P 400/BARRA Growth 13.67% | S&P 400/BARRA Value -0.57% | Russell 3000 36.80% | Russell 3000 21.82% | Russell 1000 32.85% | DJ Total Market 23.15% | Russell 2000 21.26% | Russell Mid Cap 8.25% | S&P 600/BARRA Growth -1.18% |
| S&P 500 30.47% | Russell 1000 8.93% | S&P 400/BARRA Value 13.43% | S&P 500/BARRA Value -0.64% | Russell 3000 Growth 36.57% | Russell 1000 Value 21.64% | S&P 400 32.25% | MSCI EAFE 20.00% | S&P 500 21.04% | Russell 3000 Value 8.04% | Russell 3000 Value -4.33% |
| DJ Total Market 29.78% | Russell 2000 Growth 7.77% | Russell 2000 Growth 13.37% | Russell 2000 Value -1.54% | S&P 400/BARRA Value 34.04% | Russell 3000 Value 21.59% | Russell 3000 31.78% | S&P 400 19.11% | Russell 1000 20.91% | Russell 1000 Value 7.02% | Russell 1000 Value -5.59% |
| Russell 3000 Value 25.41% | S&P 500 7.62% | Russell 3000 Value 10.88% | Russell 2000 -1.82% | DJ Total Market 33.47% | Russell 2000 Value 21.37% | Russell 2000 Value 31.78% | Russell Mid Cap Growth 17.86% | Russell 3000 20.90% | S&P 500/BARRA Value 6.08% | Russell Mid Cap -5.62% |

**Figure 3.1**  Periodic Table of Capital Market Returns

*Note:* This figure ranks the performance of iShares, which represent a variety of stock styles. The retur listed from best to worst for each calendar year.

*Source:* "Periodic Table of Capital Market Returns Size/Style and Country" printed with permission Bar Global Advisors

| | 1992 | 1993 | 1994 | 1995 | 1996 | 1997 | 1998 | 1999 | 2000 | 2001 | |
|---|---|---|---|---|---|---|---|---|---|---|---|
| | S&P 400/BARRA Growth 6.94% | Russell 1000 10.18% | Russell 3000 Value -1.95% | Russell 2000 Growth 31.04% | S&P 600 21.32% | Russell 1000 Growth 30.49% | Russell 1000 Value 15.63% | DJ Total Market 20.57% | S&P 600/BARRA Growth 0.57% | S&P 400/BARRA Growth -7.97% | High |
| | DJ Total Market 5.78% | S&P 500 10.08% | Russell 1000 Value -1.98% | S&P 400 30.95% | Russell Mid Cap Value 20.26% | S&P 400/BARRA Growth 30.17% | S&P 500/BARRA Value 14.68% | S&P 600/BARRA Growth 19.57% | Russell 2000 -3.02% | Russell 2000 Growth -9.23% | |
| | Russell 3000 Growth 5.22% | DJ Total Market 6.98% | DJ Total Market -2.35% | S&P 600/BARRA Value 30.69% | DJ Total Market 19.59% | S&P 500/BARRA Value 29.99% | Russell 3000 Value 13.50% | Russell Mid Cap 18.23% | Russell 3000 -7.46% | Russell 3000 -11.46% | |
| | S&P 500/BARRA Growth 5.06% | Russell 3000 Growth 3.69% | Russell 2000 Growth -2.43% | S&P 600 29.96% | S&P 400/BARRA Value 19.40% | DJ Total Market 29.65% | Russell Mid Cap 10.09% | S&P 400 14.72% | Russell 1000 -7.79% | S&P 500/BARRA Value -11.71% | |
| | Russell 1000 Growth 4.99% | Russell 1000 Growth 2.87% | S&P 400 -3.58% | S&P 600/BARRA Growth 29.07% | S&P 400 19.20% | Russell Mid Cap 29.01% | Russell Mid Cap Value 5.08% | S&P 500/BARRA Value 12.72% | S&P 500 -9.10% | S&P 500 -11.89% | |
| | MSCI EAFE -12.17% | S&P 500/BARRA Growth 1.67% | S&P 600/BARRA Value -4.52% | Russell 2000 28.45% | Russell Mid Cap 19.00% | Russell 3000 Growth 28.74% | S&P 400/BARRA Value 4.67% | S&P 600 12.40% | DJ Total Market -9.27% | DJ Total Market -11.95% | |
| | | | S&P 600 -4.77% | S&P 400/BARRA Growth 27.30% | S&P 400/BARRA Growth 18.41% | S&P 600 25.58% | S&P 600/BARRA Growth 2.29% | Russell 1000 Growth 7.35% | Russell Mid Cap Growth -11.75% | Russell 1000 -12.45% | |
| | | | S&P 600/BARRA Growth -5.47% | Russell 2000 Value 25.75% | Russell Mid Cap Growth 17.48% | Russell Mid Cap Growth 22.54% | Russell 2000 Growth 1.23% | Russell 3000 Value 6.65% | MSCI EAFE -14.17% | S&P 500/BARRA Growth -12.73% | |
| | | | S&P 400/BARRA Growth -6.98% | Russell Mid Cap Growth 17.01% | Russell 2000 16.49% | Russell 2000 22.36% | S&P 600 -1.31% | S&P 600/BARRA Value 3.03% | S&P 500/BARRA Growth -22.08% | Russell 3000 Growth -19.63% | |
| | | | | Russell Mid Cap 16.15% | S&P 600/BARRA Growth 16.09% | S&P 600/BARRA Growth 15.58% | Russell 2000 -2.55% | S&P 400/BARRA Value 2.33% | Russell 1000 Growth -22.42% | Russell Mid Cap Growth -20.15% | |
| | | | | Russell Mid Cap Value 15.44% | Russell 2000 Growth 11.26% | Russell 2000 Growth 12.95% | S&P 600/BARRA Value -5.06% | Russell 2000 Value -1.49% | Russell 3000 Growth -22.42% | Russell 1000 Growth -20.42% | |
| | | | | MSCI EAFE 11.21% | MSCI EAFE 6.05% | MSCI EAFE 1.78% | Russell 2000 Value -6.45% | Russell Mid Cap Value -0.11% | Russell 2000 Growth -22.43% | MSCI EAFE -21.44% | Low |

**3.1** *(continued)*

and that most new jobs are being created by an entirely new way of doing business are viewed by the investment establishment as a set of
facts unrelated to the marketing process. The importance of real diversification is not pushed down the distribution channels of many
banks, mutual fund companies, insurance companies, 401(k) vendors,
trust companies, or brokerage houses. It did not reach most investors
in time to prevent significant losses in 2000–2002. It is not reaching
most investors who need to be taking advantage of the opportunities
presented by the new dominant investment system. Readers who are
now hearing the message of real diversification for the first time
should pay particular attention to the procedures outlined in this
chapter.

For readers who work in a sector of the financial industry where
indifference to investment methodology and technique has become
commonplace, we recommend the sixth edition of *Investment Analysis
and Portfolio Management*.[3] It explores in a clear and logical manner
the reasons why real diversification is so effective in maximizing returns while controlling risk.

### Misleading Information

A cartel of some large mutual fund companies is responsible for ensuring that the assets of pension plans, retirement accounts, foundations, trusts, and personal accounts are dangerously underdiversified.

We will explain by using the example of the "Mass-Marketing Mutual Fund Company." The name is fictitious because the abomination
of management, or lack thereof, is so pervasive among some commonly
held retail mutual funds that it would be unfair to cite just one. It is
likely not only that you would recognize this mutual fund company's
name, but also that you might be familiar with the individual funds.
They are some of the most widely held investments in the United
States, so we fictionalized their names as well.

What is not fiction but frighteningly real are the dates and largest
holdings of each of the funds. We list each one's major stock positions
at the beginning of the bull market of 1997, at the peak of the bull
market in 1999, and at the onset of the formulation phase. You will see
that every fund owned practically the same stocks in each year we examined.

What is tragic is that many people who invested with this company
through their 401(k) plans at work or for their own individual portfolios spread their money across these funds assuming that they were
achieving the risk-reducing benefits of diversification. One would log-
ically assume that each fund would own different stocks. Why else
would they offer them?

---

## COMMODITIZED PORTFOLIO MANAGEMENT

Mass-Marketing Mutual Fund Company Funds
Top Holdings as of 9/30/1997

*Duplicate holdings are in italic*

**Conservative Growth Fund**
*General Electric*
*Philip Morris*
*American Express*
*Royal Dutch*
*Bristol Myers*
*Citicorp*
*Fannie Mae*
Tyco Intl.
Pepsi
Proctor & Gamble

**Middle of the Road Growth Fund**
*Fannie Mae*
*Philip Morris*
General Motors
Freddie Mac
Columbia HCA
IBM
Home Depot
Wal-Mart
Fleet Financial

**Gung-Ho Growth Fund**
Citicorp
Philip Morris
General Electric
Bank of America
American Express
Bristol Myers
British Petroleum
Allied Signal
Tsy 7%-06
Royal Dutch

**Herd Mentality Fund**
*General Electric*
*Philip Morris*
*American Express*
*British Petroleum*
*Fannie Mae*
Allstate
*Bank of America*
Bank of New York
*Wal-Mart*
Washington Mutual

**They'll Never Know the Difference Fund**
*General Electric*
Compaq Computer
Intel
*Citicorp*
*Philip Morris*
Microsoft
Merck
*Home Depot*
*IBM*
*Bank of America*

---

This is where the fantasy that "we sell mutual funds, and we are here to help" falls apart. Although glossy ads assure you that you will be "put on the right course" and that "we understand what you need," and although presumably wealthy aging baby boomers gaze into the sunset in a full-page promotion of why you can trust a company to manage your estate, know that what is frequently being sold is product that flows from a single spigot, bottled and labeled like snake oil in a variety of packages intended to appeal to every need of every consumer.

What you should do right now is demand of your mutual fund company, bank, insurance company, trust company, broker, or financial planner a list of the stocks in your mutual funds. The mutual fund in-

## COMMODITIZED PORTFOLIO MANAGEMENT

### Mass-Marketing Mutual Fund Company Funds
### Top Holdings as of 12/30/1999

*Duplicate holdings are in italic*

**Conservative Growth Fund**
*General Electric*
*Merck*
*American Express*
*Microsoft*
*Bristol-Myers Squibb*
*Philip Morris*
*Fannie Mae*
*Tyco Intl.*
Wal-Mart

**Middle of the Road Growth Fund**
*General Motors*
*Time Warner*
*Tyco Intl.*
*Wal-Mart*
*Citicorp*
*Bristol-Myers Squibb*
*Merck*
*Microsoft*
*American Home Products*
CVS Corp.

**Gung-Ho Growth Fund**
MBPOOL.6.5 FNMA
*General Electric*
*Citicorp*
*American Home Products*
Unilever
*American Express*
*Bristol-Myers Squibb*
*Merck*
Chase Manhattan

**Herd Mentality Fund**
*General Electric*
*American Express*
*Citicorp*
*Fannie Mae*
British Pet. Co. PLC
*Philip Morris*
*Wal-Mart*
Allstate
Bank of New York
*Bank of America*

**They'll Never Know the Difference Fund**
*General Electric*
*Microsoft*
*Wal-Mart*
*Merck*
Home Depot
*Bristol-Myers Squibb*
*Citicorp*
*Cisco Systems*
*Lucent Tech.*
American Intl. Group

dustry is not held to many regulatory standards. There is no requirement that the information on purchases and present holdings be current. It is likely that you will be provided with old information. If this is the case, waste no time in moving your money to someone who will provide you with complete, up-to-date lists of at least the major holdings of your funds so you know where your money is going.

*Index Funds.* Most people understand that the money invested in an index fund goes toward the purchase of an investment that duplicates, say, the S&P 500. What could be misleading about that?

Recognize that any investment index is a computer-generated

## COMMODITIZED PORTFOLIO MANAGEMENT

Mass-Marketing Mutual Fund Company Funds
Top Holdings as of 9/30/2000

*Duplicate holdings are in italic*

**Conservative Growth Fund**
*General Electric*
*Exxon Mobil*
*Fannie Mae*
*Cisco Systems*
Pfizer Inc.
*Lilly (Eli) & Co.*
*Microsoft*
*Intel*
American Intl Group Inc.
Merck

**Middle of the Road Growth Fund**
*General Electric*
*Lilly (Eli) & Co.*
General Dynamic
*Cisco Systems*
*Fannie Mae*
Exxon Mobil
Philip Morris
*Microsoft*
Walgreen

**Gung-Ho Growth Fund**
*Exxon Mobil*
*Fannie Mae*
Freddie Mac
*General Electric*
*SBC Communications*
*Lilly (Eli) & Co.*
*Citigroup*
Chase Manhattan
*BP Amoco PLC*
Bristol-Myers Squibb

**Herd Mentality Fund**
*Exxon Mobil*
*Citigroup*
*General Electric*
*Fannie Mae*
*SBC Communications*
Bank of New York
*BP Amoco PLC*
American Express
*Lilly (Eli) & Co.*
Wells Fargo

**They'll Never Know the Difference Fund**
*General Electric*
*Citigroup*
*Cisco Systems*
*Exxon Mobil*
*Microsoft*
Tyco Intl Ltd.
Home Depot
*Intel*
EMC Corp.
*Lilly (Eli) & Co.*

chimera. It is a virtual reality. It does not exist. In the real world a fund's investors are adding and redeeming money all the time. There is no possible way to mirror a static group of stocks. Different index funds solve the problem different ways. Here is an excerpt from the April 26, 2002, Vanguard 500 prospectus:

> Each portfolio of the trust may utilize futures contracts, options, warrants, convertible securities, and swap agreements. Specifically each portfolio may enter into futures contracts and options . . . provided not more than 20% of a portfolio's assets are invested in futures and options at any time.

## COMMODITIZED PORTFOLIO MANAGEMENT

### Mass-Marketing Mutual Fund Company Funds
### Top Holdings as of 6/30/2001

*Duplicate holdings are in italic*

**Conservative Growth Fund**
*Exxon Mobil*
*Federal Natl. Mtg. Assn.*
*Citigroup*
Federal Home Loan Mtg.
JP Morgan Chase
*General Electric*
*SBC Communications*
U.S. Treasury Notes
U.S. Treasury Bonds
Lilly (Eli) & Co.

**Middle of the Road Growth Fund**
*Citigroup*
*Exxon Mobil*
*Fannie Mae*
*General Electric*
*SBC Communications*
*JP Morgan Chase*
*Tyco Intl. Ltd.*
Wells Fargo
BP Amoco PLC
Bank of New York

**Gung-Ho Growth Fund**
*Exxon Mobil*
*Fannie Mae*
McDonald's
*Pfizer*
*American Intl. Group*
Berkshire Hathaway
*Viacom "B"*
CVS Corp.
Citizen Elec. Co. Ltd.
*Cisco Systems*

**Herd Mentality Fund**
*General Electric*
*Citigroup*
*Exxon Mobil*
*American Intl. Group*
*Viacom*
*Pfizer*
Tyco Intl. Ltd. New
*Microsoft*
Home Depot
AOL Time Warner

**They'll Never Know the Difference Fund**
*General Electric*
*Exxon Mobil*
*Fannie Mae*
*Microsoft*
*Pfizer*
*Citigroup*
USA Education
*Philip Morris*
*American Intl. Group*
*Bristol-Myers Squibb*

What these quotes reveal is that when you buy this index fund, you are buying some exotic securities, and a portion of the fund can be classified as a hedge fund. This is not a plain-vanilla basket of 500 stocks.

It can be argued that index funds mislead no one. After all, we were able to obtain this quote easily from the fine print of the prospectus. Still, considering all the so-called information and promotional material that has made index funds so popular, it is surprising that we have yet to meet a single Vanguard 500 index fund investor who understands that a sizable chunk of their money may not be invested in S&P 500 stocks at all.

It is undeniable that those vested in keeping the old dominant in-

## COMMODITIZED PORTFOLIO MANAGEMENT

### Mass-Marketing Mutual Fund Company Funds
### Top Holdings as of 5/30/2002

*Duplicate holdings are in italic*

**Conservative Growth Fund**
Pepsico
Colgate Palmolive
3M
Berkshire Hathaway
*Exxon Mobil*
Lockheed Martin
*Pfizer*
*BP PLC*
Alberta Energy Ltd.
Avon Prods.

**Middle of the Road Growth Fund**
*Citigroup*
*General Electric*
*Microsoft*
*Viacom Inc. CL B*
*American Intl. Group*
*Exxon Mobil*
*Wal-Mart*
*Pfizer*
Home Depot
Philip Morris

**Gung-Ho Growth Fund**
*Federal Natl. Mtg. Assn.*
*Citigroup*
*Exxon Mobil*
SBC Communications
Bellsouth
Wells Fargo
*BP PLC*
Bank of America
*General Electric*
Total FINA ELF S A

**Herd Mentality Fund**
*Microsoft*
*General Electric*
*Pfizer*
Intel
*Wal-Mart*
*American Intl. Group*
*Citigroup*
Johnson & Johnson
Wyeth
Cisco Systems

**They'll Never Know the Difference Fund**
*Microsoft*
*Citigroup*
*Pfizer*
*General Electric*
*American Intl. Group*
Bristol-Myers Squibb
*Federal Natl. Mtg. Assn.*
Gillette
Federal Home Loan Mtg.
*Viacom Inc. CL B*

vestment system's mass-marketing methods alive have been successful. Intelligent, assertive people allow themselves to be manipulated by the old investment culture in ways they would never tolerate in any other aspect of their lives. They see the stock market as crazy and unpredictable. What is crazy are the things that we are being told about the stock market, and what is unpredictable is the next scheme that will be employed to sell more product. The rest of this chapter explains the investor-friendly process of realize, capitalize, customize that must be employed to help you consistently make money over the next 12 years. As you use it, you will relieve yourself of the burden of wondering what the markets are going to do to you next.

## FINDING YOUR INVESTMENT ZONE BY REALIZING, CAPITALIZING, CUSTOMIZING: THE TWENTY-FIRST CENTURY INVESTMENT STRATEGY

A conflict of cultures occurs at this point as you decide for yourself how your money will be handled from now on. You may be a little skeptical about how successful this new approach will be. The first step may be to resolve this issue by remembering that the process we outline next is being taught right now in the best schools of financial analysis and investment strategy in the country. Its simplicity and common sense are its best features.

### Step 1: Realize

We have already explained how the realize process is used by Digital Dow[2] companies today to test the viability of new projects and assess their effect on current cash flows and the future value of the corporation. Computers allow this to be accomplished in a virtual setting where a variety of contingencies and circumstances can be analyzed. Investors can do the same. The starting point is to decide what value one's financial assets need to be on some future date.

Say, for example, that 11 years hence, enough money will need to accumulate to generate cash flow of $250,000 per year. Next, assess the current value of the assets plus how much can be contributed to achieve the target. Subtract liabilities such as inflation, taxes, mortgages, living expenses, and educational expenses and solve for an annual rate of return that will be required from the investments to achieve the desired goal.

The best people to help with this process are qualified consultants at full-service financial institutions and financial planners. Many do-it-yourself programs can be too simplistic. The ones that are not simplistic require input such as inflation rates; federal, state, and local tax brackets; cost of living adjustments; and social security calculations. Being off only a few percentage points on any of these will give a result that will be wrong by thousands of dollars, rendering the entire process useless.

#### The Diagnosis

By carefully inputting relevant data, a picture of one's financial self will materialize in front of the skilled practitioner. This process is no different from getting a thorough exam from a physician. Vital signs are analyzed; the viability of the metabolism is monitored; liabilities are dissected; and then a diagnosis is reached. The doctor's diagnosis may indicate that the cholesterol level must fall below 100. The financial diagnosis may be that an average return of 11% per year is required.

## Sample Strategic Allocation

| | |
|---|---|
| Large Growth | 17% |
| Large Value | 18% |
| Small Growth | 2% |
| Small Value | 3% |
| International Stocks | 10% |
| High Yield Bond | 10% |
| Mortgage Backed Bonds | 5% |
| Long-Term Bonds | 5% |
| Intermediate Bonds | 23% |
| International Bonds | 5% |
| Cash | 2% |
| | |
| Annualized Expected Return | 9.18% |
| Annualized Expected Standard Deviation | 9.27% |
| Probability of Achieving 8% over 5 Years | 61.2% |
| Probability of Negative Return over 5 Years | 6.10% |
| Probability of Negative Return over 5 Years | 1.34% |
| Expected Best Case over 1 Year | 27.72% |
| Expected Worst Case over 1 Year | −9.36% |
| Expected Best Case over 5 Years | 17.57% |
| Expected Worst Case over 5 Years | .89% |

*Note:* This example is for illustrative purposes only. It should not be construed as advice; nor does it provide relevant data on the allocation used in the example.

### The Prescription

A doctor will prescribe a portfolio of remedies such as changes in diet, an exercise regimen, and medication. A financial consultant will prescribe the specific amounts of money that must be invested in each style and asset class to achieve the 11% return.

A doctor will caution that the medication will have certain side effects and ask if that sounds tolerable. A financial consultant may caution that the probability is high that during one year out of the next six the portfolio may temporarily lose 9.36% and ask if that can be tolerated. If not, a different allocation will be prescribed that may deliver a lesser rate of return, but the trade-off will be a worse-case scenario of only −6.23%.

### The Science

The "laboratories" of many full-service financial institutions are where the analysis of the potential return and risk characteristics of each style and asset class is made. These laboratories have become some of their firm's most valued assets. Their budgets often pay the salaries of Phd's and certified financial analysts who study the properties of each style and asset class and sit on asset allocation committees.

It is the large financial institutions with large companies and government entities as clients that created these laboratories. They grew out of the need to have a systematic method of managing large pools of assets under rapidly changing market conditions. The revenue required to do this was spent wisely. The information generated is now being shared with entities outside the firms, such as financial planners, and by qualified financial consultants within the firms themselves who work with noninstitutional clients. Track records showing the success of recommendations should be made available upon request.

The name of the process developed by these laboratories is *optimization*. This means constructing the portfolio that will provide the optimal return commensurate with the least amount of risk.

Suppose that interest rates rise, the U.S. dollar falls in value, or emerging market stocks jump 67% in one year. Economic events like these will affect the anticipated return on each style and asset class. Future expectations must be reevaluated, and a new prescription will be required for the asset allocation. This process is called *reoptimization*. It is driven by changes in economic conditions. Sometimes portfolios do not need to be reoptimized for two years or more, and sometimes it is necessary two or three times a year. A financial advisor would be expected to know when optimizing is necessary and to perform the process in a timely and cost-effective manner.

## Step 2: Capitalize

Once an investor knows exactly what he or she is trying to accomplish and the asset allocation needed to get there, the funding of the investment program can begin. It is a good idea to seek the services of a certified public accountant or a financial planner to ensure that the program is being funded in the most effective way. Home equity loans, debt consolidation, or mortgage refinancing should be analyzed from the perspectives of both tax and cash flow.

## Step 3: Customize

The first two steps of the process have made this one easy. A portfolio is customized by investing the money according to the percentages outlined in the prescription. It is no coincidence that the portfolio that is constructed is likely to be very different from what had been done before. There is a reason why this is, in fact, very likely.

Once the process of mass marketing investments had been perfected, it was discovered that greater control over market share could be achieved by mass marketing investment guidance as well. The only way this could be accomplished was to stereotype investments and stereotype investors so that so-called help could be packaged and delivered. One of the cutest of these uniformly boxed strategies was to use an investor's age as the indicator of how much money should be in bonds. The rest of the money should be in stocks. It goes like this:

| Age | Stock Allocation | Bond Allocation |
| --- | --- | --- |
| 20 | 80 | 20 |
| 30 | 70 | 30 |
| 40 | 60 | 40 |
| 50 | 50 | 50 |
| 60 | 40 | 60 |
| 70 | 30 | 70 |

Never mind that a 60-year-old retiring in 1993 with over half of his or her investments going into bonds would have immediately lost 7.64% in 1997, another .87% in 1996, and another 8.74% in 1999.[4] Bonds are not always conservative, and they can be as volatile as stocks. Never mind that a person investing in the stock market from 1969 to 1983 would not have made any money for 14 years. This would have been devastating to a 40-year-old trying to save for retirement who, according to the logic just presented, would have been told to keep 60% of his or her money in stocks. The egregious stereotyping of investments results in recommendations that can be totally remote from the realities of the marketplace. The only thing worse is the stereotyping of investors.

We have spoken with too many upset 20- and 30-year-olds to count who were told that because of their age that they should be aggressive, that most of their money should be not just in stocks but in the riskiest stocks because they have the most growth potential. That such an investment posture was totally anathema to their temperament and lifestyle was not even considered. These individuals reacted to market declines by selling at low points and continually creating losses for themselves.

At the other end of the spectrum we have plenty of 70- and 80-year-old clients who tolerate volatility well, understand the investment process, and would fire us immediately if we told them to put 80% of their assets into the bond market.

The labels *aggressive* and *conservative* are overused and misunderstood. Most people equate aggressive with making lots of money and conservative with sticking it under the mattress. The reality is very different. A math lesson will explain.

When clients are asked which would they rather have—Investment A, which offers a 7% return each year for four years, or Investment B, which offers 15% per year for three years and then declines 15% in the fourth year (a distinct probability)—those that have been stereotyped as aggressive pick Investment B. They think it may be risky, but they can put up with it because they will be rewarded for it.

Individuals stereotyped as conservative, because of their age or because they have fewer assets, resign themselves to picking Investment A, assuming that they will end up with less.

Both investors are wrong. The conservative person selecting Investment A ends up like this:

Investment A

| Year 1 | Year 2 | Year 3 | Year 4 | Average Return |
|--------|--------|--------|--------|----------------|
| 7% | 7% | 7% | 7% | 7% |

Here is what the aggressive people wind up with after all their risk taking:

Investment B

| Year 1 | Year 2 | Year 3 | Year 4 | Average Return |
|--------|--------|--------|--------|----------------|
| +15% | +15% | +15% | −15% | 6.68% |

This is one reason why some people erode large sums of money or are unable to accumulate it in the first place. The impact of losses is not understood. It takes a 100% gain to make up a 50% loss, and then you will only be getting back to where you started.

## THE ANSWER TO LACK OF DISCIPLINE

An important benefit of a customized portfolio is that it allows the use of a technique we alluded to earlier in managing the problem of discipline. This technique, called *rebalancing,* helps to anticipate market movements and suggests the appropriate actions that need to be taken, all without changing either the customized strategy or the attitude toward risk. It works like this:

For a risk-tolerant portfolio requiring growth, the newly diversified portfolio may initially be allocated like the first column in the following table.[5]

|                                  | Initial Allocation | 1 Year Later |
|----------------------------------|:------------------:|:------------:|
| Intermediate Fixed Income Bonds  | 14%                | 10%          |
| Large-Cap Growth Stocks          | 20%                | 16%          |
| Large-Cap Value Stocks           | 10%                | 4%           |
| Small-Cap Growth Stocks          | 18%                | 28%          |
| Small-Cap Value Stocks           | 18%                | 23%          |
| International Stocks             | 7%                 | 4%           |
| Emerging Market Stocks           | 13%                | 15%          |

The second column shows that small-cap growth stocks are no longer 18% of the portfolio but 28% one year later. This is because small-cap growth stocks *rose* so much relative to the other investments. Large-cap value stocks are no longer 10% of the portfolio but only 4% because they *declined* relative to the other investments. The other investments have also taken up a greater or lesser percentage of the investment pie depending on their performance during the year.

To rebalance the portfolio, simply take it back to its initial allocation of one year previous as shown in the third column in the following table.

|                                  | Initial Allocation | 1 Year Later | Rebalance |      |
|----------------------------------|:------------------:|:------------:|:---------:|:----:|
| Intermediate Fixed Income Bonds  | 14%                | 10%          | Add       | 4%   |
| Large-Cap Growth Stocks          | 20%                | 16%          | Add       | 4%   |
| Large-Cap Value Stocks           | 10%                | 4%           | Add       | 6%   |
| Small-Cap Growth Stocks          | 18%                | 28%          | Subtract  | 10%  |
| Small-Cap Value Stocks           | 18%                | 23%          | Subtract  | 5%   |
| International Stocks             | 7%                 | 4%           | Add       | 3%   |
| Emerging Market Stocks           | 13%                | 15%          | Subtract  | 2%   |

The third column of this table shows that in rebalancing this portfolio, 10% is taken from small cap-growth stocks. The technique forces a taking of profits from the sector that went up the most. If it goes up more, it is fine—18% of the portfolio will still benefit.

The proceeds will be deposited in the areas that did not do as well during the year. This makes sense because the prices of the securities in these sectors will be cheaper.

Rebalancing forces action contrary to what the mass media may be advocating. They would be touting the incredibly good performance of small-cap growth stocks. Past performance numbers would be advertised. If you bought into the sales pitch, you would be adding money at or near the top of the small-cap growth cycle. The result is predictable.

Think of money as water. It will naturally seek the lowest levels. Rebalancing is the technique that helps to make the most out of this natural law of the financial markets. An experienced investment consultant should be able to provide an efficient and cost-effective way to implement this procedure.

Rebalancing should be done at least annually. It cannot hurt to do it more often if the initial allocation gets out of whack. In 1998 and 1999 we rebalanced our accounts three times per year because large-cap growth stocks were rising so dramatically during the discovery phase.

Since the market corrections of 2000–2002 we have heard a lot more in the financial media about value stocks, value-oriented mutual funds, and diversification. This is good. The danger is that people will fall under the mistaken impression that value stocks are inherently safer. They may not understand that much of their safety stems from the fact that their performance does not correlate with growth stocks and that they are best utilized within an optimized portfolio.

The remainder of the formulation phase could be characterized by a lot of performance rotation among the styles and asset classes of the markets. If the principles laid out in this chapter are utilized, there will be no looking back over one's shoulder and buying what should be sold and selling what should be bought. By employing the realize, capitalize, customize investment methodology, investors can stay a step or two ahead of the game, comfortably in their zone, taking advantage of the opportunities ahead.

• • •

Someone handed us a magazine recently with a feature article titled "Best Performing Funds of the Last 25 Years." The article said that any fund that has been around for 25 years has seen "every kind of market" and that from this the funds' managers can extrapolate the future. Their "historic insights" from two decades "add depth," the article said.

We have shown that not only are the last 25 years an insufficient period of time on which to base one's assumptions, but that they are the wrong 25 years. The article was off by a century. Part II explains why this is so. It provides the historic data and context for the material in this chapter. The discoveries explored in Part II inspired this book.

## NOTES

1. In terms of yearly performance, Wilshire Target Large Value was 11.25% in 1998 and −7.11 in 1999. Wilshire Target Large Growth was 42.21% in 1998 and 35.53% in 1999.

2. Source: Wilshire Target Indexes.

3. Frank K. Reilly and Keith C. Brown, *Investment Analysis and Portfolio Management* (Fort Worth, TX: Dryden Press, 2000).

4. Measurement: Lehman Brothers U.S. Treasury Index.

5. This is an example only and should not be considered a recommendation because personal circumstances and risk tolerance vary widely.

# Part Two

# HISTORICAL PERSPECTIVE

# 4

# THE NECESSARY REVOLUTION

## Why We Needed a New Dominant Investment System and How We Got One

*Although impatient for the morning, I slept soundly and had no need for cheering dreams. Facts are better than dreams.*
—Winston Churchill, *The Second World War*

The sun was not even close to rising, and already the phone was ringing off the hook. As I threw my briefcase under the desk, I saw that it was one of our private lines. It must be an important client, and it must be urgent for them to be calling the office at 5:30 A.M. I was right on both counts.

Jim C. had overcome all obstacles with integrity and determination to create his fortune. He was not easily rattled. "I want you to help me set up an offshore account," he said. "We've got to do it quickly." He had not slept all night.

Shadows of money laundering and sly foreign operatives figured into my impressions as Mr. C. went down his list of millions of dollars in stocks and bonds. The drama was no doubt enhanced by my low caffeine level.

This is a man who hung tough as the Dow lost nearly half its value in 1973 and 1974.[1] He kept his faith in the economy as the savings and loan (S&L) industry fraudulently sucked billions out of it in the mid-1980s. He rode out the junk bond scandals[2] and the market crash of 1987.[3] So what was this final straw laid atop the pile in 1989?

Before you can apprehend the significance of Mr. C.'s request, you must learn how brittle the dominant investment system of the

Dow had become by 1989. The grand old lady's resilience had diminished. Her tolerance for the rambunctiousness of a capitalist economy was exhausted. This was not the lusty Dow of 30 and 40 years previous.

The Dow was in its prime in the 1950s and early 1960s. From its level of 198.89 on January 3, 1950, it more than tripled by January 5, 1960, when it hit 685.47. Look for a date marking the pinnacle of the Dow's career as the dominant investment, and you will find February 9, 1966, when it reached 995.15. If the Dow were an athlete, this would have been like Michael Jordan's winning shot in the 1998 NBA championship. It was a marker of excellence, followed to be sure by other years of great performance, but none where the necessary pieces fit together as perfectly. The percentage gain from 1950 to 1966 was 400%, or an arithmetic average of 25% per year!

The investments of the dominant investment system will always be impacted by unforeseen political and economic events. As with us mortals, the measure of their strength is how they bounce back from them. The Dow rallied quickly from the recessions of 1953, 1957, and 1960. In 1962 the Kennedy administration's clash with the steel industry caused the Dow to fall from 726 on January 3 to 535.76 by June 26. Later that same year the Cuban missile crisis dealt it another blow, but by December 18, 1963, the Dow reached a new high of 767.21 (see Figure 4.1).[4]

Between 1963 and the Dow's peak in 1966, President John F. Kennedy was assassinated; the Vietnam War swung into full force; racial tensions broke into mob violence across the country; and Malcolm X was shot. Still, the Dow only hesitated before barreling upward. Then things changed.

The turn was so subtle that we can see it only in retrospect. It was not until December 11, 1972, that the Dow closed above its 1966 high, and then only by 41.12 points. This means that its arithmetic-average annual return between 1966 and 1972 was only .69%.

At first this seems understandable. The United States had bombed Hanoi; Martin Luther King Jr. and Robert F. Kennedy had been shot; a recession hit in 1970; and the dollar was devalued in 1971. These events were tragic, but so was World War II, the recessions of the 1950s and 1960s, and the assassination of a President—when the Dow recovered just fine. But this time, from 1966 to 1973, the Dow rose a meager 15.43 points and would go no further for 10 years (see Figure 4.2).

Why did the Dow get frozen in its tracks after 1966?

Chapter 1 explained that the Dow's performance correlates with productivity, often measured by gross domestic product (GDP). Here is a simple, common sense, economic concept:

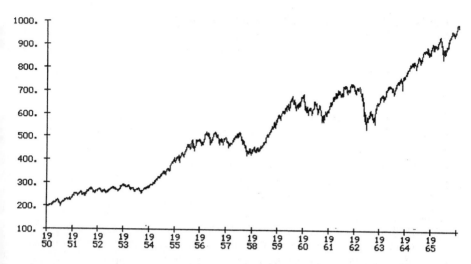

**Figure 4.1**    The Dow in Its Prime, January 1950–February 1966
*Note:* Closing prices of the Dow Jones Industrials are shown.

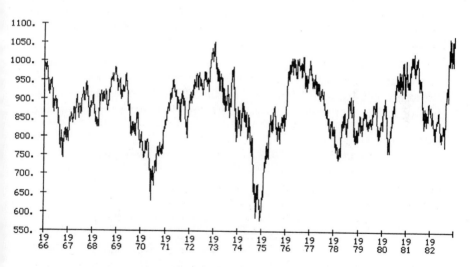

**Figure 4.2**    The Dow after Its Prime, 1966–1983
*Note:* Closing prices of the Dow Jones Industrials are shown.
*Source:* Printed with permission of Economagic, LLC and http://www.economagic.com.

The more productive
corporations are . . .

⇩

The more productive our economy
will be (higher GDP) . . .

⇩

The higher corporations'
stocks will go.

"Exceptional productivity growth characterized the years 1950–1973. Output per hour grew by almost 2.75% per year."[5] It is no coincidence that during this period the Dow reached its zenith as the dominant investment system.

Why did the energy drain out of the Dow in the 1970s, 1980s, and 1990s? Why did it take a total of 16 years from its peak in 1966 to set a substantial new high in 1983? The answer is that from 1973 to 1983, productivity growth averaged only 1.25% per year (see Figure 4.3).[6]

The declining trend of productivity, set in motion in 1973, helped to create a chain of events that included a falling stock market, rising inflation, and rising interest rates. Investment gurus advised locking up money in high yielding investments because the future returns on stocks looked dismal.

The oil embargo, recession, resignation of President Richard Nixon, and Iran hostage crisis are pointed to as reasons why the Dow could not get out of its own way in the 1970s; however, those events were nothing compared to crises earlier in the century from which the

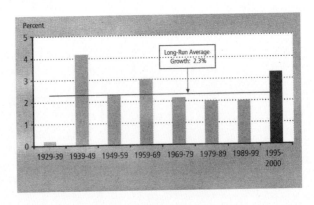

**Figure 4.3**    Per Capital Gross Domestic Product

*Note:* 10-year annualized growth rate of per capital real gross domestic product (GDP). Note that per capita GDP declines during the 1970s and 1980s.

Dow rallied brilliantly. The companies of the dominant investment system that had been firm and productive had become soggy as noodles.

## THE BULL MARKET OF THE 1980S AND EARLY 1990S?

As a recession ended in 1982, the Dow rallied from a low of 776.92 on August 12 to 1070.55 by December 27, a 37.79% increase. This signals a turning point for the Dow and the beginning of that spasm of the dominant investment system often referred to as the "Great Bull Market of the Late Twentieth Century."

The Dow blundered upward through its first significant new high in 16 years[7] to post a 27.66% return in 1985. The excitement this caused on Wall Street was not shared by Main Street.

Investors sought vehicles that would lower income taxes and capitalize on inflation. It was oil and gas or real estate investments that the well-heeled who came into our offices in the 1980s demanded. We could barely get them to consider stocks and hardly blamed them. From 1970 to 1974 stocks returned an annual average rate of –2.36%. From 1973 to 1977 the average annual return was –.21%.[8] Investors' patience for the market had worn thin. A quote from Venita Van Caspel's best-selling financial planning book of the decade sets out the limits of tolerance most people had for the Dow: "In my opinion, selected common stock equities will be a viable choice, intermittently for around 25% of your investment dollars during the decade of the eighties."[9]

•  •  •

Couples would parade into our Florida offices in high season dressed in matching white tropical shirts and slacks, the men with gold Rolexes and the women with tennis bracelets. They had stepped from a luxury car—it, too, had to be white to complete the effect—with an interior that matched a scarf, usually worn by the woman. This peacock-like display was meant to advertise their killing in real estate up north or the big score from oil out west.

They would buy their winter golf course home, then bring us the remainder to be invested in annuities, life insurance, or tax shelters. We would use quotes from Van Caspel's book to promote the advantages of owning stock, but we could seldom get them close to her 25% recommendation. Five to ten percent would be about it.

There is another story to tell. More accurately, it is the absence of a story that is remarkable. We did not see a single middle- to upper-class working person under 60 who was interested in any form of investing. This excerpt from a January 1983 article in *Dun's Business Month* will explain why:

> What's more, the official figure of 10.8% joblessness, which translates into 12 million people out of work, is a considerable understatement. It takes no account of the nearly 2 million "discouraged workers," so disheartened they have stopped looking for employment, or of 6.6 million part-time workers who want full-time jobs. Add in those people, says Allen Sinai, senior vice president of Data Resources, Ind., and the number working less than they want or not at all comes to 16.2% of the labor force. And fewer than half of those counted as unemployed are receiving jobless benefits.[10]

Add to the depressing job climate exorbitant home mortgage rates:[11]

| | | | |
|------|--------|------|--------|
| 1980 | 13.42% | 1985 | 12.27% |
| 1981 | 16.31% | 1986 | 9.91% |
| 1982 | 15.30% | 1987 | 10.16% |
| 1983 | 13.11% | 1988 | 10.49% |
| 1984 | 13.81% | 1989 | 10.24% |

The American dream was in grave danger. People were losing their homes, and it was not just the industrial white- and blue-collar workers who were in trouble:

> Last year was a bad one for Bud Leuthold. It was the first time since 1972 that he lost money growing wheat on the 4,000-acre spread near Billings, Mont., that his grandfather first farmed in 1910. Leuthold believed this year would be different. He was right: It's worse. Declining exports, expectations of bumper crops, and uncertainty over the Reagan Administration's farm policy have pushed commodity prices to their lowest levels in more than two years—promising to touch off yet another crisis when farmers sell their harvest this fall. "A third of us are broke, and a third are going broke," says Leuthold. "The rest will be going broke real soon."[12]

For the first time in U.S. history people were saying that parents should prepare their children for a standard of living beneath their own.

Inside the financial world things were no better. Stories of fraudulent S&L schemes were circulating in 1983, and by the end of the decade a bailout of the S&L industry cost the taxpayers billions. Companies too weak or lazy to be productive found a solution in illegal junk bond deals. Insider-trading scandals landed some prominent Wall Street figures in jail.

The rank and file, represented by labor unions, share the blame for the disintegration of American industry. Companies that were doing their best to be productive were often shackled by outdated contracts and forced to submit to wasteful featherbedding.

The strike against the *Washington Post* in the mid-1970s set a standard for union arrogance that was replicated by other strikes during the 1980s. While portraying themselves as victims, some union members were gorging themselves at a trough that had been filled by hard-working laborers and craftsmen before them, which these "victims" refused to take their turn in replenishing.

Some bull market—from disgruntled blue- and white-collar workers to cynical wealthy investors, dissatisfaction with corporate America was pervasive. And how does human nature react when faced with difficulties that are at least partly self-inflicted? By blaming someone else. The Japanese, with their buoyant economy and soaring stock market, were perfect targets.

Japan was building better cars, delivering manufactured goods at cheaper prices, and buying U.S. companies and making them profitable. In the second half of the 1980s commentary like this appeared in every magazine and newspaper:

> Despite all the negotiations, the U.S. trade deficit with Japan is soaring—and there's no end in sight. The Japanese are pouring their goods into the U.S., and a dangerous perception gap between Japan and the U.S. is widening.[13]

The Japanese were going to own America. There was no telling what would happen. This fear burned itself like a stick of dynamite into the American consciousness, and the explosion was ignited by the market crash of 1987.

They called it a meltdown. The Dow collapsed 22.6% in one day. It fell to 1738.74 on October 19, 1987, nearly 1,000 points from its high of 2722.40 seven weeks earlier. Today that would be like losing over 2,000 points in one session. Stocks did not fall that much even when the World Trade Center was attacked. During those dark days in the fall of 1987, hysterical investors kept our phones ringing 18 hours a day.

Of course our stoic Mr. C., who would not be caught dead in either white tropical slacks or the matching white luxury car, was calling to let us know that he would be sending more money to his account and that he hoped we would fine some bargains—which we did. But even Mr. C.'s optimism was about to be destroyed.

The Dow recovered from the 1987 crash, but investors did not. It was one more nail in the coffin of confidence in the U.S. economy. By 1988 the conventional wisdom held that the United States had forever lost its grasp on economic power.

The final straw that had Mr. C. on the phone to us before sunrise on a morning in 1989 was the purchase of the 19 buildings of Rockefeller Center by the Japanese company Mitsubishi. That a foreign country would own this symbol of American industry and financial power crystallized for many the disappointment and disillusionment that had prevailed since 1970.

● ● ●

In a large dining room in 1990, in a very large home overlooking the Gulf of Mexico, the table conversation during the entree focused on how the tax law changes had eliminated millions of dollars of write-offs. By the time we got to the cognac, the more villainous event became the falling inflation rate, which translated into falling rates of appreciation necessitating the sale of ski resorts, cattle ranches, and duck marshes. The proceeds would be used to buy gold, commodity contracts, and maybe some annuities—definitely not U.S. stocks because those silly computers were desecrating the honest work of America, which was building bigger refineries and forging more steel (take it, make it, break it).

● ● ●

In a very large boardroom in 1991 in an office building tall enough to allow a view of the cruise ships drifting like icebergs into the Port of Miami, the executive sitting next to me announced that there was no way he would allow his company's $180 million pension plan to own U.S. stocks. "High-tech is destroying American industry. Pretty soon we'll just be selling hamburgers to one another," he said. "Treasury bills were okay, guaranteed insurance contracts were okay, and we must invest in foreign stocks, especially Japan."

● ● ●

During a 1992 seminar for the rank and file on 401(k) investing on the floor of a manufacturing plant in Lexington, Ohio, questions from the audience centered on how soon we thought technology would put all of those at the meeting out of work. Isn't that why unemployment was so high? No new jobs. No new skills to learn. No room for advancement. This group was convinced that they would be the ones frying the hamburgers.

The thread that connects this diverse group of pessimists was that a second culprit—as bad as the Japanese—had emerged: new technology. The myth that it was destroying American jobs and ruining the economy was spread by the entrenched interests of what was by then the outdated dominant investment system. (Today this myth takes a new form. A company whose business involves the Internet is a dot-com with no solid foundation. This view holds that a stock with a high price per earnings ratio, using new technology to employ new business strategies, is just a gamble.)

"Get back to basics" was the inane prescription for a more productive business climate. The fact that the basics were not doing so well could conveniently be blamed on the Japanese. The truth was that by the early 1990s, spineless managers—who did little to create the golden goose that they had been living off of—and arrogant labor union tactics had done much to smother productivity.

Investors often ignored the fact that some companies and their union members (e.g., Nike) decided in the early 1990s that they must work together to toss out old systems. Heavy expenditures on new technology were viewed as just another drain on earnings that would keep stock prices from rising. Most people were not considering the positive impact that this visionary restructuring would have on future growth. Just like today, the impact on productivity that digital technology would have on the economy and the stock market was ignored by the vested interests of the old dominant investment system.

This meant that from 1990 to 1994 the financial commentary read like this: "New York has been displaced as the model of market stability."[14] By 1994 doom and gloom was pervasive: "[Robert] Prechter now recommends putting not a penny in stocks except precious metals. He's predicting a multi-year bear market with the Dow losing 90% within the decade."[15] Likewise, a *Forbes* article pointed out that a "lot of smart money thinks this is another one of those times to be long commodities."[16] In another article from that issue, Charles Allmon stated, "You're looking at the most over-valued market in this century. This thing could decline 50% from its high."[17] On January 17, 1994, *USA Today* quoted market-timer and noted financial newsletter writer Arch Crawford as saying, "I'd sell stocks now. The current status of the market is almost equivalent to the San Francisco earthquake."[18]

What seemed to be important in 1994 was for investors to understand that the dual evils of "technology" and "foreigners" had conspired against the U.S. financial markets in preventing stocks from rising any further. This assumed that we all bought into a fiction in the first place—that a bull market that raged through the 1980s and early 1990s had made us all rich and that we should now be grateful. That by 1994 it was time to take our money off the table and batten the hatches was the majority view of the card-carrying members of the old dominant investment system. To say their conclusions were wrong, that they totally missed the mark, does not begin to cover it.

•　•　•

There was a border between 1994 and 1995, and the contrasts before and after were as stark as those between East and West Germany on either side of the Berlin Wall, the last bricks of which were toted away in the early 1990s.

On the 1994 side were the dour faces of fatalistic citizens, resigned to picking their way around economic potholes and conducting their lives as best they could. It was hard to distinguish how much of the gray atmosphere was generated by the mood of the population and how much was the result of industry's gorging on resources and belching dark fumes into the air. Prosperity was reserved for an opportunistic and cynical few, grabbing their share of a shrinking pie.

After crossing the border into 1995 it was as if we were in a new country. Suddenly, the atmosphere was buoyant. There were opportunities instead of problems. The air was clearing enough to see an exciting future. One writer commented, "My favorite septuagenarian says he's never seen such a stampede for stocks among the popular pundits of the financial press."[19]

Apparently the experts were not even a little embarrassed by the total reversal of their prognostications. By 1996 the covers of financial publications were filled with headlines such as this:[20]

**MAJOR CODE RED**
**WHERE TO PUT YOUR MONEY NOW!**
**Smart strategies in:**
**Value stocks**
**News issues**
**Spin offs**

A new type of investor was coming into our offices. They did not want gold, commodities, or tax havens. They wanted to own U.S. stocks. They wanted growth. They wanted to share in the expanding economy. They heard about exciting new services and technologies, and with complete confidence in American business they were willing to wait years for their payoff until the promise could be fulfilled. They had no time for putting on airs. They were busy with their careers or were working at companies. Some were busy starting new ones, buying or selling others. They were of all ages.

## WHY THE BIG CHANGE AFTER 1994? PRODUCTIVITY SOARS

Real gross domestic product grew by 4.5 percent a year during the last half of the 1990's. Roughly a percentage point faster than its long-run average, this growth was strong enough to push the civilian unemployment rate down to 4 percent by the end of 2000, a rate not seen since 1970.[21]

The investment establishment did not see this coming because they looked at the companies of the old dominant investment system and concluded correctly that their productivity had fallen to a level insufficient to produce competitive economic growth (GDP), which in turn was insufficient to raise stock prices. So what was responsible for the compelling jump in GDP that initiated a new trend of rising prosperity? The outstanding productivity gains came from the companies of the soon-to-be-born new dominant investment system as well as companies of the old system that had adopted realize, capitalize, customize. Figure 4.4 shows this clearly.

The fact that so many experts were unable to anticipate the renaissance of American business should not be lost on us today. What was simply misunderstood then is often conveniently ignored now, for all the reasons set out in earlier chapters. The status quo must be maintained, frequently at the expense of investors like you (and us). Consequently the spin that is put on business news can be as partisan as that heard during any election campaign.

It is common knowledge among investment professionals, for example, that government statistics do not capture the output of most companies of the new dominant investment system. The Office of Management and Budget (OMB) is forthcoming about this. They know that data on the twentieth-century industrial economy does not provide a clear picture of what is happening today. The OMB has taken steps to correct this, and changes will be fully implemented by 2004.[22]

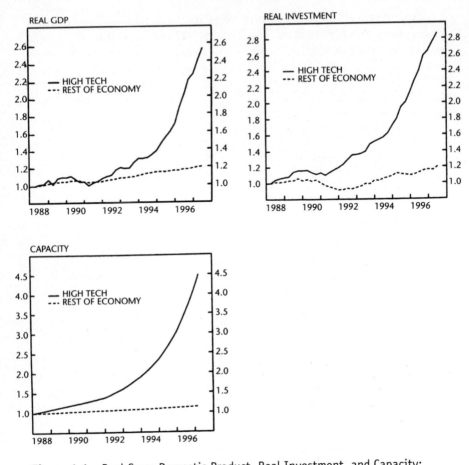

**Figure 4.4** Real Gross Domestic Product, Real Investment, and Capacity: "High Tech" versus the Rest of the Economy

*Source:* Used with permission of BCA Publications, Ltd., *The Bank Credit Analyst.*

*Note:* The realize, capitalize, customize companies were the sources of productivity in the last half of the 1990s.

Nonetheless, investment rhetoric ignores the contributions made by twenty-first century companies to the economy. It does not differentiate between the falling productivity of the twentieth-century industrial complex and the rising contribution to our national wealth by the companies of the new dominant investment system. There are more spin doctors than statesmen in the world of finance.

One statesman is Louise Yamada, senior technical analyst and vice president for research at Smith Barney. In her must-read, ground-breaking book, she explains how, in 1994, she saw the prosperity ahead by recognizing that growth was coming from a new place:

> We are experiencing the initiation of an entirely new, knowledge-based technological cycle (even a new long-wave cycle) consisting primarily of communication, information (networked intelligence), electronics, catalytic, and precision technology which renders efficiency to existing processes and defines new frontiers, and we are witnessing the dynamics of its force. It cannot be disputed that communication and information technology is a new horizon in which innovation is key and evolution into burgeoning new technologies is just beginning.[23]

## 1995: A REAL BULL MARKET BEGINS

In 1995 wages, after inflation, rose for the first time in 20 years.[24] People felt good about spending money, and consumer sentiment exploded (see Figure 4.5).

| Index | 1995 Return |
|---|---|
| Wilshire—Target Large Growth | +37.88% |
| Wilshire—Target Large Value | +43.47% |
| Wilshire—Target Small Growth | +35.19% |
| Wilshire—Target Small Value | +29.75% |

Every major style of U.S. stocks posted fabulous returns.[25]

**Figure 4.5**  Consumer Sentiment (at the University of Michigan)
*Note:* Optimism about the economy returned almost overnight in 1995.
*Source:* Survey of Consumers, University of Michigan by permission

If this turnaround were simply the result of a new technology making existing companies more productive, we should be concerned about how long the positive effects would last. If it were only the result of massive spending on computers, software, and related appliances, we should worry that it is over. But that was only one of the fortunate circumstances that were about to change things forever.

A fusion of elements in 1995 released kinetic energy with a velocity that would not only initiate the birthing process of a whole new dominant investment system but also ensure its dominance over the financial universe of the twenty-first century.

## THE ELEMENTS THAT CREATED THE NEW DOMINANT INVESTMENT SYSTEM

Discussed in detail in the following sections, these four elements created the new investment system:

- Completion of an incubation interval
- Dependable consumer economy
- Improvement in economic conditions
- Surge in foreign exports

### Element 1: Completion of an Incubation Interval

The economic scholar Joseph Schumpeter recognized periods of innovation as a necessary interruption of what would otherwise be the "static circular flow of capitalism."[26] The French historian Jacques Barzun refers to it as a preparatory period for prosperity. In *The Great Boom Ahead* Harry Dent calls it an innovation wave.[27] In *Economics in Perspective* John Kenneth Galbraith does not name it but agrees with Schumpeter that it causes "economic life to continue and enlarge."[28] We call it an *incubation interval*. It is a period of history that spawns a superabundance of new ideas that must be cultivated and developed during this interval before they become ubiquitous enough to increase productivity. An incubation interval lasts about 20 years, and one of these occurred between 1970 and 1993. Here is a short list of groundbreaking developments.

| Date | Creation |
|------|----------|
| 1970 | 747 jumbo jet |
| 1971 | Microprocessor |
| 1972 | CAT scan |
| 1973 | Skylab, the first space laboratory |
| 1975 | Sale of the first personal computer, the Altair 8800 |
| 1975 | Microsoft organized |
| 1976 | Apple Computer organized |
| 1977 | Oracle organized |
| 1978 | TGV high-speed train |
| 1979 | Walkman |
| 1979 | Compact disc |
| 1980 | Tim Berners-Lee creates Enquire, the program facilitating the World Wide Web |
| 1981 | IBM personal computer |
| 1982 | The term *Internet* is first applied to a group of networks that compose ARPANET, a Defense Department project |
| 1983 | Compact discs sold to the public |
| 1984 | Apple introduces the Macintosh and the first mouse |
| 1985 | Battery-powered automobile |
| 1986 | Laser instruments for heart and eye surgery |
| 1986 | Pocket telephone |
| 1987 | Digital audiotape |
| 1982 | Prozac |
| 1988 | Video Walkman |
| 1989 | Human Genome Project begins |
| 1992 | World Wide Web established |
| 1993 | NCSA Mosaic, the first graphic Web browser |

The incubation interval was the embryo of the dominant investment system that was growing inside our economy. The only other time more groundbreaking ideas, products, and services were conceived was during the incubation interval of the nineteenth century, which helped give birth to the Dow as the dominant investment system.

It is a testament to human ingenuity that while the world seemed to be deteriorating in the 1970s and 1980s, many people disregarded the blight and went about the business of pouring talent and energy into their visions of how to make the world work better.

## Element 2: Dependable Consumer Economy

Imagine the incubation interval taking place in an economy like Afghanistan's. Who would buy those first personal computers—generating profits that could be poured into research and development, resulting in an even better product, and eventually becoming something without which we could not live? Without that chain of events there would be no need for the Web, no need for the Internet. Without the Internet the billions of dollars of productivity increases in American corporations would not have occurred.

Each invention from the incubation interval was nurtured by the consumer economy until it could stand on its own. The cushion of the consumer supports distribution channels and marketing networks around the laboratory of capitalism that is the domestic U.S. economy. It is so constant that we speak in terms of how fast it is growing. The worst that happens is that once every 10 years or so consumers will not buy more than they did the previous year.

During the economic "slowdown" of 2000–2001 Americans spent $1.8 trillion, which was more than the entire economies of Australia, Saudi Arabia, and the United Kingdom combined.[29]

Figure 4.6 reveals that consumers failed to increase their total purchases over the prior year in only two instances, 1980 and 1990, after which a gentle, upward trend developed into 1995. This increasing momentum helped to fuel the launch of the new dominant investment system.

## Element 3: Improvement in Economic Conditions

A fact of life is that high federal deficits suck money out of the economy that would otherwise be used elsewhere. That the falling budget deficit occurred when it did left room for a surge in capital investment in new companies and technology (see Figure 4.7).

The fall of interest rates after 1994 allowed companies to borrow money for research and development, expand operations, or acquire other companies at low costs in order to improve profitability (see Figure 4.8). The low interest rates were the result of low inflation shown in Figure 4.9. A decreased government deficit, low interest rates, and inflation meant more money available in the early 1990s, just when companies of the new dominant investment system needed it (see Figure 4.10).[30]

The enrichment of the economy fueled spending by the domestic consumer who would buy the new products created during the incubation interval. This circuit of energy-producing factors was enhanced by one last critical element, foreign trade.

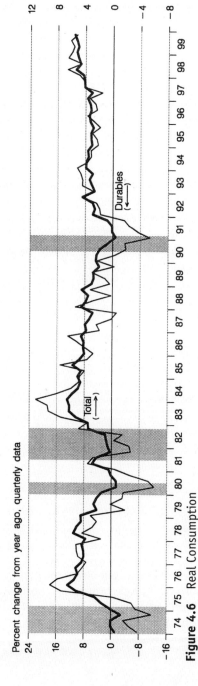

Percent change from year ago, quarterly data

**Figure 4.6** Real Consumption

*Note:* American consumers have always bought more in any given year than they did the year before. The only exceptions were the years 1980 and 1990.

*Source:* "Monetary Trends," The Federal Reserve Bank of St. Louis, 2001

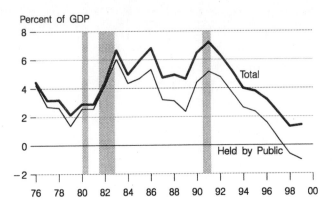

**Figure 4.7**    Reduced Government Debt

*Note:* Government debt begins to decline steeply in 1995.

*Source:* "Monetary Trends," The Federal Reserve Bank of St Louis, 2001

## Element 4: Surge in Foreign Exports

A boom in global trade occurred in the mid-1990s. In 1990 the United States sold $652.9 billion of goods and services abroad. By 1995 this jumped to $969.2 billion, almost a 50% increase.[31] The companies of what would soon be the new dominant investment system benefited the most.

Percentage Increases in U.S. Exports, 1993–1996[32]

| | |
|---|---|
| Biotech | +50% |
| Electronics | +86% |
| Digital machine tools and robotics | +115% |
| Information and communication | +51% |
| Life sciences | +51% |

There is no question that global trade played a substantial part in launching the new investment system. Why this occurred is worth exploring.

In the early 1990s every major (and minor) country came to the realization that growth in world trade had outpaced growth in industrial production.[33] Trade had become more profitable than the industries of the old dominant investment system. This moment of clarity led to the Uruguay Rounds, which had as their goal the reduction of tariffs and trade barriers. Final agreements were signed into law in 1994.

A contentious political debate enveloped the Uruguay Rounds, much of it due to the hotly contested passage of the North American Free Trade Agreement (NAFTA) the year before (1993). Trade with

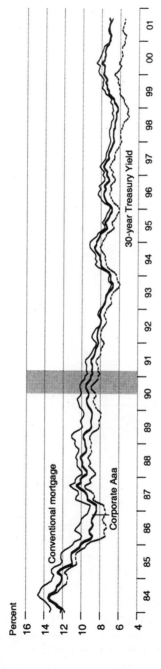

**Figure 4.8** Long-Term Interest Rates

*Note:* Interest rates begin a dramatic decline in 1994.

*Source:* "Monetary Trends," The Federal Reserve Bank of St Louis

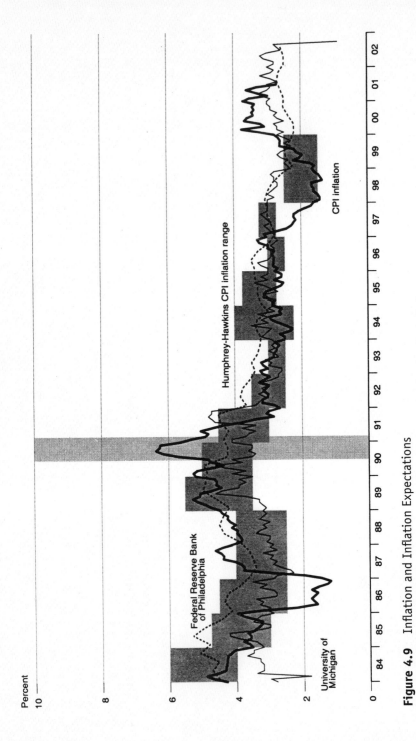

**Figure 4.9** Inflation and Inflation Expectations

*Note:* The shaded region shows the Humphrey-Hawkins Consumer Price Index inflation range.

*Source:* "Monetary Trends," The Federal Reserve Bank of St. Louis, 2002

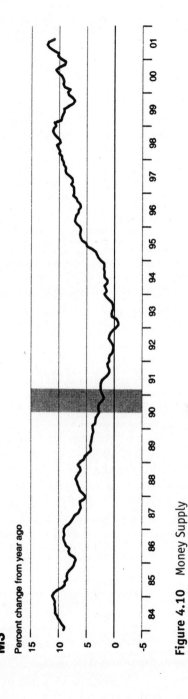

**M3**

Percent change from year ago

**Figure 4.10**   Money Supply

*Note:* The money supply begins a rising trend in 1994.

*Source:* "Monetary Trends," The Federal Reserve Bank of St Louis, 2001

Mexico was supposed to ruin us; of course, it did not. In 2000, Mexico imported more U.S. goods than did Japan, China, and the United Kingdom combined.[34]

It was not just the dropping of trade barriers that provided the export windfall. Falling global interest rates and confidence in the American economy, as a result of the declining deficit, played their part. None of this would have had any effect had we not had something new to sell—the goods and services developed during the incubation interval.

The smallest things can change our lives—the chance meeting because you wait a little longer at a counter to get your change or the book you picked off the shelf because on that particular day its blue jacket held more appeal than the yellow one next to it. It should be easy to understand that when the four major economic events just described—which by themselves could shift the balance of the investment universe—converged with a laser intensity on a fixed point in time (the mid-1990s), the investment world was sent spinning in a new direction.

That we sorely needed a new direction is not a part of any financial dialogue. That 1995 was a pivotal year in which prosperity for many Americans only just got started is not part of the rhetoric. That twentieth-century industrial companies, as represented by the Dow, had failed for 25 years to be sufficiently productive to enhance our economy—and an entirely new corporate organization had surfaced to create wealth—is obscured.

Instead, the story has been framed in such a way as to preserve the status of the old dominant investment system. In Calvinistic style we are reminded that we should be grateful for the great bull market the Dow gave us in the 1980s and 1990s. That the wealth created *after* 1995 was not derived from the old dominant investment system is glossed over. That any wealth that was created by the old dominant investment system *prior* to 1995 was not sufficient to keep our standard of living from declining for the first time in half a century was overlooked. If the early 1980s initiated a bull market, it was a party to which only a select few were invited.

## IF IT WAS NOT A BULL MARKET, WHAT WAS IT?

Unquestionably, the Dow rose at a higher rate from 1982 to 1994 than in the 1970s. More people were buying stock than had done so for a decade. This is not saying much. A new perspective is required to understand what created that counterfeit bull market, and Figure 4.11 shows that perspective clearly.

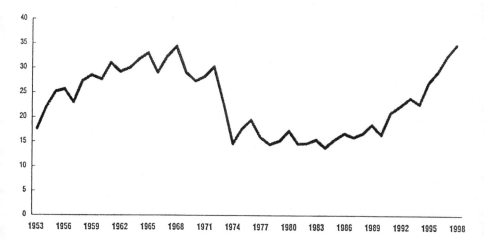

**Figure 4.11**   Household Ownership of Equities, 1953–1998 (percentage of U.S. household financial assets)

*Source:* Federal Reserve Board, Employee Benefit Research Institute, and the Investment Company Institute.

*Note:* 1953 is the earliest date for which data are available. It is not until the end of the 1990s that stock ownership by individuals reached the levels of the 1960s.

Ownership of stock dwindled so badly after 1967 that a cavity is created in Figure 4.11. It was money dribbling into this cavity that caused stocks to rise in the 1980s. The so-called bull market was merely stocks returning to some meager level of ownership by the investing public. You can see that it was only in that pivotal year of 1995 that stock ownership began to approach the levels of the 1960s, when the Dow was in its prime.

"If your cab driver, plumber, electrician (or whoever) talks about buying stock, the opportunity has passed. It's time to sell." This cliché is often put forth as a reason why stocks will do poorly in the twenty-first century. Figure 4.11 shows that household ownership of stocks in the 1950s and 1960s remained above the level reached in 1995 for 15 years. A similar stretch today would take us to about 2011, right to the projected end of the acceleration phase. In other words, we have a long way to go before we must be concerned that too many people own stock or that we should take that fact as a signal of deteriorating prices.

Imagine what would happen if the new dominant investment system, which saved our necks, was regarded with the same reverence as the old one that nearly ruined us. It would mean the new dominant investment system would be the source of job data, economic output, and corporate performance. This would mean that the financial news would suddenly become more positive. It would be like taking off a pair of sunglasses after the sky had clouded up. What had appeared stormy turns out to be only fluffy big clouds over a brilliant blue background.

If companies like AdvancePCS or Fiserv were given as much press as Disney, we would understand better what these companies do and how important they are. The formulation phase would not take as long, and clarity would come to the financial markets sooner. In spite of our supposed sophistication, this process does not seem to be happening any faster than it did 100 years ago.

You will learn in the next chapter that the circumstances surrounding the birth of our new dominant investment system are all too familiar. You will read that the birth of the Dow's dominance mirrors events today. We can use the parallels as a guide to our own future.

## NOTES

1. On January 11, 1973, the Dow was at 1051.73. On December 6, 1974, the Dow was at 577.60.

2. Ivan Boesky plead guilty in spring 1987.

3. On August 25, 1987, the Dow was at 2722.42. By October 19, 1987, the Dow was at 1738.74.

4. The Dow recovered equally well from Word War I and II. The Dow went from a low of 65.95 on U.S. entry into WWI and despite a recession reached a new high of 119.62 on November 3, 1919, less than a year after the war's end. The strike on Pearl Harbor in December 1941 caused the Dow to sink to 92.92 by April 28, 1942; but even before the war ended, the Dow hit a new high of 152.53 on December 16, 1944. By the war's end in 1945 the Dow reached a new all-time high of 195.82 on December 11.

5. Kevin L. Kliesen and David C. Wheelock, *The Regional Economist* (2001, July).

6. Ibid.

7. The Dow was at 1287.20 on November 29, 1983.

8. Topline Investment Graphics, Standard & Poor's 500.

9. Venita Van Caspel, *Money Dynamics for the 1980's* (Reston, VA: Prentice Hall, 1980), p. 60.

10. John Frank, Patrick Houston, Pary Pitzer, and Jeffrey Reyser, "The Farm Rut Gets Deeper," *Dun's Business Month* (1983, January), p. 48.

11. *Chase Investment Performance Digest* (Concord, MA: Chase Global Data & Research, 1994), p. 58.

12. John Frank, Patrick Houston, Pary Pitzer, and Jeffery Reyser, "The Farm Rut Gets Deeper," *Dun's Business Month* (1983, January), p. 48.

13. James B. Treece, William J. Holstein, Boyd France, and Ronald Grover, "The Widening Trade Gap: Is Tokyo Calling Congresses' Bluff," *Business Week* (1985, June 17), pp. 50–51.

14. "Tokyo Market: Now a Leader," *New York Times* (1990, January 1), p. L31.

15. "Stocks Up, Stocks Down," *Forbes* (1994, January 3), p. 49.

16. "Are Hard Assets the Next Big Play?" *Forbes* (1994, April), p. 49.

17. Charles Allmon, *Forbes* (1994, April), p. 46.

18. Retrieved from www.astromoney.com.

19. Editorial, *Forbes* (1995, October 23), p. 334.

20. *Forbes* (1996, June 17), cover.

21. Kevin L. Kliesen and David C. Wheelock, "The Microchip Flexes Its Muscle," *Regional Economist*, p. 6.

22. *National Economic Trends,* August 2001, Federal Reserve Board of St. Louis.

23. Louise Yamada, *Market Magic* (New York: Wiley, 1998), p. 144.

24. *National Economic Trends,* August 2001, Federal Reserve Board of St. Louis.

25. Wilshire Associates Incorporated. Data used with permission.

26. Robert Heilbroner, *The Worldly Philosophers* (New York: Simon & Schuster, 1953), p. 295.

27. Harry Dent, *The Great Boom Ahead* (New York: Hyperion, 1993), pp. 138–139.

28. John Kenneth Galbraith, *Economics in Perspective: A Critical History* (Boston: Houghton Mifflin, 1987), p. 181.

29. *National Economic Trends,* July 1, 2002, Federal Reserve Bank of St. Louis.

30. M1: the sum of currency held outside the vaults of depository institutions, Federal Reserve banks, and the U.S. Treasury; travelers checks; and demand and other checkable deposits issued by financial institutions, except demand deposits due to the Treasury and depository institutions, minus cash items in process of collection and Federal Reserve float.

M2: M1 plus savings deposits (including money market deposit accounts) and small-denomination (less than $100,000) time deposits issued by financial institutions; and shares in retail money market mutual funds (funds with initial investments of less than $50,000), net of retirement accounts.

M3: M2 plus large-denomination ($100,000 or more) time deposits; repurchase agreements issued by depository institutions; Eurodollar deposits, specifically, dollar-denominated deposits due to non-bank U.S. addresses held at foreign offices of U.S. banks worldwide and all banking offices in Canada and the United Kingdom; and institutional money market mutual funds (funds with initial investments of $50,000 or more).

31. U.S. Department of Commerce Bureau of Economic Analysis, Survey of Current Business. Retrieved from www.bea.doc.gov.

32. *Statistical Abstract of the United States* (Washington, DC: U.S. Department of Commerce, 1997), p. 802.

33. World Trade Organization. Retrieved from www.wto.org.

34. National Economic Trends, Federal Reserve Bank of St. Louis.

# 5

# A PARALLEL UNIVERSE
## Why the Beginning of the Dow Can Be Our Guide for Today

*The basic human motivation that underlies all economic behavior has proved remarkably unvaried over time and across space and culture.*
—Jeremy Atack and Peter Passell

### SHORT PEOPLE

It was an October Saturday afternoon in Tennessee when we ushered our two bored adolescent children to the rear of the main hall and up the sweeping staircase of the Hermitage, President Andrew Jackson's home 10 miles from Nashville. We would point to a silver inkstand or mahogany sewing table and say, "Isn't it fascinating to see how people lived?" and affirm our parental wisdom in insisting that they both attend this family outing.

At the top of the staircase, the first bedroom on the right was furnished with antiques from the 1870s and 1880s. The bed displayed there elicited the first sign of interest in Americana that afternoon. "How could a grown man sleep in that?!" This starts the conversation, held by almost anyone who has visited historic homes, about how much shorter people were in previous centuries. It is reasoned that mankind's march of progress increasingly elevates lifestyles, thereby promoting good health, which results in ever more robust physiques. The part about the height and prosperity correlation is true;[1] the increasingly elevated lifestyles part is not.

It is natural for us to believe that progress is linear, that we advance along a continuum where there is comfort in the belief that tomorrow will always be better. We conclude that chronology and sequence must dictate similarities and seek clues to the future by spotting a trend. But the evidence shows that sometimes transformation can double back. One of these times was the 1970s and 1980s, when America's growth stalled and then reversed itself, until we no longer had the world's leading economy. Another time was the 1870s and 1880s, when in similar fashion prosperity and living conditions deteriorated to a level well below that of the preceding decades.

The evidence to substantiate this lies in the bedrooms of places like the Hermitage in Nashville, Tennessee. That is where you will find beds that only have to be long enough to accommodate males who are 5½ feet tall, the average height in 1870 and 1880. The operative fact is that a century earlier, at the time of the American Revolution, people were considerably taller.

Height data on recruits into George Washington's army gathered by Robert Fogel of the University of Chicago[2] attest to the imposing carriage of Revolutionary War and post–Revolutionary War Americans, reflective of their abundant lifestyle. That after decades of progress the quality of life in America regressed so sharply as to affect even the stature of its citizens is a result of the decline in prosperity that existed between 1870 and 1896. Fortunately, this turned out to be the period of an incubation interval that would rescue the economy by providing it with a new dominant investment system represented by the Dow. As seen in Figure 5.1, the height of young American males finally returned to the level of the early 1800s by the beginning of the Dow's acceleration phase in the 1920s.

The decline in living standards that threatened Americans in the second half of the nineteenth century must have seemed even more intolerable because of the abundance that preceded it. The expectation that a permanent condition of prosperity had set in was created by railroad expansion that had made self-sustained economic growth surge. In 1810 there were about 75,000 workers in American industry. By 1860 there were over 1.3 million.[3] From 1830 to 1850 railroad track mileage soared by 36,567%.[4] Americans enjoyed a productivity growth rate of 2.6% per year.[5]

These were the decades of the pick it and ship it business model and the first dominant investment system. Its peak years came between 1830 and the 1860s. If not for the Civil War, its prime years may have lasted even longer. Nonetheless, productivity remained higher for a longer period of time than it did during the 1950s and 1960s, the peak years for the second dominant investment system represented by the Dow. At least one of the reasons for this has to be the fearlessness, energy, and celebration of independent thought and action that typified Americans

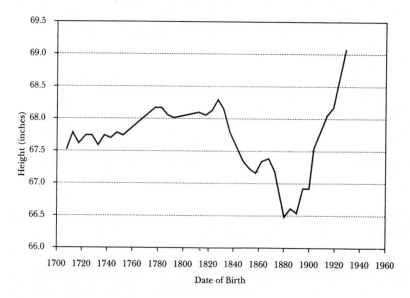

**Figure 5.1**   Height of American-Born White Males, 1710–1960

*Source:* Robert Fogel, "Nutrition and the Decline in Mortality since 1700," in Stanley Engerman and Robert Gallman, eds., *Long-Term Factors in American Economic Growth* (Chicago: University of Chicago Press, 1986), Table 9.A.1.

*Note:* The height of American males declined dramatically in the late 1800s and did not return to Revolutionary War levels until the acceleration phase of the second dominant investment system in the 1920s.

during those years. (Chapter 8 explains how a similar generational personality will define our own new dominant investment system.)

It is a dynamic culture that could hold Davy Crockett and Jim Bowie at the same time as John James Audubon and Charles Darwin—and that had the Texas Rangers tracking down gunslingers at the same time that many of the nation's colleges and universities were being built (see the box).

With a literacy rate surpassing today's, Americans traveling in covered wagons entertained themselves with new books like *Moby Dick* by Herman Melville and stories like "The Pit and the Pendulum" by Edgar Allan Poe. The vigorous new writings of Henry David Thoreau reinforced their conviction in personal liberty and independent thought. While pioneers clattered across the prairie, the New York Knickerbockers donned the first baseball uniforms in 1852, and the word *lingerie* came into general circulation. Pioneers, farmers, and intellectuals across the country attended lectures on self-reliance by Ralph Waldo Emerson. After Alexis de Tocqueville visited America in those years, he used the country as a model for the ideal democratic state of the future.

## Major Colleges and Universities Founded During the Nineteenth-Century Incubation Interval

*1832*
Dennison University
St. Louis University

*1834*
Oberlin College
University of Delaware

*1836*
Illinois College
Marietta College
Spring Hill College

*1837*
DePauw University
Emory University
Knox College
University of Michigan
Mount Holyoke
Mercer University

*1839*
Wake Forest College
Greensboro College

*1840*
University of Missouri

*1841*
University of Richmond
Howard College

*1844*
Cumberland University
University of Notre Dame
University of Mississippi

*1845*
Baylor University
U.S. Naval Academy

*1847*
Colgate University
Fordham University
Grinnell College
Lawrence College
Taylor University
Tulane University
State University of
   Iowa

*1848*
University of Wisconsin

*1851*
Northwestern University
Ripon College
University of Minnesota
Westminster College

*1853*
Duke University
College of the City of
   New York
Willamette University
Illinois Wesleyan
Washington University
Louisiana State University
Ohio Wesleyan
Loyola College

*1854*
Antioch College
Pennsylvania State
   University
Pacific University
Cornell

*1856*
Santa Clara University
College of California

*1859*
Massachusetts Institute of
   Technology

*1861*
University of Colorado
University of Washington
Vassar College

*1863*
University of Massachusetts

*1864*
Gallaudet College
University of Kansas

*1865*
Purdue University
University of Maine
University of Kentucky

*1866*
University of New
   Hampshire

Everyone had an opinion and openly fought for it—feminists, Mormons, Catholics, abolitionists, slave owners. Indians were massacred, and settlers were massacred. There was justice and there was no justice, but there did not seem to be a lot of whiners. In the poem "Mediums" Walt Whitman described the Americans he saw like this:

They shall arise in the States.
They shall report Nature, laws, physiology, and happiness,
They shall illustrate Democracy and the kosmos,

They shall be eliminative, amative, perceptive,
They shall be complete women and men, their pose brawny and
   supple, their drink water, their blood clean and clear.
They shall fully enjoy materialism and the sight of products,
They shall enjoy the sight of beef, lumber, breadstuffs, of Chicago the
   great city. . . .[6]

The accomplishments of the era inspired Thoreau to write, "I know of no more encouraging fact than the unquestionable ability of man to elevate his life by conscious endeavor."[7] "Conscious endeavor" was taken seriously. By 1857 the major cities in the East and in the Great Lakes region were connected by rail. By 1867 John Augustus Roebling had designed the Brooklyn Bridge, and the first Belmont Stakes was run.

Then, just as it would exactly 100 years later, the high level of sustained productivity dropped below 2% in 1870 and remained in this depleted state for nearly the rest of the century.[8]

## THE BEGINNING OF THE END FOR THE FIRST DOMINANT INVESTMENT SYSTEM

The economic boom following the Civil War ended in the depression of 1873. "One-fifth of the railroad mileage in the United States was sold under foreclosure. The New York Stock Exchange closed for 10 days, and banks suspended specie payments."[9] This began 24 years of excesses followed by periods of recovery followed by economic retribution. The cycles of panics and depressions were so routine that they became the subject of intensive study by nineteenth-century economists, and the concept of the business cycle was born.

Today, most economic texts refer to the last third of the 1800s as the peak years of the Victorian equilibrium. Authorities like Alfred Marshall concluded that the cycles of business contractions were necessary for maintaining fiscal balance, or equilibrium. Marshall explained the environment of boom and bust in mathematical terms that are still required reading in many courses of economics to this day.

The term *equilibrium,* implying some sort of stability, was lost on the stunted Americans of the late 1800s. What were business cycles to academics was straw after straw threatening to break the backs of the majority of U.S. citizens. The Pollyanna view of the situation that came down from the rarified air of academia calls to mind the 1980s, when Wall Street jauntily declared that we were in a bull market while personal bankruptcies rose 60%, billions of tax dollars were bailing out the savings and loan industry, and the United States became a debtor nation for the first time in 71 years.

While economists were busy identifying so-called cycles in the 1870s, those closer to the situation described it like this: "Every man of affairs wears an unpleasant reproachful look day in and day out, with no signs of change for the better," reported the *New York Times* on October 23, 1873. On February 5, 1878, the paper reported, "Speculation in the stock market was dull. The ursine fraternity utters the gloomiest of prognostications as to the future of values."

•  •  •

If you had known the diminutive and disappointed Lyman Frank Baum when he was stranded penniless in South Dakota, you never would have suspected that he would eventually leave a legacy that would touch us all.

He was born in the 1850s to a family whose oil business had thrived in a booming economy. He grew to manhood expecting, like most Americans of the period, that prosperity was a permanent and reasonable entitlement for hardworking, ambitious young men. By the late 1860s there were ominous signs that things would not work out as he had expected.

Railroad bonds slumped in value in 1866[10] as profits declined. To compensate, railroads raised rates, which in turn angered farmers needing to get their crops to market. The Granger movement was formed by farmers banding together to apply pressure on state legislatures to intervene. The first Granger laws were enacted in Wisconsin in 1874 to curb price gouging.

The new laws did not stop the frequent, and often violent, protests that continued for the next 20 years—the situation being compounded by falling agricultural prices. In 1870 corn sold for 70 cents per bushel and then declined steadily to 30 cents per bushel by 1890. Wheat and oat prices fell 30%.[11]

One by one the railroads went bankrupt. We found in the literature that historians often blame the railroad's problems on the falling agricultural prices. The fact is that between 1870 and 1890, the pick it and ship it business model was weakening, and less and less railroad freight was agricultural. By 1890, less than 25% of all freight carried by rail came off the farm.[12] Agricultural products were slowly being replaced by capital goods and commodities, but the prices of these were falling as well. Between 1870 and 1896 copper prices fell 70%, steel rails 84%, and coal 33%.[13] As the purveyors of these products made less money, and as demand fell, less product was shipped, further impacting railroad profits.

Those desperate to preserve the take it, make it, break it business culture while it deteriorated in the late twentieth century (and continues to deteriorate in the twenty-first) must have taken a lesson in misguided pigheadedness from the pick it and ship it gang a century before. Then, too, instead of taking shrinking profit margins as a sign that old business structures needed replacing, it was decided that the status quo must be preserved at all costs. The railroad industry became highly leveraged and speculative.[14] Financing schemes, crooked political land giveaways, and shifty debt arrangements were rationalized as sophisticated business tools but in the end did nothing to slow the rate of railroad bankruptcies.[15]

Layoffs and wage cuts incited protests, riots, and strikes beyond just the rail industry. Unrest extended into mining and manufacturing as declining prosperity filtered through America. The term *hobo* entered the lexicon. In 1875 the American Federation of Labor (AFL) was born. By 1888, when the optimistic 32-year old Baum opened his first store in Aberdeen, South Dakota, shocking events like the Haymarket massacre[16] were destroying Americans' spirit, and a lower standard of living was destroying their health (see Figure 5.2).

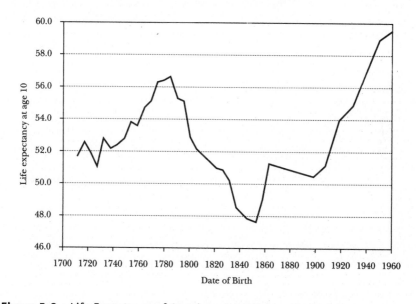

**Figure 5.2** Life Expectancy of American-Born Males, 1710–1960

*Source:* Robert Fogel, "Nutrition and the Decline in Mortality since 1700," in Stanley Engerman and Robert Gallman, eds., *Long-Term Factors in American Economic Growth* (Chicago: University of Chicago Press, 1986), Table 9.A.1.

*Note:* Life expectancy of American males declined in the latter half of the 1800s and did not return to the levels of the late 1700s and early 1800s until the acceleration phase of the second dominant investment system in the 1920s.

## "TOTO, WE'RE NOT IN KANSAS ANYMORE"

A privileged upbringing, within a culture and economy where all things seemed possible, must have helped to fortify Baum against the far less productive conditions he faced as an adult when the faltering economy overwhelmed even the government framework that had helped to create it.

> One might search the whole list of Congress, Judiciary, and Executive during the twenty-five years 1870–1895, and find little but damaged reputation. The period was poor in purpose and barren in results.[17]

As a young man Baum tried, but failed, to make a living as a playwright, actor, traveling salesman, and the owner of Baum's Castorine Company, which produced axle grease.

While he probably didn't get much comfort from it, Baum was not alone. In 1882 there had been 6,738 business failures, not including farms, railroads, and their bankers. By 1893 the bankruptcies of the businesses related to the pick it and ship it economy more than doubled to 15,242.[18] Frustrated citizens watched the development of electricity, which most could not afford to access.[19] Rapid communication and its promise of higher productivity arose with the spread of telephones,[20] but their actual use was limited to the very wealthy. A book by Jacob Riis titled *How the Other Half Lives* was published in 1890 and became a bestseller. It exposed the poverty and squalor of life in New York City. The Sierra Club was founded in 1892 to curb the destruction of the environment by the coal, oil, and steel industries.

If Baum never gave up because he believed in a more prosperous future, he must have been encouraged by the first million-share trading day on the New York Stock Exchange in 1886.[21] Whether he correctly saw this as a sign of a new source of productivity that was percolating just beneath the surface, we do not know. But in 1888, at the age of 32, he boldly moved his wife and his children to Aberdeen, South Dakota, and opened Baum's Bazaar, which did not last long before it fell into bankruptcy and he turned to publishing.[22]

Baum finally found himself unable to support his family when his newspaper, the *Aberdeen Saturday Pioneer,* went under because of the sinking local economy. He would be forced to move his family to Chicago and find work—first as a newspaper reporter, then as a commission salesman.

That not only Baum but also the fiscal condition of the nation

## TIMELINES OF PAINFUL TIMES, 100 YEARS APART

**1980**—7.6 million unemployed; Prime rate 21.5%
**1979**—Gas rationing begins; Chrysler loses $1.1 billion (biggest loss for American company); Divorce rate up 69% in 10 years
**1978**—Oil prices soar
**1977**—New York City blackout affects 9 million
**1976**—The term *misery index* enters the lexicon
**1975**—Dow begins the year at 632.04, the lowest start in 14 years; vandalism and violence increase; New York homicides up 20%; rapes and robbery up 40%
**1974**—President Nixon resigns
**1973**—Stock market falls, recession begins

→

**1873**—Stock market panic and depression
**1874**—Ulysses S. Grant presides over most corrupt administration of the nineteenth century
**1875**—Farm prices collapse, record number of foreclosures
**1876**—18,000 Businesses go broke, 4 times as many in 1871
Immigration reverses: 45% more people leave the U.S. than enter it
**1877**—Erie Rail goes broke, massive strikes against railroads
**1878**—U.S. currency plunges to lowest point

**1986**—National debt passes $2 trillion (double that of 1981)
**1984**—United States becomes a debtor nation first time since 1913
**1983**—Record crime wave in New York City
**1982**—20,265 Business bankruptcies, highest figure since depression; Silicone Valley begins first layoff
**1981**—General Motors reports first loss since 1921

→

**1881**—American Federation of Labor forms to combat unfair practices
**1882**—Strike against the iron and steel industry (lasts four months); freight handlers close entire railroad system
**1883**—Panic of 1883, railroad overbuilding causes more failures and strikes
**1884**—Knights of labor shut down Gold Rail Line
**1885**—Riots in Cincinnati lasts 6 days, 45 killed
**1886**—Chicago Haymarket riot kills 60; 1,400 strikes

---

## TIMELINES OF PAINFUL TIMES, 100 YEARS APART

**1990**—Drexel Lambert goes bankrupt, housing values fall, personal bankruptcies up 60%, U.S. enters recession

**1989**—Congress passes bill to bail out S&L industry; Dow drops 190 points, largest drop in history

**1988**—Homeless estimated as high as 2 million

**1987**—STOCK MARKET CRASH; $500 billion in equity lost

→

**1887**—10 year cycle of drought, causes many farm failures

**1888**—Best-selling book proposes government to control production and distribution of all goods

**1889**—Farmers and Labor Union of North America agree on graduated income tax, government-owned railroads, and breakup of large landholders

**1994**—U.S. stocks predicted to underperform for rest of decade

**1992**—Poverty rises to 14.2%, highest in 9 years

**1991**—Disposable income falls

→

**1892**—Homestead Steel strikes, biggest strike of nineteenth century

**1893**—Crash of 1893; depression lasts 4 years; Philadelphia and Reading Railroads go broke

**1894**—Coxey's Army of unemployed march on Washington, D.C.

**1895**—Gold reserves sink to 41 million

**1896**—Farmers commodity prices have now declined for 33 years

---

would be transformed into something wildly successful was not apparent to our hero as he stood penniless on the prairie in South Dakota. It was not apparent to manufacturers of equipment, rubber products, chemicals, hardware, forest products, leather products, or household goods. It was not apparent to newspaper publishers, doctors, lawyers, farmers, or bankers. And just like a century later, in 1994, on the eve of another explosion in productivity and prosperity, it was conspicuously not apparent to those on Wall Street, supposedly with their hands on the pulse of America's financial future. As reported in the *New York Times* on January 1, 1896, "It began with a depression, ran into buoyancy, held the advance long enough for the enthusiasts to liquidate . . . and finally, in its closing days, witnessed a panic. To the investor the year has been a trying one."

• • •

## THE TURNING POINT

In 1897 Baum was on the road selling glass, bakery, and cookware. He was surprised to find that for the first time in his life he was making a good living. This did not stem from a suddenly elevated appreciation for crockery, but from a reinvention of the economy, like the one we witnessed in the mid-1990s. A stockbroker at the firm of Cuyler, Morgan, and Company had this to say in January of 1897:

> Among investors and people from all parts of the country I find a very hopeful feeling. There is a general confidence in the future. And this, by the way, is in marked distinction to the lack of such confidence which existed before. Then everyone was frightened. Now all are sanguine.[23]

The positive new trend didn't stop there: "Failures for the year which closed last night have been smaller and average liabilities per failure smaller than in any year during the last 23 years except four."[24]

The new prosperity allowed Baum to recapture some of the affluence of his childhood. He moved his family into an elegant new home. For the first time in his adult life he had some disposable income and time to cultivate his creative gifts, which he put to good use. In 1898 he finished writing *The Wonderful Wizard of Oz*.

A number of authors and sources have remarked on this new prosperity: "The final years of the century found a dynamic reversal in economic conditions."[25] In *From Dawn to Decadence*, Jacques Barzun stated, "The turn of the century was a turning indeed; not an ordinary turning *point* but rather a turntable on which a whole crowd of things facing one way revolved until they faced the opposite way."[26] "A retrospect of 1897 is much more pleasing than was a similar retrospect of 1896. The year was marked by a decisive recovery of business . . . and at the year's close we find the outlook more hopeful than for many years past."[27] And the *New York Times* noted on January 17, 1897, that the "stock market became active. It is strong. Both activity and strength promise further development. Even something like enthusiasm is developing. The Wall Street week has closed with a show of what—contrasted with recent experiences—is outright buoyancy."

This was a dramatic turnaround, and it was caused by the same set of factors that would synchronize an economic and cultural shift of similar proportions in 1995. The fact that both of these turning points occurred just in time to usher in new centuries may seem a little too convenient. That the same set of factors that rejuvenated the economy of 1897 and rekindled prosperity converged again in the twentieth century may be suspect.

A variety of theories have been put forth to explain the happy reversal in America's fortunes in 1897, not one of which commands universal agreement. Supporters of William McKinley's candidacy for president attributed his winning of the election to the new prosperity. Historians have pointed to the discovery of gold in the Klondike river valley in 1896, and the Alaskan gold rush that followed it, as the source of new wealth. But the facts show that many huge gold strikes had occurred earlier with no economic effect, one in Colorado as early as 1890. To quote David H. Fischer, "These events were part of a long continuum of gold discoveries that had happened through the nineteenth century without raising prices."[28] It follows that gold strikes alone did not start the economic boom in 1897.

Some economists contend that an increase in the money supply created the turnaround in 1897. They cite data showing that the annual growth of money was 6% from 1879 to 1897 and that it increased to 7.5% from 1897 to 1914. Other economists point out that using only a slightly different set of years to calculate averages shows that there was not appreciable change before or after 1896 in the money supply.[29]

What no one questions is that Americans stepped into an entirely different world in 1897. That world brought with it a new dominant investment system. The same four factors that created our own new system in 1995 converged in 1897 to send America on an exciting new course.

## THE ELEMENTS THAT CREATED THE SECOND DOMINANT INVESTMENT SYSTEM REPRESENTED BY THE DOW JONES INDUSTRIAL AVERAGE

### Element 1: Completion of an Incubation Interval

*The suggestion that two decades, and not one, be called the Nineties, arises from the rush of new ideas and behavior that took place between 1885 and 1905.*

—Jacques Barzun, *From Dawn to Decadence*

In Chapter 4 we defined an incubation interval as a period of history that spawns a superabundance of new ideas that must be cultivated and developed during the interval before they become ubiquitous enough to increase productivity. The incubation interval for the third dominant investment system occurred between 1970 and 1994.

In a capitalistic economy, things must either grow or die, and historians and economists have pointed out the intrinsic importance that these periods of innovation have in advancing a healthy economy.

The incubation interval for the second dominant investment system occurred between 1870 and 1896. Just as they would a century later, long periods of prosperity stood like bookends on either side of it. A characteristic of both intervals was the breaking down of confidence in the capabilities of established authorities. That the canons of behavior and frameworks of action—which worked during the first two-thirds of each century—no longer worked in the last third, was not grasped by those in power until the point was forcibly driven home by those who had to live with the decisions that were handed down. In the 1970s and 1980s a short list of challenges to the status quo included Vietnam War protests, race riots, and the women's liberation movement. In the 1870s and 1880s examples include the labor and granger movements and the feminist movement (Baum's mother-in-law was Matilda Joslyn Gage, who coauthored *History of Women Suffrage* with Susan B. Anthony and Elizabeth Cady Stanton).

In *The Victorian Frame of Mind,* the historian Walter Houghton says of the years prior to 1870 that it "was still possible to adopt this or that theory of Church or State with full confidence that it might be true—though not that it was." He proceeds to comment on the shift that occurred: "But less possible after 1870. For about that time a number of things converged to suggest relativity of knowledge and the subjective character of thought. This radical change, bounding the mid-Victorian temper, is documented in the popular work of Walter Pater."[30]

Out of this stew of change came innovations that would change how life was lived: "In a word, between 1870 and 1900 the pattern of working-class life which the writers, dramatists and TV producers of the 1950's thought of as 'traditional' came into being. It was not 'traditional' then, but new. It came to be thought of as age-old and unchanging."[31]

The first lesson to be taken from this incubation interval is its far-reaching and culture-altering effects. The second is that the extent to which an innovation will impact society may not be known for decades. That something as innocuous as barbed wire would change the culture of a continent by allowing cattlemen, farmers, the transportation industry, and the residents of towns and cities to cohabit large blocks of land was not foreseen on its invention. Nor can it be foreseen how innovations may develop when used in concert with others. An inflatable rubber tire is one thing. Who would have predicted that it would become an intrinsic element in establishing a culture in which two or

## Products of the Nineteenth-Century Incubation Interval

| Date | Creation | Date | Creation |
|------|----------|------|----------|
| 1870 | Pneumatic subway | 1885 | Skyscraper |
| 1871 | Pneumatic drill | | Transformer |
| 1872 | Electric typewriter | | Gasoline-powered automobile |
| 1873 | Car coupler | | Adding machine |
| | Barbed wire | 1886 | Aluminum reduction |
| 1874 | Structural steel bridge | | Halftone engraving |
| 1875 | Internal combustion engine | 1887 | "Platter" record (horizontal flat |
| | Electric dental drill | | disc) |
| | Mimeograph | | Monotype |
| 1876 | Telephone | | Air inflated rubber tire |
| | Gas engine | 1888 | Credit card |
| 1877 | Phonograph | | Kodak camera |
| | Refrigerator car | 1889 | Dishwasher |
| | Glider | | Aspirin |
| | Electric welding | | Steam turbine |
| 1878 | Electric railway | | Bolt-action rifle |
| | Arc lamp | 1890 | Milk test |
| | Potato chip | 1891 | Peepshow, kinetoscope |
| | Microphone | | Tesla coil |
| | Incandescent lightbulb | 1892 | Escalator |
| 1880 | Lipstick | | Diesel engine |
| | Hearing aid | 1893 | Movie projector |
| 1882 | Electric flat iron | | Photoelectric cell |
| | Electric fan | 1894 | Automatic loom |
| 1883 | Linotype | 1895 | X ray |
| | Automatic machine gun | | Hot dog |
| 1884 | Steam turbine | | Safety razor |
| | Flexible roll film | 1896 | Self-powered model airplane |
| | Roller coaster | | Wireless telegraphy |
| | Fountain pen | | |
| | Hamburger | | |

three cars per family make the automobile America's main mode of transportation? Not enough time has elapsed since the end of the twentieth-century incubation interval for us to appreciate all that it can deliver. But what the nineteenth-century incubation interval tells us is that we have a long and exciting journey ahead.

## Element 2: Dependable Consumer Economy

Just how Americans' devotion to consumerism developed would make an interesting topic for a book all by itself; because as tough as things were from the 1870s to 1896, the American consumer kept the economy from collapse. The number of people engaged in retail trade grew 52% between 1864 and 1874 and jumped another 63% by 1889. Advertising volume grew 300% from 1867 to 1880 and another 171% by 1900.[32]

In 1872 Aaron Montgomery Ward established the first large-scale mail-order business. He opened up a consumer pipeline by winning the public's trust when he proved that he had the ability to get household items to isolated farmers and remote communities. In 1875 1,138 new brand names and trademarks were registered with the U.S. Patent Office, and the number rose exponentially every year. Everything from malted milk (invented in 1886 by William Horlick of Racine, Wisconsin) to baseballs was delivered across America.

In 1878 the American Cereal Company mass-marketed the first breakfast food, Quaker Oats, and in 1879 Frank Woolworth opened the first five-and-dime. The Armour Brothers were making Chicago Beef and Pork famous. John Deere figured out that farmers would buy manufactured plows, and the Pillsburys of Minneapolis–St. Paul figured out that their wives preferred to buy ready-to-use flour.

In 1883 the *Ladies Home Journal* became a hit with housewives and a great place to introduce new products like Coca-Cola, which was created in 1886, the same year *Cosmopolitan* magazine became a new advertising outlet for fashion and cosmetics.

In 1892 *Vogue* magazine began publication, and Sears, Roebuck, and Co. mailed out 8,000 postcards across the country introducing their new services. Two thousand orders were immediately received. With the promise, "Satisfaction guaranteed or your money back," items as diverse as washing machines, plows, tools, watches, baby carriages, bicycles, harnesses, and stoves were sent out across the country.

## Element 3: Improvement in Economic Conditions

The single most harmful factor at the root of the economic hardship of the 1870–1896 period was a decade-long deflation. Wholesale commodity prices bottomed in 1896.[33] When prices began to inch up in 1897, this improvement in economic conditions brought relief to farmers, merchants, and manufacturers.[34] Real wages rose for the first time that most laborers could remember (see Figure 5.3).[35]

Economists debate the reasons for the economic turnaround. Because there was no controlling agency like the Federal Reserve to govern the money flow, the improvement could only come from market forces. The logical explanation seems to be that an accelerating population increased demand. In 1850 the total U.S. population was esti-

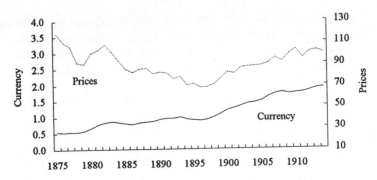

**Figure 5.3** The Price Revolution of the Twentieth Century, 1875–1914

*Note:* Wholesale prices reversed their deflationary trend in 1896. The money supply had been gradually increasing since 1875 even as prices kept falling and could not have caused the end of the damaging price declines (Milton Friedman and Anna Jacobson Schwartz, *A Monetary History of the United States, 1857–1960*).

*Source:* "The Great Wave: Price Revolutions and the Rhythm of History" by David Hackett Fischer, © 1996 David Hackett Fischer. Used by permission of Oxford University Press

mated at 17,312,533. Even though difficult times caused immigration to reverse in 1876 (45% more people left the United States than entered it), the U.S. population by 1890 had soared to 45,979,391.[36] This 165.58% increase in population drove the need for goods and services allowing for higher prices.

## Element 4: Surge in Foreign Exports

The first modern Olympic games were held in Athens, Greece, in 1896. This was a harbinger of the happy circumstance that was to follow. In 1896 European countries began to buy U.S. agricultural products in record amounts:

> The government's annual statement of international trade balances—showing more than a million of dollars to our credit for each day of 1896—is an ample answer to every doubt or quibble about our financial condition. Such a record is unprecedented in the history of our nation.[37]

In 1896 and 1897 European wheat crops were shrinking while American crops were twice as large.[38] This is when America earned the title "bread basket for the world." American wheat that sold for 51 cents in 1895 sold for 72 cents in 1896 and 81 cents in 1897,[39] a 59% increase. U.S. wheat exports had doubled.

Agricultural products initiated the export boom, but it seemed to open a channel for other American products as well. The export value of automotive parts and engines grew from $2,000 in 1895 to $10,000 in 1896; sawmill products from $14,000 in 1894 to $22,000 in 1897; petroleum products from $3,000 in 1895 to $19,000 in 1897; machinery from $22,000 in 1894 to $44,000 in 1898; copper products from $16,000 in 1895 to $34,000 in 1897. In total, the export of U.S. merchandise jumped from $793,000 in 1895 to $1,032,000 in 1896 and $1,210,000 by 1898, a 52.58% increase over the three-year period.[40]

> After a whole year of entire freedom from disturbance or alarm, in which the country has paid heavy foreign indebtedness, taken and paid many millions for stocks sent from abroad, and accumulated credits against other countries represented by merchandise balances of more than $320,000,000 in its favor for the past five months, with deferred exchanges for more than $20,000,000 held by New York banks alone, while great industries have been pushing their way into foreign markets with unprecedented success, the monetary situation is no longer a matter of anxiety.[41]

From the end of the discovery phase in the spring of 2000, through the market volatility of 2002—as most of the stocks of the new dominant investment system tumbled in value—there was a lot of talk about how this stampede out of stocks meant the end of the new twenty-first century (realize, capitalize, customize) company. All one has to do to prove how incorrect this conclusion was would be to turn to September 24, 1900, when the Dow Jones Industrial Average had fallen 31.76% from its high of 77.61 on September 7, 1899—the end of its own discovery phase. The dramatic decline in value of what was then the new take it, make it, break it–style company did nothing to prevent those stocks and others like them from being the driving forces of American productivity for decades to come. It did nothing to stop those companies from helping America to form a "pattern of life . . . that would come to be thought of as typical of the 1950's."[42]

To comprehend that we are only just beginning to walk down a parallel road of prosperity, we only have to appreciate that the interlocking of the same four elements that converged in 1897 to send the twentieth century on a new course, did the same for us in 1995.

• • •

The fluctuations of the financial markets today are made to seem as mysterious as the rites of a secret male society. Its actions are viewed through a screen of complexities, maintained by a variety of forces with their own agendas, and rooted in rigid principles and traditional conventions. This approach is not unappealing to many people. A lot of us prefer the feeling of stability conferred by established precepts, even if we do not understand them. To know they exist inspires confidence, an important requirement for participants in the financial marketplace.

The problem is that the financial markets exist within a capitalistic economy that can only survive through a course of evolution. The markets are a body that is kept healthy only by the continual mitosis and metamorphosis of its cells of stocks and bonds. Its life depends on the process of change. This makes the application of long-lasting, hard and fast rules of security analysis and market performance a lot like nailing down Jell-O: Eventually it will transform itself and follow its own natural course.

All of this makes the study of change more helpful in understanding the future of stocks and bonds than the brooding over, or creation of more, intractable analytics. Placing stocks and bonds in their historic and cultural context afforded us the ability to examine their changes, and we have learned the following (see also Figure 5.4):

- There is a process at work that causes an omnipresent method of doing business—pick it or ship it; take it, make it, break it; realize, capitalize, customize—and the investments that represent that method of doing business; to go through almost human stages of birth and early development. They will thrive during

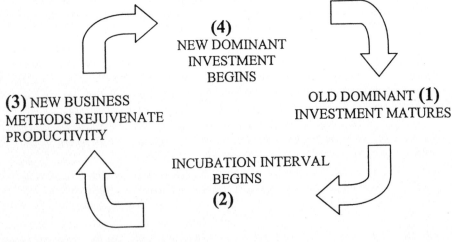

**(4)**
NEW DOMINANT
INVESTMENT
BEGINS

**(3)** NEW BUSINESS
METHODS REJUVENATE
PRODUCTIVITY

OLD DOMINANT **(1)**
INVESTMENT MATURES

INCUBATION INTERVAL
BEGINS
**(2)**

**Figure 5.4**  The Cycle of a Dominant Investment

their prime years of productivity and performance and then eventually pass into several decades of aging:

| | |
|---|---|
| Birth and development | First four decades |
| Prime years | Middle decades: 50s and 60s |
| Years of aging | Last decades 70s, 80s, and early 90s |

- The last 25 years or so of the aging process are stressful and difficult as the mature business model, and the dominant investment that represents it, are no longer strong enough to drive economic productivity.

- Curiously, these last 25 years are also a time when old rules are challenged and an abundance of new innovations are created and developed that will eventually be the new drivers of productivity and result in a new dominant investment system. We call this period the incubation interval.

- The convergence of four elements sparks a dramatic and lengthy economic turnaround that signals the birth of a new dominant investment system: (1) end of the incubation interval; (2) dependable consumer economy, (3) improvement in economic conditions; and (4) surge in foreign exports.

Stewards of the old dominant investment system have told us that it is impossible for the securities markets to cycle in this way because people are so different in the twenty-first century than in the nineteenth or even in the twentieth century. When asked to explain how they came to this conclusion, the response ranged from "my gut tells me" to "it's just something everybody knows." One person said with a straight face that he was well acquainted with the habits of nineteenth-century Americans because he never misses a rerun of *Bonanza* or *Wagon Train*.

The importance of the written word to the highly literate nineteenth-century American citizen results in a plethora of material giving us insight into their thoughts and feelings. The language is more flowery, but what is expressed is uncannily familiar: "The eminent lawyer, the physician in full practice, the minister . . . even the literary workman, or the eager man of science—are one and all condemned to an amount and continued severity of exertion of which our grandfathers knew little."[43] According to Mark Patterson in *The Age of Reason,* "Even apart from personal ambitions, the very existence of hundreds of objects, once unknown or within the reach of a few, now made widely available and therefore desirable, increased the size of one's expenses and the load of his work."[44] W. R. Greg wrote, "Not only the tempo of work but the tempo of living had increased with striking impact, so much so that one observer thought that 'the most salient characteristics of life in this latter portion of the 19th century is speed.'"[45]

By the end of the incubation interval in 1896, the rush of human traffic created problems like our own: "Parents fretted more about the behavior of their teenagers . . . the concerns focused on the nation's youth problem . . . pilfering, vagrancy, roaming the streets, larceny, drinking, begging and fighting"[46]

Cocaine was popular among the upper classes, and morphine was not yet illegal. The term *seven-percent solution* was coined because it was well known that this was what the famous detective Sherlock Holmes injected himself with from time to time.

The improvement in the economy after 1897 created a higher level of disposable income and some leisure time, but like today, "many middle class Americans could play only if they were persuaded they were improving themselves and not wasting time."[47]

The old health spas of Saratoga Springs and White Sulphur Springs were inundated with a new clientele interested in becoming physically fit through more active pursuits than merely lolling in soothing waters. The health craze instigated the opening of new spas for the middle class in Frenchlick, Indiana; Hot Springs, Arkansas; Colorado Springs, Colorado; and Asheville, North Carolina. A popular diet discouraged carbohydrates and recommended a breakfast of bacon, eggs, beefsteak, or sausage.[48]

Nineteenth-century investors were as enthralled with companies of the new Dow Jones Industrial Average during its discovery phase as we were with NASDAQ stocks during our own discovery phase. Stocks like American Tobacco rose from $66.50 in 1896 to $221.50 by April 1899, a gain of 233%.[49] Their bubble of irrational exuberance burst when Dow stocks plummeted 25% in just the last four months of 1899. We explained in Chapter 2 how this was followed by another decline of 31.76% in 1900, and then another drop of 46% between 1901 and 1903. But these frightening market reversals neither stopped the Dow from becoming the dominant investment nor kept it from nearly doubling in value over the next decade.

It should not be lost on us today that as the Dow rose in its early years to become the dominant investment, America was engaged in two wars, the Spanish American War and the War in the Philippines. The assassination of President McKinley and the distrust of the Robber Barons of corporate America surrounded the financial markets with uncertainty. Just as things began to look better, investors had to put up with additional market declines of 48.54% in 1906. The message in this is that none of these setbacks kept the Dow from becoming the new dominant investment then, nor will similar struggles keep NASDAQ-type stocks from thriving as the dominant investment now.

The biggest threat to our investment health will not stem from the inevitable crises—always striking when we least expect—that will temporarily impact stock prices. The real threat lies closer to home and derives from any inclination there may be to dismiss the changes that have occurred.

The twenty-first century investment transformation has already affected pension benefits, 401(k) plans, and the financial services industry. It could materially affect benefits promised by insurance and mutual fund companies. The next chapter explains why individuals, state, and federal regulatory agencies must acknowledge the important reconfiguration of the financial markets and act immediately to address these changes.

## NOTES

1. Jeremy Atack and Peter Passell, *A New Economic View of American History* (New York: W.W. Norton, 1994).

2. Ibid.

3. *Historical Statistics of the United States* (Washington, DC: U.S. Department of Commerce, Bureau of Census, 1975).

4. Ibid., p. 588.

5. Jeremy Atack and Peter Passell, *A New Economic View of American History* (New York: W.W. Norton, 1994), p. 445.

6. Walt Whitman, *Leaves of Grass* (New York: W.W. Norton, 1973), p. 480. Reprinted by arrangement with New York University Press.

7. Brooks Atkinson, ed., *Walden and Other Writings of Henry David Thoreau* (New York: Random House, 1965), p. 81.

8. Jeremy Atack and Peter Passell, *A New Economic View of American History* (New York: W.W. Norton, 1994), p. 445.

9. Sydney Homer, *A History of Interest Rates* (New Brunswick, NJ: Rutgers University Press, 1963), p. 282.

10. Ibid., p. 312.

11. *Historical Statistics of the United States* (Washington, DC: U.S. Department of Commerce, Bureau of Census, 1975), p. 735.

12. *Historical Statistics of the United States* (Washington, DC: U.S. Department of Commerce, Bureau of Census, 1975), p. 431.

13. *Historical Statistics of the United States* (Washington, DC: U.S. Department of Commerce, Bureau of Census, 1975), p. 208.

14. Jeremy Atack and Peter Passell, *A New Economic View of American History* (New York: W.W. Norton, 1994), p. 431.

15. Samuel Morison, *The Oxford History of the American People* (Cambridge, UK: Oxford University Press, 1965).

16. At a labor meeting in 1886 at Haymarket Square in Chicago, police opened fire on the crowd. Seven police were killed, and a total of 70 people were injured.

17. Henry Adams, *The Education of Henry Adams* (New York: Random House, 1931), p. 294.

18. *Historical Statistics of the United States* (Washington, DC: U.S. Department of Commerce, Bureau of Census, 1975).

19. Edison perfected the lightbulb in 1879. Electric power lines reached most homes during the next 25 years, but cables had to be installed from homes to the lines at the street. The cost of these cables and the power was paid by the consumer. Chris Scarre, ed., *Smithsonian Timeline of Inventions* (New York: Darling Kindersley, 1993), p. 43.

20. The telephone was invented in 1876.

21. Jeremy Atack and Peter Passell, *A New Economic View of American History* (New York: W.W. Norton, 1994).

22. David Traxel, *1989: The Birth of the American Century* (New York: Random House, 1998).

23. Benjamin Graham, *New York Times* (1897, January 12).

24. Dun and Bradstreet, *New York Times* (1989, January).

25. Milton Friedman and Anna Schwartz, *A Monetary History of the United States* (Princeton, NJ: Princeton University Press, 1963), p. 138.

26. Jacques Barzun, *From Dawn to Decadence: 1500 to the Present—500 Years of Western Cultural Life* (New York: Harper Collins, 2000), p. 615.

27. David Hackett Fischer, *The Great Wave* (Cambridge, UK: Oxford University Press, 1996), p. 182.

28. Ibid., p. 184.

29. Ibid.

30. Walter E. Houghton, *The Victorian Frame of Mind 1830–1870* (New Haven, CT: Yale University Press, 1957), p. 14.

31. Eric Hobsbawm, *Industry and Empire: The Birth of the Industrial Revolution* (New York: New Press, 1999), p. 142.

32. *Historical Statistics of the United States* (Washington, DC: U.S. Department of Commerce, Bureau of Census, 1975).

33. Ibid.

34. David Hackett Fischer, *The Great Wave* (Cambridge, UK: Oxford University Press, 1996).

35. Jeremy Atack and Peter Passell, *A New Economic View of American History* (New York: W.W. Norton, 1994)

36. *Historical Statistics of the United States* (Washington, DC: U.S. Department of Commerce, Bureau of Census, 1975).

37. *New York Times* (1897, January).

38. Milton Friedman and Anna Schwartz, *A Monetary History of the United States* (Princeton, NJ: Princeton University Press, 1963).

39. *Historical Statistics of the United States* (Washington, DC: U.S. Department of Commerce, Bureau of Census, 1975).

40. Ibid.

41. Dunn & Co., *New York Times* (1898, January 1).

42. Eric Hobsbawm, *Industry and Empire: The Birth of the Industrial Revolution* (New York: New Press, 1999), p. 142.

43. Walter E. Houghton, *The Victorian Frame of Mind, 1830–1870* (New Haven, CT: Yale University Press, 1975), p. 6.

44. Ibid., p. 6.

45. Ibid., p. 6.

46. Thomas Schlereth, *Victorian America* (New York: HarperCollins, 1991).

47. Ibid., p. 209.

48. Ibid., p. 219.

49. *Wall Street Journal,* May 28, 1996.

# Part Three

# RECONSTRUCTION

# 6

# ARTIFICIAL INTELLIGENCE

## Why You Cannot Count on Your Pension Income Retirement Money or Foundation Grant and What to Do about It

*The fates lead the willing and drag the unwilling.*
—Seneca

### PLAY IT AS IT LAYS

"I'd like to thank you all for coming," said our host, the president of a $780,000,000 company, as he raised his glass to toast our dinner at the Bellagio Hotel, one of the planet's more lavish casino-resorts. Even though we were there on our own dime—finding out later that the two actuaries, who also brought their wives, had their expenses paid by our host—we were surprised that this relatively small Florida company would foot the bill for its pension committee to meet at such a lavish location, particularly considering the circumstances.

The purpose of the meeting was to discuss the company's pension plan, which promised to reward long-term employees by paying them a retirement benefit equal to 30% of their annual pay. Because there was not enough money in the plan to do this, meetings were scheduled, reservations were made, and we all found ourselves—very apropos as it turned out—in Las Vegas, the city built to escape reality.

The appropriateness of a destination like Las Vegas to the examination of a pension plan, specifically categorized as a defined benefit plan, arises from a pension system that condones stacking the deck against those whom it was intended to benefit. The same sleight of hand that put Social Security in danger runs amuck in the arcane world of pension plans. No one asks too many questions. We see what we expect to see and hear what we want to hear.

What we heard from the company's president during the morning meeting the next day was that revenues and earnings were way down. We heard about lousy cash flow and increasing competition. It would be a hardship for this company to make enough of a contribution to its pension plan to ensure that it could make good on its promises to continue to pay current retirees, plus those in line to retire, the income benefits that they have been promised in the years ahead.

This announcement was not unexpected. Most companies face the same dilemma. Do you report cash flow as earnings, which can boost your stock price? Do you use it for bonuses to reward that new chief financial officer (CFO) or maybe yourself? Do you use it to expand and buy that new equipment to make you more competitive, or do you dump it in the pension plan?

We thought we had been summoned because the company had decided to do the latter. Why else would we have been invited? After all, this company was not presently a client, but a prospective client, to whom we had laid out the new procedures that must be implemented to operate pension plans in this new investment culture in which we find ourselves. The infusion of cash, coupled with the new strategy we would help to put in place, would put things in order so that the company could keep its promises of paying retirement benefits. That the financial advisors who currently handled the plan were not in attendance led us to assume that they would soon be out of the picture.

What actually took place is what happens every day in boardrooms, committee meetings, and hotel conference rooms across the country when the topic of discussion is an underfunded pension plan. The solution decided upon was as shifty as any card trick but more insidious, not only because it would affect people's lives, but because it is dressed up in a comfortingly conservative suit of actuarial procedure which never seems to come under scrutiny. Here is how it works.

Assumptions about the pension plan's financial condition are made based on

- The number of employees who will receive benefits
- The benefits to which these people will be entitled
- How long the beneficiaries will live and require payments
- The disability rate for nonretired participants who may require benefits
- Turnover rate (how many people leave the company before they are entitled to benefits)

- The age at which people can retire
- The investment return (the higher the investment return assumption, the less money the company needs to put in the plan; said another way, the more money the plan makes for itself, or is *projected* to make for itself, the better it is for the company that sponsors it)

Once a year the actuaries selected by the company lump all of this together and pick a number to represent the hodgepodge. This is called the *actuarial assumption*.

The other task appointed to the actuary is to select a *cost method* for funding the plan. The cost method is simply the way the amount of employer contributions to the plan are determined.

So while those of us gathered around the conference table at the Bellagio munched our continental breakfasts, upon a command from the company's president, the actuaries pushed aside their gooey Danish and stood to present their actuarial assumption and their cost method. The sleight of hand comes next. You will understand how the trick is done if we give you a little background.

The actuaries are advocates for the company. Just like any other vendor they are selected and paid by their clients to perform a service. That service is to ensure that the company that hires them gets to put as little money as possible into the pension plan.

In the text *Planning for Retirement Needs* you can read this: "The most important decision the plan actuary advises on is what cost method to use for a defined-benefit plan. . . . The right cost method should provide the plan sponsor with flexibility in funding and also meet the employer's tax objectives."[1]

Here is where reality and perception part. The reality is that actuaries do not wake up each morning worrying that retirees will have enough to live on. They worry that their clients will not be happy if they actually have to put any money toward the benefits they have promised their employees. They worry that they will be fired if they don't provide "flexibility": "What the actuary does is set up a situation where there is flexibility. . . . The actuary can maximize flexibility by setting up past-service liability vs amortizing past-service and future-service costs together."

Dodge, weave, juggle—whatever it takes is okay. All that is required is that the funding standard account required by IRS regulations be satisfied in the end. It is no different from the corporate tax return prepared by the accountant. Because every available loophole and strategy are used to reduce the tax bill, what ends up on the return bears little, if any, resemblance to a company's real earnings. There is nothing illegal about this. We all do the same with our personal tax returns. The difference is that the way we do our tax returns will not affect anyone's promised retirement benefits.

*Planning for Retirement Needs* is not some renegade publication, but a balanced and thorough book that was required reading for us to obtain some continuing education credits. Within the industry it is understood that the actuaries' allegiance is to the sponsor of the plan. It is understood that their projections are meaningless as they relate to anyone actually collecting any money upon retirement. "Neither the plan actuary nor the choice of an actuarial cost method bears any relationship to the cost of the plan."[2]

It is most plan sponsors themselves, like our host at the Bellagio, who misunderstand the actuary's role. The solution he had ready at that breakfast meeting had nothing whatsoever to do with getting his company's plan to where it would be able to keep its promises. Instead he asked the actuaries to provide a solution by changing their "assumption" and their "cost method." Obviously, this had all been discussed ahead of time because two new scenarios were quickly produced, neither requiring the use of any company cash. With no discussion necessary, a motion was made and voted on.

Next, we were invited to take 10 minutes to discuss "the market." The following was entered in the minutes of the quarterly pension committee meeting: "Proposals were presented for our consideration by two vendors [meaning us, who both represent the same company]. Their recommendations were analyzed and reviewed and found inferior to the services we are presently receiving. We will continue to review all new services available in the marketplace to ensure that our employees receive the best possible return on their investment dollars." The meeting adjourned, and the president headed for the casino.

## LEAVING LAS VEGAS

States, municipalities, nonprofit organizations, and public and non-public companies all can offer defined benefit plans. Many plan sponsors, either for fear of lawsuits or because they truly wish to do the right thing, do not adopt the position taken by the gambling company president we just described.

In a lot of cases we have found that the actuary's role is simply misunderstood. The actuarial assumption is perceived as a target growth rate for the assets. For example, most plans in the late 1990s had actuarial assumptions ranging between 7% and 8%. Between 1995 and 1999 the average annual rate of return for pension plans in the United States ran between 15% and 28% per year. So in good market years most plan sponsors assumed that they were accumulating huge surpluses. What was not talked about were the liabilities that were also increasing at a record rate. This is no different from the problem we face with Social Security. We have an aging baby-boomer population that is going to live longer than any other generation so far. As Social Security will be drained, so will pension benefits. Furthermore, any perceived surpluses disappeared as 2000 went down as the "worst year in pension history."[3] While liabilities grew at 25.96%, average pension assets fell 2.50%,[4] putting employee benefits in the hole 28.46%—this as the clock keeps ticking on boomers who are going to want their money from these plans.

Compounding the problem even further is that corporate and noncorporate (states, municipalities, nonprofit organizations) America is watching their balance sheets closer than ever. The path of least resistance is to rely on actuarial manipulation to keep as much cash flow as possible from being siphoned off into a pension plan.

At a moment when funds in Social Security, Medicare, and prescription drugs are drying up—when corporations, states, municipalities, and nonprofit organizations are pinching pennies and are unable to supplement employee benefits—we are being thrown a lifeline in the form of a new dominant investment system. The strategy a pension plan needs to employ to take advantage of it will not only help to ensure a plan's solvency and ability to continue to pay its beneficiaries, but will legitimately maximize the plan's growth and lower the amount of contributions, or costs, that fall in the lap of the plan sponsor.

**Table 6.1**  Overall Returns of Defined Benefit Plans Surveyed (as of December 31, 2001) versus Target Return

|  | Return (%) | Target Return (%) |
| --- | --- | --- |
| Under $10M | −2.80 | 8.23 |
| $10–49M | −3.50 | 9.07 |
| $50–199M | −2.66 | 8.59 |
| $200–499M | 1.02 | 8.09 |
| $500–999M | −2.44 | 8.89 |
| $1–9.9B | −3.84 | 8.51 |
| Over $10B | −3.42 | 8.68 |

*Source: PLANSPONSOR*, "Defined Benefit Survey," 2002.

*Note:* Return targets for defined benefit plans are similar across all plan sizes, at 8.65% on average. Actual returns, however, are a different story, with an average overall return in 2001 of −2.78%. Returns in 2001 were a far cry from their targets but were nonetheless stellar as compared to the S&P 500.

The solution to the problem is outlined in the following. Over $200 billion of pension assets have already adopted this strategy. It takes advantage of the new investment culture while protecting promised benefits. Like all things productive, simplicity and common sense are what makes it effective.

## Step 1

We obtained census data from our clients that allow us to segregate both the active and retired employees into age groups according to how old they are and how long before they retire. For most companies we came up with at least four "cells" or categories that look like this:

| Cell | Duration | Description of Employee |
| --- | --- | --- |
| Short | 0–1½ years | Already receiving benefits or will be soon |
| Intermediate | 1½–8½ years | Preretirement age |
| Long | 8½–14 years | The boomers |
| Very long | 14–60 years or more | Youngest and furthest from retirement |

## Step 2

The amount of money that is owed to each group is calculated. In financial jargon this is the future value of present liabilities. From this data an index can be constructed, specific to the plan, telling us day by day what the true liabilities are.

## Step 3

Now that we know exactly what money is owed and when, investments are selected accordingly. This is called matching assets with liabilities.

This is a common-sense approach. It is no different than if you had a balloon mortgage coming due in eight years. You simply set aside money in the appropriate investment to ensure that the funds are available to cover that liability. A financial planner or accountant helps determine how much money should be set aside and how fast it needs to grow to meet this obligation. This is called the discount rate. Because a pension plan has so many obligations, the liability index monitors all of them together. Just as you would check the performance of the investment made for the balloon mortgage, to be sure it was growing at the rate it is supposed to, the pension plan compares

| Cell | Investment Goal | Style and Asset Class Prescription (Dependent on Economic Conditions) |
|---|---|---|
| Short | Cash flow | Treasury and agency bonds; mortgage-backed securities |
| Intermediate | Cash flow Some growth | Same as above plus foreign and corporate bonds, value, growth, and international stock |
| Long | Growth Some cash flow | Small- and large-cap growth and value stock; international and domestic fixed income; some emerging markets stock |
| Very long | Growth | Value, growth, focus on small- and mid-cap stock, international and emerging markets |

its performance against its liability index. The plan's discount rate is determined by using the rate of high-quality zero-coupon bonds.

The Financial Accounting Standards Board (FASB) and the Securities and Exchange Commission (SEC) have been saying for years that the method just outlined is a very good idea:

> The objective of selecting assumed discount rates is to measure the single amount that, if invested at the measurement date in a portfolio of high-quality debt instruments, would provide the necessary future cash flows to pay the accumulated benefits when due. Notionally, that single amount, the accumulated post-retirement benefit obligation, would equal the current market value of a portfolio of high-quality zero coupon bonds whose maturity dates and amounts would be the same as the timing and amount of the expected future benefit payments.[5]
>
> The SEC staff believes that the guidance that is provided in paragraph 186 of FAS 106, for selecting discount rates to measure the post-retirement benefit obligation also is appropriate guidance for measuring the pension benefit obligation. . . .
>
> Rates that cannot be justified or are just too high will be passed on to the SEC's enforcement division for further action. The enforcement division could require restatement of the company's financial statements, as well as seek to impose civil or criminal penalties.[6]

Why is the method we have outlined for managing pension plans new if guidance mandating it was set up over a decade ago? The answer is that pension plans were given a 15-year grace period to get into compliance. That period is over.

When FAS 87 was enacted, corporate pension funds were allowed to amortize(straight line) their current surplus or deficit over the remaining service period of employees, or 15 years whichever was greater, starting between 1/1/85 and 1/1/87. For most companies, they had a pension plan surplus back in the middle 80's since liabilities had higher discount rates then and equities had performed well. This surplus amortization has boosted earnings for the last 15 years. The year 2000 financials saw the end of this amortization for many companies suggesting 2001 earnings and beyond would suffer accordingly due to the loss of this earnings support.[7]

That there has been no rush on the part of pension plans to create liability indexes and invest the assets in accordance with a prescription of accepted investment methodology can be explained by referring back to our anecdote at the outset of this chapter. You saw how far we got in Las Vegas.

The Department of Labor (DOL) is supposed to enforce the rules, but there are over six million private pension plans with over $5 trillion in assets covering over 150 million beneficiaries.[8] The DOL is not given the resources to enforce the rules. Plan beneficiaries, however, have the right to know how the pension plan is being managed. They have the right to see investment policy statements, how the plan is being invested, and what the strategy is for addressing all the issues we have discussed. A plan beneficiary does not have to rely—and should not—on an annual statement (some participants do not even get this) derived from an actuarial report that projects what their cash flow at retirement will be. The number could have been created with smoke and mirrors, and the promised benefits could evaporate into thin air.

There is an agency called the Pension Benefit Guaranty Corporation (PBGC) that charges companies a flat rate premium per employee that is intended to insure pension benefits. The intentions of this government agency are good, but as is true of Social Security, the money may not be there to cover the scope of the problem that looms ahead.

The solution is for every pension plan to adopt the procedures that we have outlined. An alternative course would be to hope one gets at the head of the line when the guaranteed payments are handed out. Roll the dice.

## THE MATRIX

There is a careless belief on the part of legislators, economic leaders, and—most dangerously—plan participants themselves that the 401(k) has come of age as a "sound investment tool and the average

American's best hope of assuring themselves a steady flow of retirement income." Or so 401(k)s were described in the opening remarks of a congressman's speech at one of the thousands of forums on retirement planning that are held every year in the United States.

The confidence in this view flows from our democratic convictions that people should have the responsibility for controlling their own destiny because they alone know what is good for them. Of course this is true. So a retirement plan that puts workers in control and allows them to "assume responsibility for their retirement income . . . by directing their own investments"—as it is described on the first page of a booklet on 401(k)s published by the U.S. Department of Labor's Pension and Welfare Benefits Administration—has definite appeal as a solution to the retirement planning crises. That in most cases the control that workers have over their 401(k)s is an illusion and that the investments that they are given permission to direct are circumscribed by a twisted mass of self-interest that grows like an abscess on an originally well-intentioned concept is where perception and reality part company.

If we are talking about a 401(k) plan where the total account balances of all the employees that participate add up to a sizable sum of money, you will find in many cases that even as the participating workers are told over and over that they are in charge, their collective assets are used to pull strings, grant favors, boost egos, and advance careers in a total disregard for the effect this will have on the growth of the employees' money.

This is not to say funds are being misappropriated or pilfered from workers' accounts. That would be easier to detect and to punish. The problem is far more insidious. It occurs when decision makers directly involved with the plan (this may be company owners, CFOs, CEOs, company administrators, treasurers, or human resource people) grant the business of handling the 401(k) account to financial services merchants without regard for the investment needs of the participating employees. The fact of the matter is that plan participants can invest only in what is offered in their menu of investment options. The selection of these investments and the vendor that is contracted to provide them is as highly charged a political football as any presidential election. Often those in charge of a company's 401(k) know that they are rubbing up against more money than they will ever see in one place at any time again in their lives, and they use it to advance their own agendas.

We have seen 401(k) businesses awarded to golfing buddies, relatives, and in one case to the girlfriend of the married-with-children owner of a company. Frequently the people being gifted with this business know nothing of investing. In one case a new CFO of a company with a $120,000,000 401(k) plan gave the account to his brother-in-law who had been a surveyor eight weeks before. (This is legal. By passing a simple test and paying a fee, you can go to work at many mutual fund, bank, brokerage, and insurance companies.) Although it is allowed to happen every day, clearly these people are not equipped to be decoding what sorts of things 401(k) plan participants have a "choice" of investing in.

The other group of people who decide what employees can invest in are the 401(k) decision makers at the sponsoring company. Only the largest corporations may have their own in-house investment advisors, experienced and trained to do nothing but watch over their company's 401(k) options. At most companies it is the treasurer, CFO, chief operations officer, vice president of administration, or a human resources manager who is already overworked and has the additional responsibility of the 401(k). The people in these capacities with whom we work on a daily basis rely on us to assist them in selecting the investment options for their 401(k) plans. They readily admit that they do not have the time or, if they do, the qualifications to make such decisions on their own. At bottom they truly have the best interest of their employees at heart.

Another attitude prevails among corporate 401(k) decision makers. For each one that is well intentioned, there seem to be two prima donnas who set themselves out as investment gurus. They study the faddish magazines of pop finance, become the groupies of mutual fund companies, and try out their experiments on their company's 401(k) plans. They dimly understand that executing the investment process is hard and difficult work when the needs of just a single individual must be considered, much less trying to accommodate hundreds or thousands of employees. Instead of a systematic process, they rely on their gut—we hear this a lot—or the research they do during their break to determine the investments their employees will be able to use to ensure that "steady flow of retirement income" as promised in the U.S. Department of Labor booklet.

The mocking of 401(k) participants takes a different form when a menu of 30, 50, or over 100 mutual funds are offered. This confers not control but confusion. It is unfair to encourage people to put hard-earned dollars into a 401(k) when there is no rhyme, reason, or process available to them to manage that money. Participants in these plans were told to "hang on, 'themarket' always comes back," during the volatility of 2000–2002. Many are still waiting because they do not know that there is no longer a "themarket"; they don't know we are in a new investment culture; and if they did, they cannot be sure where the funds they have invested in put their money.

To give the appearance that plan sponsors are taking seriously their fiduciary responsibility that affords their employees control over their retirement assets, an interesting bit of theater is often carried out. The players will be those in charge at the company, who will often include a few of the rank and file just to demonstrate how democratic the system is. Usually these people are so intimidated by being able to rub elbows with management that they play along, not knowing what the game really is.

The other players will be representatives from two or three financial services companies who are invited to explain how their 401(k) programs work and why they are superior to the competition. The idea is to demonstrate that the company has no conflicts of interest and is trying to select the best set of investments and services for its 401(k). The production will be noted and recorded in company minutes just in case some renegade employee actually wants to know how his or her money wound up where it did.

Of course, the whole production is a sham. It had already been decided which investment company would get the business, long before the other vendors were invited to perform. The paperwork had probably already been signed.

It is in this way that 401(k)-plan business is given in exchange for favorable mortgage rates or corporate loans, a better deal on insurance, either corporate or private, or maybe just to return a favor.

## REAL CONTROL

The 401(k) concept is sound. Encouraging people to take responsibility for their own wealth is the right approach. But the only way this can be accomplished fairly is by actually giving employees the control that they are being told they have.

The conflicts of interest that are bound to occur cannot be legislated out of the system. There are already regulations in this regard that are not being enforced. What we propose is that no single corporate 401(k) account be allowed to accumulate more than $2,000,000. What needs to happen is that payroll systems should funnel employee deductions directly into a participants' IRA accounts, which they can set up wherever they wish. This account should be called "John Doe's 401(k)/IRA."

If the employer makes matching contributions, this money should be directed in the same way to an adjoining account labeled "XYZ Corporation/Match for the Benefit of (FBO) John Doe." A profit-sharing contribution would be directed to a parallel account labeled "XYZ Corporation/Profit Sharing FBO John Doe." In this way money would revert back to the company if the employee left before they were vested.

The technology is available to do this. A secondary benefit would be that the plan sponsor would no longer have to be responsible for whether an employee contributed too much money, failed to pay back a loan, or needs a distribution. All of this would be dealt with at the financial institution that held the employees' accounts and reported directly on the employer's tax return.

The investment of the money would truly be under the employee's control and under the guidance of a personal financial advisor.

Until the system we have proposed can be adopted, the following steps should be taken by all sponsors of 401(k) plans. These ideas are not new. For example, the requirement that an investment policy statement must be drafted has existed for years. The problem is, most people we talk to who are responsible for 401(k) plans still do not even know what it is. The Profit Sharing/401K Council of America estimates that only half of all 401(k) plans have one.

The retirement triad is made up of Social Security, pension/defined benefit plans, and 401(k)s. We know Social Security is in question; we have explained why pension plans look dubious; and unless the steps outlined next are adopted by all 401(k) plans immediately, the unfolding of the new dominant investment system will be lost on 401(k) plan participants as well.

### The 401(k) Business Plan

1. Together with an experienced investment advisor all companies should adopt an investment policy statement for their 401(k). Topics covered should include

   - Age and dynamics of the workforce
   - The fact that the fund menu selected must enable each plan participant to achieve an investment allocation that will fit into what we call their *investment zone*
   - A list of all styles and assets classes to be included
   - The parameters by which a fund will be selected for or terminated from each asset class
   - The methodology by which the funds will be monitored on both a qualitative and quantitative basis
   - The mechanism that will allow employees to rebalance and reoptimize their portfolios
   - How all of the above will be communicated to employees

2. The investment policy statement becomes the action plan for the 401(k). It should be executed immediately.

3. Once the plan is set up correctly, participants can follow the investment guidelines from Chapter 3 to manage their 401(k) just as they do the rest of their assets.

• • •

# SAMPLE 401(k) INVESTMENT POLICY STATEMENT

### Courtesy of Profit Sharing/401(k) Council of America (PSCA)

### Part I. THE PLAN

The ABC Company sponsors the ABC Defined Contribution Plan (The Plan) for the benefit of its employees. It is intended to provide eligible employees with long-term accumulation of retirement savings through a combination of employee and employer contributions to individual participant accounts and the earnings thereon.

The Plan is a qualified employee benefit plan intended to comply with all applicable federal laws and regulations, including the Internal Revenue Code of 1986, as amended, and the Employee Retirement Income Security Act (ERISA), as amended. (Optional: The Plan is intended to comply with ERISA Section 404c.)

The Plan's participants and beneficiaries are expected to have different investment objectives, time horizons, and risk tolerances. To meet these varied investment needs, participants and beneficiaries will be able to direct their account balances among a range of investment options to construct diversified portfolios that reasonably span the risk-return spectrum. Participants and beneficiaries alone bear the risk of investment results from the options and asset mixes that they select.

### Part II. THE PURPOSE OF THE INVESTMENT POLICY STATEMENT

This investment policy statement is intended to assist the Plan's fiduciaries ensuring that they make investment-related decisions in a prudent manner. This outlines the underlying philosophies and processes for the selection, monitoring, and evaluation of the investment options and investment managers utilized by the Plan. Specifically, this Investment Policy Statement

- Defines the Plan's investment objectives
- Defines the roles of those responsible for the Plans' investments
- Describes the criteria and procedures for selecting investment option investment managers
- Establishes investment procedures, measurement standards, and monitoring procedures
- Describes ways to address investment options and investment management that fail to satisfy established objectives
- Provides appropriate diversification within investment vehicles
- (Optional) Describes the Plan's approach to unrestricted investment options (mutual fund window and self-directed brokerage), company stock, and advice

This Investment Policy Statement will be reviewed at least annually, and when appropriate, can be amended to reflect changes in the capital markets, plan participant objectives, or other factors relevant to the Plan.

*(continued)*

## Part III. INVESTMENT OBJECTIVES

The Plan's investment options will be selected to

- Maximize return within reasonable and prudent levels of risk
- Provide returns comparable to returns for similar investment options
- Provide exposure to a wide range of investment opportunities in various asset classes
- Control administrative and management costs

## Part IV. ROLES AND RESPONSIBILITIES

Those responsible for the management and administration of the Plan's investments include, but are not limited to the following:

"The ABC Company, which is responsible for selecting the trustee(s); hiring the record keeper and/or investment advisory consultants; and appointing the members of the investment committee (if one exists). If there is not investment committee the ABC Company is also responsible for

- Establishing and maintaining the Investment Policy Statement
- Selecting investment options
- Periodically evaluating the Plan's investment performance and recommending investment option changes
- Providing Plan participant investment education and communication

"The Plan's trustee(s), which is responsible for holding and investing plan assets in accordance with the terms of the Trust Agreement.

"The investment managers, which are responsible for making reasonable investment decisions consistent with the stated approach of the Plan, and reporting investment results on a regular basis as determined by the Plan fiduciaries.

"The record keeper, which is responsible for maintaining and updating individual account balances as well as information regarding plan contributions, withdrawals, and distributions.

"The Investment Committee (if there is one), which is responsible for

- Establishing and maintaining the Investment Policy Statement
- Selecting investment options
- Periodically evaluating the Plan's investment performance and recommending investment option changes
- Providing Plan participant investment education and communications

## Part V. SELECTION OF INVESTMENTS AND MANAGER

The selection of investment options offered under the Plan is among the ABC Company/investment committee's most important responsibilities. Set forth in the following are the considerations and guidelines employed in fulfilling this fiduciary responsibility.

*Investment Selection*

The Plan intends to provide an appropriate range of investment options that span the risk-return spectrum. Further, the Plan investment options will allow all Plan participants to construct portfolios consistent with their unique individual circumstances, goals, time horizons, and tolerance for risk. Major asset classes offered will include the following:

(This is where the classes of investments to be included in the Plan are to be listed. The appropriate benchmark and peer group for each investment will be noted.)

After determining the asset classes to be used, ABC Company/the investment committee must evaluate investment managers and choose managers to manage the specific investment options. Each investment manager must meet certain minimum criteria:

1. It should be a financial services provider, investment management company, or an investment advisor registered under the Registered Investment Advisers Act of 1940.
2. It should be operating in good standing with regulators and clients, with material pending or concluded legal actions.
3. It should provide detailed additional information on the history of the firm's investment philosophy and approach, and its principals, clients, locations, schedules, and other relevant information.

Assuming the minimum criteria are met, the particular investment under consideration should meet the following standards for selection:

1. Performance should be equal to or greater than the median return for an appropriate, style-specific benchmark and peer group over a specified time.
2. Specific risk and risk-adjusted return measures should be established and agreed to by ABC Company/the investment committee and be within a reasonable range relative to an appropriate style-specific benchmark and peer group.
3. It should demonstrate adherence to the stated investment objective.
4. Fees should be competitive compared to similar investments.
5. The investment manager should be able to provide all performance holdings and other relevant information in a timely fashion, with specified frequency.

## Part VI. INVESTMENT MONITORING AND REPORTING

The ongoing monitoring of investments must be a regular and disciplined process. It is the mechanism for revisiting the investment option selection process and confirming that criteria originally satisfied remain so and that investment option continues to be a valid offering. While frequent changes are neither expected nor desirable, the process of monitoring investment performance relative to specified guidelines is ongoing.

*(continued)*

Monitoring should occur on a regular basis (e.g., quarterly) and utilize the criteria that were the basis of the investment selection decision. It will include a formal review annually. Further, unusual, notable, or extraordinary events should be communicated by the investment manager immediately to ABC Company/the investment committee. Examples of such events include portfolio manager team departure, violation of investment guidelines, material litigation against the firm, or material changes in firm ownership structure or announcements thereof.

If overall satisfaction with the investment option is acceptable, no further action is required. If areas of dissatisfaction exist, the investment manager and ABC Company/the investment committee must take steps to remedy the deficiency over a reasonable period. If the manager is unable to resolve the issue, termination may result.

### Part VII. MANAGER TERMINATION

An investment manager should be terminated when ABC Company/the investment committee has lost confidence in the manager's ability to

- Achieve performance and risk objectives
- Comply with investment guidelines
- Comply with reporting requirements
- Maintain a stable organization and retain key relevant investment professionals

There are no hard and fast rules for manager termination. However, if the investment manager has consistently failed to adhere to one or more of the previous conditions, it is reasonable to presume a lack of adherence going forward. Failure to remedy the circumstances of unsatisfactory performance by the investment manager, within a reasonable time, shall be grounds for termination.

Any recommendation to terminate an investment manager will be treated on an individual basis, and will not be made solely based on quantitative data. In addition to those listed previously, other factors may include professional or client turnover or material change to investment processes. Considerable judgment must be exercised in the termination decision process.

A manager to be terminated shall be removed using one of the following approaches:

- Remove and replace (map assets) with an alternative manager
- Freeze the assets managed by the terminated manager and direct new assets to a replacement manager
- Phase out the manager over a specific time period
- Continue the manager but add a competing manager
- Remove the manager and do not provide a replacement manager
- Navigate the manager to a brokerage window (if available)

### Part VIII. PARTICIPANT EDUCATION AND COMMUNICATION

The Plan will communicate to employees that they control their own investments, permit investment changes at least quarterly, and provide efficient educational materials allowing employees to make informed decisions.

### Part IX. COORDINATION WITH THE PLAN DOCUMENT

Notwithstanding the foregoing, if any term or condition of this investment policy conflicts with any term or condition in the Plan, the terms and conditions of the Plan shall control.

### Part X. FURTHER GUIDELINES (optional)

*Mutual Fund Windows*

In an effort to provide some (but not total) investment flexibility, a mutual window option is offered as a way of providing additional investment options to Plan participants. In developing and maintaining the Plan's mutual fund window, ABC Company/the investment committee will evaluate the window provider for reasonable cost, fund availability, competitive service capability, and participant satisfaction. There will be an annual review to confirm competitiveness.

*Self-Directed Brokerage*

In an effort to provide total investment flexibility, a self-directed brokerage option is offered in the Plan. The Plan's self-directed brokerage option allows participants to invest in any publicly traded security, including stocks, bonds, and mutual funds, with the following exceptions: short sales, options, future limited partnerships, currency trading, and trading on margin. In developing and maintaining the Plan's self-directed brokerage option, ABC Company/the investment committee will evaluate the self-directed option provider for reasonable cost, competitive service capability, and participant satisfaction. There will be an annual review to confirm competitiveness.

*Company Stock*

ABC Company stock is offered as an investment option pursuant to the terms of the Plan. Plan fiduciaries will be responsible for managing the investment Plan's assets in company stock according to the Plan document. ABC Company/the investment committee will monitor the performance of ABC Company stock but not for the purpose of recommending levels of company stock investment in the Plan or the elimination of company stock as a Plan investment as they may have access to inside information.

*Advice*

As with any designation of a service provider to the plan, the designation of a company or individual to investment advice to plan participants and beneficiaries is an exercise of discretionary authority and control with respect to management of the plan. Therefore, ABC Company/the investment committee will act prudently and solely in the interest of the plan participants and beneficiaries both in making such designation(s) and in continuing such designation(s).

   At a minimum, the investment advice by the selected provider should be unbiased and be based on sound asset allocation theory and in-depth fund analysis. It should also be tailored to each participant's circumstances. Monitoring will occur on an annual basis and utilize the same criteria that forms the basis of the investment advisor selection decision.

Two weeks ago our team presented our 401(k) services to a potential new client. We were given two hours to speak to the committee. The investments topic ran five minutes over, and two committee members left. Here's how the agenda unfolded.

| Topic | Minutes Actually Allotted | Percentage of Time Spent |
|-------|-------|-------|
| Introductions | 5 | 4 |
| Compliance and plan design | 50 | 42 |
| Record keeping and administration | 46 | 38 |
| Employee communications | 14 | 12 |
| Investments | 10 | 4 |

This shows another aspect of the matrix in which 401(k) plans are entangled. It is the labyrinth of regulations so complex that entire industries have grown up within the legal, accounting, and computer science fields to support it. The allocation of time devoted to these issues in the agenda just shown is likely to reflect the expenditure of time and energy during any given period that is spent on these different areas. We have no study to support this, but most of our colleagues in the 401(k) business agree with our assessment.

The percentage of time and effort devoted to proper investment methodology is miniscule compared to what is spent in regulatory, compliance, and technical issues. This could be justified if it served to protect employees, but it does not. The excessive amount of regulations that already exist did not protect Enron employees in 2002 from losing their retirement assets. A full grounding in the facts of the new Dominant Investment System, and the techniques that must be used to invest in it as outlined in Chapter 3, would have. But there is no time for that.

The dismantling of the large pools of 401(k) assets should be accompanied by a repeal of at least two-thirds of the legislation in which they are mired. Most of it looks like this:

Top-heavy status is measured on a "determination date," which is generally the last day of the preceding plan year (December 31 for calendar-year plans). Prior to EGTRRA [Economic Growth and Tax Reconciliation Act of 2001], distributions made over the preceding five years are included in the top-heavy calculation (first-year "look-back"). However, under EGTRRA, certain changes will take effect starting in 2002 regarding the top-heavy calculation. First of all, the five-year look-back will, in most cases, be replaced by a one-year look-back. So, effective for the 2002 year, with the exception of in-service distributions, only distributions made during the one-year period ending on the determination date will be included when determining the value of the non–key employee's account.

Second, a participant who was not an active employee at any time during the year ending on the determination date would have his or her balance excluded from the top-heavy calculation. Because non–key employees (generally nonowners) are more likely to terminate employment or take a distribution, excluding their distributions from the account value will likely reduce the accounts of non–key employees more than the accounts of key employees. For most plans, this will increase the likelihood, and the plan will be top-heavy.

Keeping up with these constantly changing complex regulations is an unnecessary burden on human resources departments and corporate administrators. Much of it centers around preventing highly compensated employees and owners from avoiding taxes by putting an unfair share of their income into retirement accounts. In the new customized environment in which we live, this can easily be dealt with on a person-by-person basis through individual tax returns.

## NO FOUNDATION, FOUNDATIONS, AND ENDOWMENT FUNDS

Two members picked themselves up off the floor and called our office after the bomb had been dropped. They were new to the board of this popular foundation, and like many volunteers who generously give their time and their talent to jobs for which they do not get paid, they found themselves thinking that they may have bitten off more than they could chew.

The bomb was figurative, but it was as destructive as a real one would have been. The new building that the foundation's paid staff had to occupy in 30 days had no roof, no drywall, no plumbing, and no electricity. The assets of the foundation had sunk to a level so low that feeding cash into the building project was no longer possible without permanently depleting the corpus of the foundation's assets. Subcontractors were not getting paid, and construction stopped.

We were asked to figure out what happened. Statements were faxed and projections reviewed. In just 15 minutes it became clear how a prominent charity, supported by a constant flow of money from society's upper crust, could regress into a downhill slide toward the financial equivalent of homelessness.

Between 1998 and 2000 the money that poured in from fundraising efforts during a booming economy was invested 60% in so-called blue-chip growth stocks and 40% in bonds. This allocation was arrived at so arbitrarily that no one could recall its source: "Langford C. may have told Bentley R., 'That's how this other organization in town does it.'" While no one will admit to it, this approach is so ubiquitous that what we found on a deeper inspection of the portfolio did not surprise us.

Here is a short list of the so-called blue-chip purchases and what happened to their values by the spring of 2002:

**Table 6.2**   Value of Blue-Chip Purchases, Spring 2002

| Security | Purchase Price | Purchase Date | May 2002 Price[a] | Percentage Decline |
|---|---|---|---|---|
| American Express | 63 | 10/00 | 41.68 | 33.84 |
| Bristol Myers | 79 | 10/99 | 30.27 | 61.68 |
| Campbell Soup | 32 | 3/96 | 27.70 | 13.44 |
| Coca-Cola | 88 | 3/98 | 54.60 | 38.00 |
| John Deere | 64 | 3/98 | 47.50 | 25.80 |
| Dow | 46 | 12/99 | 33.80 | 26.50 |
| DuPont | 84 | 5/98 | 46.10 | 45.00 |
| Eastman Kodak | 87 | 7/98 | 35.25 | 59.00 |
| General Electric | 60 | 9/00 | 32.00 | 46.66 |
| Gillette | 64 | 3/99 | 35.13 | 45.00 |
| Merck | 95 | 12/00 | 56.00 | 41.00 |
| Pfizer | 48 | 4/99 | 34.80 | 27.50 |

*Note:* Bristol Myers, Merck, and General Electric together represented 25% of the portfolio because these were thought to be the bluest of the blue chips.

[a] Closing prices as of April 27.

Frightened by the market declines of 2000 and 2001, donations received by the foundation were put into bonds that then declined in the fourth quarter of 2001 and dropped further in the first quarter of 2002.[9] This exacerbated the foundation losses by another $720,000.

Another emotional, knee-jerk reaction was the doubling up on positions in the companies just listed and those like them. The justification for this was that they were supposedly cheap because the price per earning ratios were low, and history was thought to prove that they would soon bounce back. Large profits would be achieved with little risk by buying Merck at 50 and watching it soar back to 90. This panicked effort to make up for losses only drove the portfolio further into a hole.

The situation with this foundation is not unlike that of many others. The contributions of donors are going toward subsidizing an old dominant investment system, and a shrinking piece of the pie remains to do the work of the charity. Had the same situation occurred in the

1950s, 1960s, or even 1980s, reliance on the historic performance of so-called blue chips would have paid off. But the ending of an old investment culture also ended the effectiveness of the old fixed ideas of how foundations and endowments should manage their money.

When, in an effort to learn how best to guide boards in the handling of the money to which they have been entrusted, we ask members to explain the basis on which decisions have been made in the past, someone usually points toward the *prudent man rule*. This can be a solid basis on which to build an investment strategy, as long as one recognizes that what is "prudent" today is not what was prudent 20, 50, or 100 years ago. Here is Justice Samuel Putnam's definition of the prudent man rule:

> All that can be required of a trustee to invest is that he shall conduct himself faithfully and exercise a sound discretion. He is to observe how men of prudence, discretion, and intelligence manage their own affairs, not in regard to speculation, but in regard to the permanent disposition of their funds, considering the probable income as well as the probable safety of the capital to be invested.[10]

Putnam's original statement has been amended and enhanced, but the key word *prudent* has stuck. This is peculiar in that "prudent" is a fluid concept. Proof that any definition of a prudent investment cannot be an enduring proposition lies in the fact that Putnam wrote his opinion in 1830. No doubt, in 1830 Justice Putnam's idea of a prudently managed portfolio would have been one that consisted of bonds, predominately railroad bonds.

So who were the more prudent fiduciaries in 1903? Those who kept buying railroad bonds, or those who adopted a methodical approach to investing in a new dominant investment?

The only prudent course that a twenty-first century fiduciary can follow when making decisions on money that does not belong to them is to adopt the investment methodology outlined in Chapter 3.

The process should begin with an investment policy statement spelling out whether the fund's primary goal is to last into perpetuity, provide bequests (and if so, to whom), or provide cash flow for projects, operations, or emergencies. A liability analysis should be performed much like that which is required for a defined benefit plan. After this is completed, the optimal portfolio can be prescribed and the rebalancing technique employed.

The unique dynamics at work on the boards of charitable or nonprofit organizations can turn the collective best intentions of its members into a formless, makeshift affair unless the methodology we outlined to manage money is employed. The rotation of board members interrupts continuity as experienced members are replaced by new ones. Big donors may get a prestigious board seat in exchange for the tacit approval to make the decisions—like directing the investments to the bank that just agreed to some personal financing. Deference may be given to a celebrity or high-powered business executive who neither wants nor asks for it, resulting in the investment strategy of the funds shooting off in a new direction, out of context with arrangements that were just beginning to come together. In this way ambitious plans are continuously recycled but seldom achieved.

The investment committee of Denison University included some high-powered financial people: John Lowenberg, a former Robinson Humphrey fund manager; John Canning, president of the Chicago private equity firm Madison, Dearborne Partners; and Mark Dalton, a Connecticut financier. In 1999 they permitted 12% of the University's endowment fund to be invested solely in Cisco stock. Half of the endowment was invested in illiquid funds with no disclosure or investment return requirements. Long periods went by when no one knew how much money they had or what it was invested in. On the assets to which they could assign a value, they lost $105 million in six months.[11]

The reason for this gross mismanagement? "We decided it was time to get some decent returns here, and that meant being a little more aggressive,"[12] says Jim Oelshlager, an alumnus of the University and a principal of Oak Associates, a mutual fund company that—no surprise here—was given a large chunk of the endowment's money to manage. The word in Oelshlager's sentence that gives weight to our contention that boards and finance committees have a dynamic all their own is *we*. The fact that Oelshlager was not a member of the finance committee but was permitted to weigh in on asset allocation decisions that would directly benefit him and his firm shows the willful disregard for even the appearance of propriety that exists. That Oelshlager does not seem embarrassed by this—since his quote using the "we" appeared in a nationally distributed magazine—points to the shortage of regulations and surplus of ego that can meet around the conference tables of certain organizations.

Denison University did have an investment policy. This is of no use if it is carelessly enforced. They had high-profile investment people making decisions. This is of no use if none of them has any sense of discipline or are ill informed about basic investment methodology, as the committee members at Denison seemed to be.

Those who are concerned with what happens to their charitable donations should ask to see an investment policy statement that governs the pool of money into which their contribution will go. The document should outline clear objectives, spending policies, liabilities, and investment guidelines. A composite statement should be available listing all the endowment's assets and how they are broken down by percentages. This should be accompanied by comments on why each manager was selected. This should include not just performance numbers but qualitative issues as well. Things like the size of the firm or their unique research methods might be included.

The composite statement should be compared to the investment policy statement. In this way one can determine whether the policy is being followed. A potential donor may prefer to give the information to his or her financial advisor. An experienced person can size up the situation quickly to determine whether the charity in question is worthy of a donation.

The board or finance committee that adheres to the investment policy mandate has a much easier job. Their task becomes simply to ensure that stated guidelines are being met. Those with minimal investment experience do not need to be intimidated by those who lay claim to knowledge of finance (less experienced investors have no need to be intimidated anyway; a case in point is Denison University). The committee's job is to see that objectives are being met and that guidelines are being honored. If they are not, ask why not. If a suitable answer is not delivered, refer to the investment policy statement for direction. The answers to how and why to remove a board member, fire a money manager, or amend an asset allocation strategy should have already been spelled out.

●　●　●

*There is bound to be a flaw in the participant's perception of the fundamentals. The flaws may not be apparent in the early stages but it is likely to manifest itself later on. When it does, it sets the stage for a reversal in the prevailing bias.*
—George Soros[13]

George Soros has been described by the *New York Times* as "the most powerful and profitable investor in the world today." Soros's success comes from finding "the flaw in the prevailing perceptions" about the financial markets and then backing up his convictions with large sums of money.

The flaw in perceptions that prevails in the markets today is the disregard for the fact that a new investment culture has replaced an old one. It is those who participate in the early stages before there is a reversal in the prevailing bias that will be most successful. Those entrusted with the responsibility of making decisions for pension plans,

401(k) plans, foundations, and endowments can accomplish this in an orderly and business-like fashion by adopting the methods set down in the book. The management of money, as we describe it, operates no differently than that of any other profitable business. A plan should be realized, capitalized, and customized. If its conception is realistic and it is executed with a military discipline, it will work. As the assets of their large pools of money fall in step with the new dominant investment system, the beneficiaries can feel confident that promises made to them will be kept.

Those willing to recognize and act on the reversal in the prevailing bias that is occurring will be naturally led into it. Those unwilling to adapt to the new investment culture will be dragged along, fulfillment of expectations always just out of each. Then, somewhere near the end of the acceleration phase, they will decide, "It's time to get some better returns here." As impulsive as two-year-olds, they will try to accomplish this by being a little more aggressive with their makeshift plans and arbitrary decisions. As they indulge old habits and rationalize away the inevitable losses, they will take comfort in the fact that, "Oh well, at least it wasn't my own money."

## NOTES

1. Kenn Tacchino and David Littell, *Planning for Retirement Needs* (Bryn Mawr, PA: American College, 1997).

2. Ibid. Here the term *cost* means the amount of money that a plan sponsor has to contribute to the plan so that it can pay its promised benefits.

3. Courtesy of Ryan Research, Ryan Labs.

4. Ibid.

5. FAS 106, paragraph 186.

6. SEC Guidelines on FAS 87 (June 1993 letter to all corporations).

7. FAS 87 Transition Amortization, courtesy of Ryan Labs.

8. "Plan Sponsor Defined Benefit Plan Survey, 2000." *Plan Sponsor Magazine,* March 2001.

9. The Lehman Brothers Government Corporate Bond index return in the first three months of 2002 was −1.2%.

10. Consulting Group, "Endowments and Foundations," 2000.

11. Ron Suskind, "On Dangerous Ground," *Smart Money* (2001, September), 117–124.

12. Ibid., p. 120.

13. George Soros, *The Alchemy of Finance* (New York: Wiley, 1994).

# 7

# NEW LOGIC

## Reading the Messages and Using the Tools of the New Investment Culture

*Numbers alone confer no advantage.*
—Sun Tzu, *The Art of War*

"Existing theories about the behavior of stock prices are remarkably inadequate," says George Soros, by way of explaining how he has made billions in the financial markets. "They are of so little value that the fact that I could get by without them speaks for itself."[1]

That the methods Soros uses, which make him the planet's most successful investor, do not derive from some rigorous application of what we have been told to accept as basic fundamental principles of financial analysis demonstrates just how wispy these supposedly fundamental principles can be. The reason for this is the evolutionary nature of the financial markets, the path of which we showed in earlier chapters. Soros explains that the momentum behind the markets' perpetual state of transformation is caused by the bandying between two forces: (1) market events that affect supply and demand and (2) people's perceptions and reactions to these events. He calls this *reflexivity*.[2] Reflexivity renders the financial markets the epitome of change. People, as a rule, do not like change.

In the especially change-averse investment community, the reluctance to move on can slow progress. An example of how an institution for understanding can turn into a cult of justification is the consensus formed by economists about the incubation interval of 1870–1896.

Ideas and forces were being churned up in those years that would reinvent the global economy. But rather than see the volatility this created as a by-product of evolutionary renewal, the opposite view was promoted—and it prevailed. This view held that instead of being the inevitable precursor to positive change, volatility was a necessary agent of the status quo, putting everyone in their place, fighting each new idea, and moving toward an ordered world of theoretical equilibrium.

It seems that equilibrium theories stem less from actual fact than from a very human desire to believe in some inevitable conventional condition to which we will eventually always return: "Won't we be glad when things get back to normal!"

The "seize the day before" approach is exacerbated today by our ability quickly to collect, organize, and transmit heaps of data about the financial markets to anyone who wants it. Unrestricted access to information is a necessary ingredient of the new investment culture, but we have not learned to use it very well—especially when statistics are involved. That we should be less preoccupied with data and more concerned about the set of circumstances from which they issue becomes disconcertingly obvious when we examine numbers that update us on the health of the economy.

## MIXED SIGNALS

When we talk about data explaining changes in the growth of businesses, the productivity of various sectors of the economy, or any combination of these, we are talking about numbers gathered by the federal government. These data are projected to us on a daily basis and cause us to reach conclusions about the country's present and future financial health. It moves or does not move markets. It may cause us to build or not build a new home, change jobs, retire, have a child, buy a new washing machine, or invest in stock.

As these words are being written, most people are nervous about the economy, and consequently nervous about the stock market. If not the sole instigator of the uncertainty, the economic numbers definitely tend to support it. Here is the joke: The output of most of the companies of the new dominant investment system is not included in these economic numbers that are broadcast to us daily.

The types of companies whose productivity and growth are not counted in measurements of economic health include computer software reproduction, fiber-optic cable manufacturing, cellular telecommunications, environmental consulting, credit card companies, and shopping warehouse clubs.[3] Even this short list represents products and services that most of us are intimately connected with each day and that can be viewed as necessities. They are important drivers of national economic health. Why don't they count?

The economic data we receive most often receive come from the Standard Industrial Classification (SIC) system that was put in place in 1930. Except for an update in 1987, the methodology for collecting data has not changed since. It is an accurate measure of the fading take it, make it, break it economy. With the old dominant investment system in critical condition, the SIC system has become the monitor of its vital signs.

The Office of Management and Budget (OMB) has begun replacement of the old SIC system with the North American Industry Classification System (NAICS). The intent is to make the system relevant to the twenty-first century, but implementing it is arduous and time-consuming. The transition will occur in stages. The Federal Reserve will be using some of the new NAICS data in 2002. The Bureau of Labor Statistics will initiate reporting of employment numbers under the new system some time in 2003. Producer price indexes will be revamped and reported under a new system in 2004. The schedule could be too optimistic. Substantial reclassification of U.S. businesses will be necessary. This raises the issue of how breaks in data will be handled as one system transitions to another. It will not be as simple as drawing a line between the twentieth century and the twenty-first.

Maybe we have missed it, but we have yet to see or hear in the general media any qualifying remarks that the economic statistics being reported are coming out of a time warp. No disclaimers and no explanations are offered. Does this mean that as we transition to the new system, and the numbers get better—because they will be coming from companies of the new dominant investment system—the companies of the old investment system will get the credit? Will it be as if the leads attached to a critical patient were furtively removed and re-attached to some healthy body so that the doctor can point to the monitor and tell the grieving relatives, "Don't worry about a thing—he'll be back to normal any day now"?

## NUMEROLOGY

The fact that in order to monitor corporate productivity accurately, the OMB found it necessary to rebuild the entire economic monitoring network by installing NAICS proves that the apparatus that makes businesses productive, and therefore profitable, has undergone a complete conversion. Setting this evidence of change aside, anyone who was invested in stocks or mutual funds as we entered the twenty-first century had to suspect that something important was going on, if only because of the contradictory explanations put forth to explain the transformation of the markets.

Other than investors themselves, those in a position to experience that transformation most acutely are those of us whose career classifications fall under the umbrella of investment advisor. Ushering money every day among individuals and institutions and the stocks and mutual funds they invest in administers healthy doses of reality to our assumptions about the financial markets. This intimate contact with the markets often makes most of our colleagues and ourselves the first to discard ineffectual theories and the statistics that support them. But many in the financial services industry persist in relying on irrelevant and outdated information. It is curious that a government bureaucracy like the OMB would recognize a fundamental shift affecting investors and act upon it, long before some investment counselors who have the advantage of viewing the situation from a much better vantage point. Likewise, it is troubling when we see investment advisors relying on market data and investment statistics that are 5, 10, or 20 years old when assisting clients in making investment choices.

In the academic world there is considerably more interest in rethinking old assumptions. The debate between Jeremy J. Siegel, professor of finance at the Wharton School of the University of Pennsylvania, and Robert J. Shiller, professor of economics at Yale University about how properly to evaluate the markets is a very public example. Less public is the important work being done by Robert D. Arnott and Ronald J. Ryan discussed in earlier chapters.

Yet the application of old data to new sets of circumstances goes on. Irrelevant statistics are handed down like totems to clients and potential customers, becoming the source of much misguided investment advice.

## Past Performance Becomes Irrelevant
## in Analyzing Investment Talent

When the Dow was strongly dominant it made some sense to look at the 5-, 7-, or 10-year track records of mutual funds. Until that old system began to weaken, there were two constants that made measurement of past performance somewhat useful. The first was the fact that the take it, make it, break it business model was the major source of corporate productivity; the second was that most methods of stock analysis revolved, in one way or another, around that business model.

Any valid analytical comparison must have its set of controls. The two constants created that controlled environment where one money manager's methods could be compared against others during good times and bad. A 5- or 10-year track record that encompassed a manager's performance during the Dow's dominance showed their strengths and weaknesses at different points in an economic cycle. As long as the constants remained in place, perhaps some assumptions could be made about how a manager's methods would work under similar conditions as the cycle repeated. It was even valid to compare a manager's performance against the Dow itself to establish how much value was added over the index.

By the 1990s, as the Dow's dominance was weakening, it was clear that past performance analysis was no longer able to offer any clues about what could be expected from a manager's methods of analyzing and buying securities. We can see now that the reason past data became invalid is that the constants had changed as a new dominant investment system took over. Several studies were done in the 1990s that prove how irrelevant historic performance data had become to the portfolio manager or mutual fund selection process.

In 1994 Lipper Analytical Services examined the top-performing mutual funds the year after they were recognized as the best performers in their category. To conduct the study, Lipper used Morningstar, a company that ranks mutual funds between one (lowest) and five (highest) stars, based on past performance. The study looked at the list of five-star funds at the beginning of each year and measured their performance in the following twelve months.[4]

The study concluded that when most funds do so well that they are labeled top performers, their returns are below average the following year.

Percentage of Five-Star Funds Whose Performance Was Below Average the Following Year

| Year | Stock Funds | Taxable Bond Funds | Tax-Exempt Bond Funds |
|------|-------------|--------------------|-----------------------|
| 1990 | 52.6 | 10.5 | 50.0 |
| 1991 | 71.1 | 95.7 | 66.7 |
| 1992 | 56.0 | 63.6 | 60.7 |
| 1993 | 63.6 | 55.9 | 47.8 |

Another study that proves how unreliable numbers have become in evaluating a mutual fund was conducted by Burton Malkiel of Princeton University in 1996. Malkiel, a former dean of Yale University's graduate business school, examined the overall performance of the Forbes "Honor Roll" of mutual funds to determine the value of Forbes's historical data as a predictor of a fund's future success.

This study differs from Lipper's Morningstar study in that Forbes's requirement for making the honor roll is above average, but steady, long-term performance through both bull and bear markets. "Short-term bursts of glory will not get a fund on the Forbes Honor Roll. Consistency of performance and toughness in tough times will." So while Forbes, too, looks at past data, it views those data for a different purpose than Morningstar does—by focusing on lower volatility. But the results of the study show that even when the historical data are viewed in a different light and for a different purpose, they are still an irrelevant predictor of future performance.

Malkiel's findings showed that the year following a fund's selection for the Forbes Honor Roll, the fund would underperform the Standard & Poor's (S&P) 500, and sometimes significantly.

The following table summarizes the study's findings by comparing the Forbes Honor Roll funds to the S&P 500 the year after they appeared on the Honor Roll.[5]

Total Percentage Return of Mutual Funds the Year after They Made the Honor Roll

| Year | Composite Return of the Funds of the Forbes Honor Roll | Standard & Poor's 500 Index Performance |
|------|--------------------------------------------------------|------------------------------------------|
| 1983 | −7.45 | 6.22 |
| 1984 | 24.19 | 31.64 |
| 1985 | 10.66 | 18.62 |
| 1986 | 2.25 | 5.18 |
| 1987 | 14.96 | 16.50 |
| 1988 | 24.83 | 31.56 |
| 1989 | −8.60 | −3.11 |
| 1990 | 29.96 | 30.39 |

• • •

Over the last decade, as evidence mounted that historic data were becoming increasingly useless as a predictor of future investment returns, a countervailing force encouraged the reliance on these useless statistics. This was the proliferation of eye-catching computer programs filled with data that could be easily sorted, filtered, and printed in colorful charts, graphs, and PowerPoint presentations. Boutique consulting firms sprung up to advise individuals and companies on the best money managers in which to invest. Elaborate brochures contained colorful pages decorated with reams of useless data, which we have seen presented by people who have never actually spoken to, or had any contact with, the investment managers they were claiming to have so thoroughly analyzed. Computers created the self-proclaimed expert.

The do-it-yourself investor was also downloading supposed analytical tools. Lists of so-called honor-roll funds, top-performing funds, and 5-star funds were easily accessible.

Between the pseudoconsultants and the individual investors, the flow of money into top-performing funds was phenomenal. Even though it did not work, past performance became the overriding criteria for selecting a portfolio manager. Financial Research Corporation, a mutual-fund consulting firm located in Chicago, analyzed the amount of cash flowing into funds ranked by Morningstar. In 1996 the study revealed that 75% of all cash flowing into stock mutual funds was being invested in funds with a four-or five-star Morningstar ranking.[6] We can conclude that most of that money experienced inferior returns almost immediately.

In 1996, a survey of over 3,300 mutual fund investors performed by researchers at Columbia University's Graduate School of Business discovered that people overwhelmingly chose an investment's published record of past performance as the single most important basis on which an investment decision is made.

On a scale of 1 (lowest) to 5 (highest), those surveyed gave past performance a score of 4.62. It is extraordinary and disappointing that no other criteria even came close. Fees were judged to be the next most important criteria with a score of 2.28. Investment style scored a meager 1.68, barely beating out the importance of checking and brokerage services at 1.38. Confidentiality scored 1.35.[7]

How portfolio managers functioned during the old investment culture has nothing to do with how they will function in the new one. The question that needs to be asked is not, "What did you do five or ten years ago?" but, "Where will you invest my money today?" This seems obvious, but apparently it is not. What is a fund's research process? Where does the research come from? How is the decision of what to invest in ultimately reached? What sorts of people are investing the money—patient plodders, aggressive trading types? What is the tone of the firm or mutual fund company itself? These are the questions that should be asked. This is how Morningstar should be used because it does offer some analysis of those qualitative issues. The quantitative, or numerical, data are practically useless in comparison.

Understanding the qualitative issues surrounding the portfolio manager at an investment firm or mutual fund company will lead to the superior performance that is being sought. There are many ways to get from point A to point B. Within the mutual fund and investment management industries there are hundreds of research methodologies and hundreds more ways to carry them out. There are different personalities with differing views of political and social conditions. What is needed is confirmation that the money manager under consideration has a system that digests this amalgamation of factors in a consistent way. Once the methods used by different managers are understood, a cross section of them can be selected to manage the assets in question. In this way, real diversification will be achieved, leading to less risk and superior performance.

The alternative to making qualitative matters the primary concern in comparing money managers is to fall back on past performance and become vulnerable to the manipulation of numbers that we demonstrate in the following:

After a difficult several months when stocks have been volatile you see an advertisement for a mutual fund that boasts an annual return of 25%. The immediate assumption is that the fund's managers clearly know something other people do not. A closer look shows that it is not managing money that they are good at—they are good at knowing how to play the past performance game.

| | |
|---|---|
| Investment beginning in year one: | $100,000 |
| After one great year of performance the money grows to: | $200,000 |
| Terrible returns the next year create losses. The portfolio is back to: | $100,000 |

Your average annual return is 25%, but you have not made a dime.

Explanation: $100,000 to $200,000 = 100% return year 1
$200,000 to $100,000 = –50% return year 2
Net return = 50%
50% ÷ 2 years = 25% average

## Market Averages Become Immaterial

Even without the inception of a new dominant investment system, the use of market averages as a guide to whether stocks are over- or underpriced is a dicey exercise. But this has not been the majority view.

The generally accepted notion holds that because large-company U.S. stocks, adjusted for inflation, grew at 7.43% annually between

1925 and 2001, this must be their inherently normal growth rate. In support of this theory many statisticians believe that this average is arrived at through the market's ability to account fully for all available information at a given point in time, in an objective fashion. This means that one year's events have no effect on the next; each year is an independent random realization (the *random walk theory*). According to this view, there are no fundamental shifts that can occur that are not already fully discounted in the market's price. Yet the statisticians seem to contradict themselves by believing that the markets are shaped by an inexplicable equilibrium force that will always cause the stocks of large companies to revert to an average annual return of 7.43%.

Frank Schmid, writing in *Monetary Trends,* a publication of the Federal Reserve Bank of St. Louis, compares the logic of market averages to that used in predicting the flip of a coin.[8] By flipping a coin an infinite number of times, the long-run average of heads will be 50%. This is not because, as some believe, a law of nature mandates a reversion to the mean. It is that an infinite number of coin flips eventually smooths out any deviations. Those who believe some natural phenomenon will cause Dow-type stocks or the old dominant investment system to revert to its 7.43% average annual return are no different from those who apply cryptic notions to coin tossing. The erroneous belief in reversion to the mean in coin tossing is called the *gambler's fallacy*.

Those who peg "themarket's" return at 7.43% will say it is "cheap" when its performance falls below 7.43% and that therefore stocks should be purchased. "Themarket" is "expensive" when the performance average rises above 7.43%, and therefore stocks should be sold. Perhaps after the Dow ended its discovery, formulation, and acceleration phases and found its rhythm, the 7.43% number could have been an accurate indicator of the market's normal and expected rate of return. But at least one authority will not even concede that much ground any longer to the old reliance on market averages.

Economists theorize that in a capitalistic system the laws of supply and demand inevitably create a state of equilibrium. (Recall that the economic view of the equilibrium state developed in the 1800s.) Fundamental stock analysis grows out of this equilibrium theory. Stocks are also supposed to have a true fundamental value, so their market price will eventually move toward equilibrium and reflect that value. Taken collectively, all stocks of the market will do the same. The equilibrium state of the market will be its average. George Soros disagrees: "There is little empirical evidence of an equilibrium or even a tendency for prices to move toward an equilibrium. The concept of an equilibrium seems irrelevant at best and misleading at worst."[9]

In Part I we quoted experts who explained why big-cap stocks can no longer be counted on to maintain an average growth rate of 7.43% per year. This is a problem not only for the change-averse investor, but also for many insurance and mutual fund companies—and to a much greater extent. They have created popular investment products that allow participation in the growth of the S&P 500 while guaranteeing investors' principle. The guarantees are based on the kinds of market averages we have been discussing. In asking an insurance company representative what would happen if the S&P 500 did not perform as expected and his company was forced to have to make good on all the guarantees, he told us: "Not only will I not be around to talk to you anymore, the whole company will disappear." He said this with a haughty condescension, as if a commandment of biblical proportion has precluded this from ever happening.

It is nonsense to expect the market to "average" a return that is independent of the growth rate of the stocks that comprise it. It follows that because we have a new investment culture that defines the kinds of stocks that represent the market differently, we should be wondering what new sorts of average returns we can expect. To do this we will need to find ways to differentiate the expectations of the companies of the old dominant investment system from those of the present system. This will not be easy because current protocol requires all companies to report the same kinds of data, regardless of whether it bears any relevance to the type of business in question.

One corrective measure would be to free companies using new business models from the encumbrances of the quarterly earnings report. Rituals like the preannouncement of quarterly corporate earnings, followed by the announcement of what is put forth as actual earnings, should be eliminated. Gimmicks like this serve only to put a positive spin on weakened old companies while being a shortsighted and inhibiting way of judging the progress of companies working hard at adapting to, and prospering in, the twenty-first century. If it is frightening to picture a world with no quarterly earnings reports, if it evokes suspicious feelings because these vital gems of data are being withheld, we counter that for 20 years now, successful portfolio managers have told us that they have developed their own data-collecting methods because they view things like earnings reports and balance sheets with a jaundiced eye.

Another way of getting the new investment culture out of the shadow of the old is to delineate analysts specializing in the new dominant investment system from those who focus on the companies of the previous (Dow Jones) dominant system. Just as the community of bond (the first dominant investment system) analysts separated themselves in the twentieth century from stock analysts—because their perspective differs—the new, third group would be free to develop their own analytical tools. This would make it more likely that twenty-first century companies would be viewed in their proper perspective. The three groups of analysts, just like the two groups (bond and stock) we have now, would be equally important to investors who will always need to have portfolios diversified across all three groups.

• • •

## NO FEAR

The disciplines of war and business are not far apart. The classic *Art of War* written in 500 B.C. in China by Sun Tzu has been studied by business executives who have told us that it offers valuable insights into strategy, leadership, and victory. Sun Tzu believes that "the only constant of war is constant change."[10] (No doubt the investment community needs to study this book as well.) Once it is universally apprehended how skillfully the companies of the new investment culture embraced change and broke out of the constraints imposed by convention, it will become apparent why they are so important to our twenty-first century economy.

Sun Tzu also says victory is achieved with "serenity, subtlety, and control." Many companies of the new investment culture have succeeded with such serenity and subtlety that most of us have not even heard of them, much less understand what they do. A description of a handful of these companies, selected at random from our list of Digital Dow$^2$ stocks, is offered in the following pages. Understanding how they fit into the economic sector in which they operate will benefit investors more than any sterile set of irrelevant financial calculations and should prompt readers to learn more about the other Digital Dow$^2$ companies.

Just as the new ways of doing business that gained momentum in the 1890s created a new way of life that would last through the 1900s, the new businesses that gained momentum in the 1990s are shaping the way we will live in the twenty-first century. Many of these companies are already indispensable to us. We should be grateful for the courage with which they have stepped in to rebuild the different parts of our economy that the old dominant investment system no longer had the strength to serve.

## The Fuel of the Consumer Economy

Electronic transactions have evolved from being simply a convenient way to access cash and pay for merchandise and services, to being the semiconductors of our reliable consumer economy. Credit and debit cards used to be a handy way to buy the item that you had not foreseen you could not live without—until you spotted it one Saturday afternoon in your favorite department store. Today, a credit or debit card is as important as a driver's license.

We use plastic to prove the tax deductibility of products or services when we file our tax returns. It is a prerequisite for anyone with an expense account, and, ironically, we are often asked to provide a credit card along with a driver's license when we want to write a check. You cannot rent a car, or any other item, without a valid credit card. The use of plastic as security and identification, which serves to protect merchants, has greased the wheels of the economy in such a way that almost any item anyone desires is now available 24-7. Finally, credit cards make possible the billions of dollars worth of transactions that take place on the Internet.

As we take for granted the importance of the credit or debit card transaction, we overlook the companies that make the whole process function efficiently—so efficiently that we never think to ask why it never breaks down.

### Concord EFS

Nine and one-tenths billion transactions annually at supermarkets, gas stations, stores, and automatic teller machines—that is the number of electronic transactions processed by Concord EFS (see Figure 7.1) in a slow year. (Their annual report says that they faced some challenges because the recession "slowed volume" in the second half of 2001.) Add modesty to the list of this company's positive characteristics because their slow year did not prevent them from racking up one more year on top of 14 consecutive years of record earnings. Between 1986 and 2001, Concord EFS stock outperformed every publicly traded company of both the NASDAQ 100 and the S&P 500.

When listening to Ed Labry's matter-of-fact way of describing the evolution of the company, of which he is now president, it is easy to disregard (as he seems to) the vision he possessed in the 1980s to see where the company could be by the turn of the twenty-first century. At a time when credit and debit card transactions required handling carbon copies to keep records, Concord EFS set up an electronic draft system. In 1990 everyone from Wall Street to Main Street told Ed Labry that putting credit cards in grocery stores would never work. In 1996

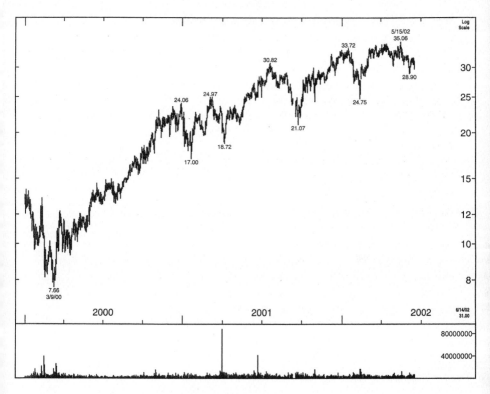

**Figure 7.1** Concord EFS (NYSE symbol: CE)

he was assured again that his pay-at-the-pump idea for purchasing fuel was a nonstarter. As it turned out, most of this book's readers have, during the past week, had a transaction processed by Concord EFS either at a gas station or a grocery store, and that is in addition to having Concord's help in getting cash from an ATM or paying for goods at retail or convenience stores.

Ed Labry and chairman and CEO Dan Palmer have made tough choices and stuck with their decisions. They foresaw that Personal Identification Number (PIN) systems were superior to having cardholders sign receipts. When an item is purchased with a signature, the merchants must collect the day's receipts and send them to a bank where it may take two days to clear them before the merchant gets paid. Signatures can be easily forged. When a customer enters a PIN number, the transaction is completed immediately, and the merchant gets paid the next day. Additionally, a PIN is more secure than a signature.

Setting up a PIN-based network was a huge investment for Concord EFS, but it is paying off. Merchants prefer it because of the real-time nature of the transaction and the reduction in exposure to fraud. To reduce fraud, Great Britain has mandated that by 2005 all debit and credit card transactions must use PINs instead of signatures. This trend toward PINs opens up another potential source of increasing revenue for Concord EFS.

In 2001 Concord began assembling the components of a comprehensive risk management service. Retailers annually lose between $12 billion and $15 billion because of check fraud. Identity theft, the fastest growing crime in the United States, is expected to cost financial institutions $8 billion by 2004. Concord EFS understands that by building a system that provides real-time access to multiple data sources, combined with cutting-edge technology, Concord can become indispensable in helping to reduce the drain that these crimes have placed on the economy.

Concord EFS is in position to capitalize on an important shift in the way consumers pay for transactions. Payment systems can be divided into three general categories: paper, cards, and electronic. Their market share in 2001 was as follows:

| Paper | 69.4% |
| Cards | 28.6% |
| Electronic | 2.0% |

Within 20 years payment methods will be dramatically different (according to the *Nilson Report,* 2002):

| Paper | 35.8% |
| Cards | 48.2% |
| Electronic | 16.0% |

This shift represents trillions of dollars of transactions moving to card-based systems of the type monitored by Concord EFS. The volume of debit card transactions alone is expected nearly to double from 6% of all transactions in 2000 to 10.8% by 2005, then jump to 14.8% by 2010. Concord EFS has anticipated this important trend and has the systems in place to capitalize on it.

## Improving Health Care in America

With the possible exception of education, there is no other sector of the U.S. economy more in need of an infusion of energy from the companies of the new dominant investment system than health care. The problems are so thoroughly rehashed in the media that no explanation of them is required here: too many Americans with no access, inconsistent and unfair distribution of services, soaring and inconsistent costs, and so on.

The part of the U.S. health care system to which these problems most conspicuously attach themselves is drug treatment, the worst possible place. Drugs are the most critical factor in preventing, controlling, and curing disease.

The problems do not stop at our inability to make drug therapies available to everyone with a need for them. It extends to how they are most appropriately prescribed, how they are used in concert with other drugs the patient is taking, and how the patient is using the medication. The underdiscussed fact on which these problems turn is that there are so many new drugs available now, and the list is increasing each day—this just from the traditional sources of pharmaceutical science. Add the new therapies coming out of the science of biotechnology, and the tide of new products becomes a storm surge.

Overworked physicians need easy access to prescribing guidelines based on nationally accepted treatment standards. Hospitals, emergency rooms, and physicians need access to the portfolio of drugs a patient is taking. The primary care physician, given the ultimate responsibility for the patient's health, needs to know the effect of treatment and that it is being used correctly. That there are severe breakdowns in this treatment chain is evidenced by the 7,000 deaths and hundreds of thousands of hospitalizations that occur as a result of drug interactions. $1.5 billion is spent each year just on hip fractures resulting from falls due to patients taking the wrong mix of drugs.

Too often, doctors are blamed for the overmedication of their patients. This is an unfair assessment given the fact that the potency of today's drugs (which makes them so effective in the first place) means that some patients' medicine cabinets have become arsenals of little time bombs that, when used inappropriately, can go off in their bodies. Many patients do not take this seriously. Sometimes it is because they are too ill to do so.

This convergence of problems creates a challenge that only a company of the new dominant investment system would be capable of taking on.

### AdvancePCS

Like many other visionaries, David D. Halbert, chairman and chief executive officer of AdvancePCS (see Figure 7.2), did not set out to

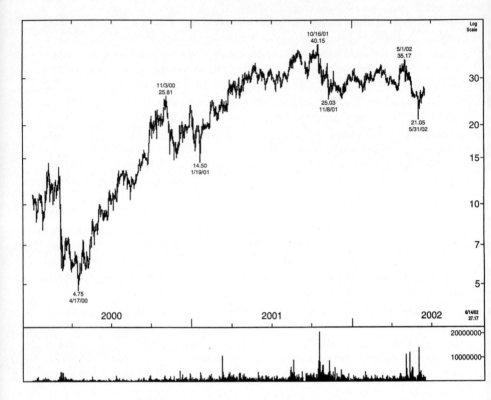

**Figure 7.2** AdvancePCS (NASDAQ symbol: ADVP)

rebuild an entire sector of the economy. The son of a physician and the grandson of an entrepreneur, he grew up in a medical household where ways to improve patient care were discussed around the dinner table. He becomes passionate when he explains how his company's mission is to improve the state of health care in America. He has already done a good job, and he is just getting started.

In 1987 David D. Halbert and Jon S. Halbert founded the company that eventually became AdvancePCS. The company focused on delivering exceptional value and service. Just 15 years after signing its first client, AdvancePCS served more than 1,000 of the nation's largest health plans, employers, and other providers of pharmacy benefits. Growing rapidly with the addition of new services and a series of strategic acquisitions, AdvancePCS established itself as an innovative leader in its industry. It was the first to process prescription claims online for pharmacy benefit programs and make extensive use of computer technology to improve the quality of care delivered to health plan members while reducing costs for its client-payers.

Today, the company offers health plans a wide range of products and services at a level that extends well beyond claims processing and other traditional pharmacy benefit management functions. That is why AdvancePCS is known as a health improvement company, a business that CEO Halbert says is a new model for the future of health care. Technology is at the center of this effort, as AdvancePCS works to help connect a fragmented health care system with information and services that benefit patients, payers, physicians, and pharmacies.

Halbert also says that AdvancePCS has the ability to inject the most important factor missing in health care today: competition. AdvancePCS serves more than 75 million Americans, or one out of every four people in the country. It is likely that anyone reading these words who has ever obtained a prescription drug through a corporate or insurance company benefit program has used AdvancePCS. This gives the company incredible bargaining power over drug manufacturers, creating billions of dollars of savings every year. AdvancePCS does what a patient alone cannot do—get the best deal. In this way the company attracts more insurance companies and other payer groups as clients. But injecting competition into the pharmaceutical drug industry is only a secondary benefit of improving the quality of health care.

Halbert says patient safety is the most important priority. Using its vast information technology capabilities, AdvancePCS is able to provide pharmacies and physicians with information about a patient's prescription drug history, which helps to thwart drug interactions. AdvancePCS also monitors patients' compliance with drug therapies and can help pharmacists and physicians follow up with those who are not taking medications properly. The benefits of technology do not stop there.

A diabetes management program was begun by AdvancePCS when it discovered that one of its clients had a high percentage of beneficiaries who were diabetic. A diabetic education program was instituted for the patients, and physician treatment programs were upgraded. The scientific validation of the successful outcome, as well as the data from the ongoing monitoring of the programs, will be used to enhance the database for the benefit of other clients whose beneficiaries need assistance with the management of diabetes.

One of AdvancePCS's clinical pharmacists conducted a study to confirm the effectiveness of a drug regime that treats immunocompromised patients. Immediately, the study revealed that some patients were not using the right drugs. This led to an analysis of organ transplant patients to see if they were on the correct regimen. By notifying patients, hospitals, and physicians before side effects appeared, patients were saved from permanent disability, or worse.

AdvancePCS has posted a compounded revenue growth of 138% per year over the past 14 years. Continued growth will come from the often-cited aging baby-boomer population who will need increasing amounts of medical care. Another revenue source is the burgeoning biotech industry. AdvancePCS is expected to generate over $200 million in biotech drug distribution revenues in 2002. Its goal is to be the largest distributor of biotech products within just a few years. Accomplishing this goal will raise AdvancePCS's biotech revenues to over $1 billion per year.

Halbert says that they are just getting started. Emergency rooms and clinics should have instant access to the medical data of an injured or unconscious patient. There should be greater access to cheaper drugs. There should be more intensive monitoring of a drug therapy's usefulness and more intensive study of high incidences of specific diseases among geographic and demographic groups. The company that can facilitate this is indispensable to the fair and effective administration of health care in the United States.

## Keeping the Money Flowing

The commerce of the twenty-first century economy crosses continents, cultures, and time zones. The traffic of financial transactions cannot become tied up in knots. Its integrity cannot be compromised. Money must be able to flow freely between mortgage banks, savings institutions, brokerages, financial planners, investment advisers, insurance companies, agents, leasing companies, ATM machines, large money-center banks, small local banks, and the point-of-sale credit card machine. That this process has never bogged down and that it runs so smoothly that no one questions how it all works or who makes it work are a tribute to the companies that are indispensable to America's productivity and the new business culture that supports it.

### Fiserv

"We are to financial institutions what electricity is to a home," says Les Muma, president, CEO, and visionary, about the company he co-founded with George Dalton in 1984. Muma is a theoretical mathematician who ran the data processing unit of Freedom Savings and Loan in Tampa, Florida, in the 1960s. About to lose his position when Freedom Savings no longer saw the need for a data processing department, Les, as he says, "bought his job." He automated the operations of his new acquisition, turning it from solely a data center into a business that could provide a variety of services to financial institutions. After meeting Dalton, who ran his own data processing firm, the two decided to pool their talents, and Fiserv (see Figure 7.3) was born. They made their first acquisition in 1985 and went public in 1986. To-

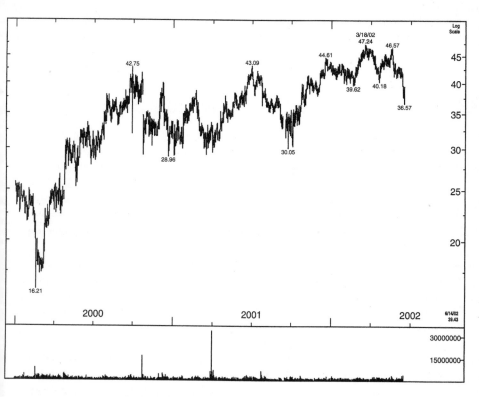

**Figure 7.3** Fiserv, Inc. (NASDAQ symbol: FISV)

day Fiserv provides products and services—the company has more than 200 distinct offerings—to more than 13,000 financial services companies in over 90 countries. Some key products and services include:

Core account processing

Check processing and imaging

Call center solutions

Treasury management

Mortgage origination and servicing

Health insurance management

Loan closing

Vehicle lease and loan management

Insurance policy/claims management

Employee education seminars

Bank branch servicing

ATM solutions

Statement presentment and imaging

Internet banking

Plastic card production and fulfillment

Credit card servicing

Flood insurance processing

E-commerce transactions

Trust processing and
services

Operations support systems

Brokerage transaction processing

Customer management solu-
tions

Private banking solutions

Fraud detection systems

Muma correctly anticipated that the modernization of the financial services industry would occur through mergers and acquisitions.
When the Glass-Steagall Act was repealed in 1999, the regulatory
walls prohibiting interaction among commercial banks, investment
banks, and insurance companies came down. Coupled with the necessity for these institutions to upgrade their systems to operate in a customized, online world, an $80 billion per year market opened up.

Financial institutions are eager to outsource their operations to
Fiserv rather than face the time and costs associated with establishing their own account processing and information management systems. A passionate belief that "clients make paydays possible" and
that the most advanced technology is worthless without service means
that Fiserv has a 99% client retention rate.

Fiserv contracts with its clients for periods of three to five years.
Coupled with the high client retention rate, a very attractive stream of
recurring revenue results. Fiserv uses this for acquisitions and product development.

Superior customer service can be delivered only by contented employees, and Fiserv needs 18,000 of them to deliver their unusually
broad range of products. By offering superior benefits, including sab-
batical leaves, employee turnover is below 20%. It is significantly less
among the ranks of management, helping to ensure continuity in the
delivery of services and product development.

A point was reached early in the twentieth century when electricity turned from being a luxury to a necessity that was taken for
granted. The modernization of capitalism has created another such
turning point. This time we have become dependent on financial utility companies like Fiserv. Just as before, we take all that this new utility offers us for granted. From an investment point of view this is a
mistake.

Where twentieth century utility companies served only a section of
the country, a financial utility like Fiserv has customers around the
globe that depend upon it. Free from regional restrictions, Fiserv's
strong reputation and global reach mean that it can easily continue to
add to its customer base year after year.

## Empowering Intelligence

The communication technology needs of the federal government are so vast that meeting them is like integrating every profession, institution, corporation, or utility in New York City under one system. The situation is made more complex because the government was among the first to develop and utilize information technology. Its different branches—military, executive, and administrative—must now upgrade old systems and get them to interact. To do this the proposed budget for information technology in 2003 is $52.1 billion, up from $37.6 billion spent in 1999. Like many corporations, the job of modernizing the government's communications systems will be outsourced to a great degree. A company that is experienced in managing data flow for scientific, legal, military, engineering, and commercial institutions would be a major beneficiary of the government's need to expand and upgrade its networks.

Intelligence and homeland security are most often mentioned as areas in desperate need of improved networks and upgraded systems. It has been made abundantly clear that it does not matter how much information can be collected; if it cannot be organized, analyzed, and shared, it is worthless. The science of semiconductors offers the tools to make better use of military and intelligence agency data. But this sensitive area requires more than technology skill from any company that intends on winning government contracts. The company must demonstrate an understanding of military and intelligence community culture and have employees that have already met high security standards. CACI International (see Figure 7.4) qualifies on all counts.

### CACI International

When we asked Jack London how he was able to turn CACI, a small and highly specialized computer consulting firm, into such a dynamic leader in providing information technology and network solutions needed to prevail in today's new era of defense and noted that *Forbes* magazine lists CACI among the top 200 "Best Small Companies," he sheepishly offered, "I guess I always had a kind of knack for being a little ahead of the curve." Indeed he does.

Jack London has transformed CACI into a company with diverse capabilities, one of which is the maintenance of databases for the U.S. Department of Justice. CACI provides the event databases that allow attorneys to access technical data and develop case points in an automated format allowing for the global sharing of insights and information. This tool was invaluable in the Exxon-Valdez oil spill case and the Challenger explosion. We can only guess at the scientific data in areas

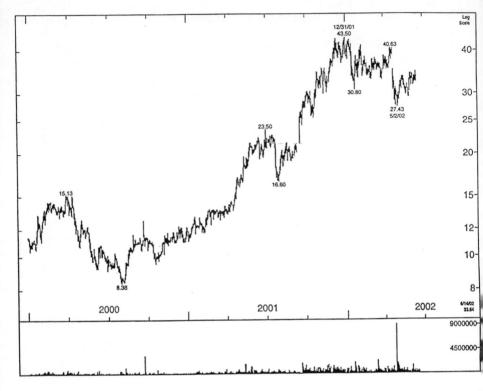

**Figure 7.4**    CACI International Inc. (NYSE symbol: CAI)

of physics, chemistry, the environment, and engineering that must be organized when these kinds of cases are investigated.

"The General Dynamics A12 lawsuit was really a big one," said London. Litigation was the result of the government's cancellation of the A12 Stealth aircraft contract. This case exhibits another important dimension to CACI, the ability to address situations complicated by security issues. A majority of CACI personnel have security clearances at a variety of levels permitting them to solve problems relating to highly classified material.

CACI, formerly known as the California Analysis Center Inc., was originally founded in 1962 by Herb Karr, whom London described as a "visionary businessman," and Harry Markowitz, a programming genius, who has also made significant contributions to the investment community. These are discussed in the next chapter. Karr and Markowitz developed Simscript, a computer language for the U.S. Air Force that addressed inventory problems and analyzed weapons capabilities. They recognized that their new software language had other applications that led them to the creation of a consulting company to train and support its new users.

London graduated from the U.S. Naval Academy in 1959, began his military career as a Naval aviator, and then joined a Navy Hunter-Killer Task Force—the kind of antisubmarine unit made famous in the movie *Hunt for Red October*. He finished his full-time Naval career as an engineer and joined CACI in 1972. He remained in the Naval Reserves and retired as a Captain in 1983, all the while moving up the CACI ranks from vice president to division president in 1982. He became president and CEO in 1984 and chairman in 1990.

Jack London watches trends. A decade ago he saw the need for special-purpose networks at agencies like the Federal Aviation Authority and the intelligence community, where passwords and firewalls were critical to its operation. CACI built a seismic detection system, for example, for the U.S. Air Force to monitor nuclear tests by rogue nations.

The momentum of attacks and threats against the United States that had been building for over a decade was not lost on him either. He recognized that national security would require the integration of government networks across a diversity of agencies from the Border Patrol to the CIA.

CACI's expertise has always been instrumental in helping to protect the nation's security, but in the post–World Trade Center attack environment it has become even more of a necessity. Significantly, however, London's first response to the question of how homeland security should be addressed was to stress the importance of people. "Well-trained operatives are a necessity. Everything can't be done by technology," he said. While that most certainly is true, he has crafted CACI into an entity that is especially qualified to assist those well-trained people in being more productive. CACI's core competence has been augmented by 18 astute acquisitions over the last nine years, adding powerful new capabilities and talented employees.

Like every other Digital Dow[2] company, CACI lays its success at the feet of its 5,600 employees located in 90 offices around the world. They helped CACI to post record revenues during the economic slowdown of 2001 and maintain a contract retention rate of over 90%. The company's reputation for quality, efficiency, and accountability will no doubt result in new contracts as the federal government develops its security initiatives.

Even without the federal government's new focus on intelligence gathering, CACI would have been likely to continue its 40-year track record of revenue growth. The enormity of the federal landscape makes it an entire planet unto itself that must be connected by information systems. A hardworking company grounded in the issues of defense, law, engineering, and science—as CACI International is—can be counted on to get the job done.

## Humanizing Human Resources with Technology

The burden of employment regulations that falls on corporations in America today is staggering. Just to ensure that an employee gets a paycheck, these tasks need to be performed: file with the Equal Employment Opportunity Commission (EEOC); comply with Social Security Administration regulations; set up tax filing and reporting; meet medical and insurance requirements for medical savings accounts, flexible spending accounts, and the Family Medical Leave Act; and set up 401(k) deductions and, when applicable, the deduction of insurance and nonqualified plan contributions. A single violation of any of these functions could result in considerable fines.

The paycheck is just the beginning. Employees need to be found, recruited, and trained. Then they need help in filing insurance claims, staffing, relocation services, travel and expense reimbursement, administration of retirement and postretirement benefits, performance reviews, and career development. This short list becomes more complicated by the need for companies to deal with different regulations in a variety of states and foreign countries. It gets worse when companies have several divisions that they may have acquired that will have different insurance carriers, benefits, and corporate policies.

All of these tasks fall to human resources (HR) departments whose chief responsibility is to maintain equilibrium between corporate and regulatory policy and employee motivation and morale. Where companies of 10,000 or more employees are concerned, it is becoming an impossible and costly task. According to data from the Saratoga Institute, Hackett Group, and Gunn Partners, human-resources costs per employee can average $1,200 per year but can range as high as $4,400 per year, and the employees' level of satisfaction is not rising with those costs.

A new level of corporate productivity can be added by lightening the administrative burden carried by HR departments. The company that takes the lead in providing such HR solutions to other companies will become as indispensable as office furniture.

### Exult, Inc.
"There are 300 companies in the United States and the United Kingdom, averaging 60,000 employees each, that spend $1,600 per year on administration, operational, and technological HR functions that we can do for them cheaper and better," says Jim Madden, chairman, president, and CEO of Exult (see Figure 7.5). And he has proved it. Un-

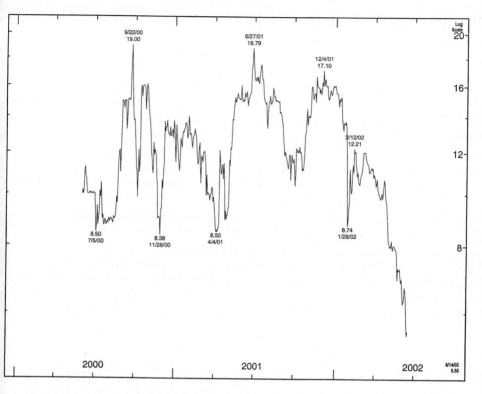

**Figure 7.5**  Exult, Inc. (NASDAQ symbol: EXLT)

der his guidance Exult has not only created an important new service but also met or exceeded the performance standards the company has guaranteed its clients.

The niche Exult has found is enormous. The 300 companies that are Exult's target market represent $290 billion of business. Studies have revealed that companies are ready to outsource this business. Indeed, one of Exult's first clients, BP PLC (formerly BP Amoco), had wanted to outsource much of its HR work for some time but could not find the right provider, until Exult came along.

Like many companies of the new investment culture, Exult could not accomplish what it does if the science of semiconductors had not enabled the storage and delivery of data. But providing employee benefits is not accomplished with technology alone. A complete understanding of the universe of HR issues with which a company must deal on a daily basis is critical to keeping employees happy in a field steeped in bureaucratic regulation. There are bigger companies than Exult that can throw money and technology at HR problems, but none that are as grounded in employee services. The company's innovative Advisory Council includes HR thought leaders such as David Ulrich, professor at the University of Michigan's School of Business Administration, who has been described by *BusinessWeek* as the "Best Educator in HR." Lynda Gratton, another council member, directs the London Business School's Human Resource Strategy Program and is recognized as a global authority on HR issues. The combination of HR intelligence and technology means that Exult's clients can not only outsource their root HR functions but also get advice on how HR can function at its highest level, and then customize these functions according to the company's special needs.

Exult does not insert itself into its clients decisions about which benefits vendors they should use. The client can employ whichever insurance company it wants, for example, and Exult will do all the enrolling and claims processing. Their expandable platform has eliminated boundaries and can accommodate any client preference.

The list of services shown in the box does not do justice to the value Exult adds to the efficient management of a workforce. An example of a unique benefit is a system that maintains a skills inventory for each employee. When a new team is needed for a project, the manager can filter out people with the required skills, schedule, and personal goals that would make an effective group. Getting the right people involved benefits the company as well as the new team members.

Services like this make Exult's clients more employee-friendly. This atmosphere is further enhanced by relieving HR departments of mundane chores so that they can spend more time in contact with em-

## Services Offered By Exult

| Advice and Information | Payroll/ Production | Rewards | Life Events | Finance and Accounting |
|---|---|---|---|---|
| HRIS/HRIT | Payroll | Health and welfare benefits | Recruiting/ resourcing/ staffing | Accounts payable |
| Performance management | Data administration | Retirement income benefits | Training/ e-learning | Travel and expense reimbursement |
| Employee data and records management | Systems administration | Salary/bonus administration | Expatriate administration | HR procurement |
| Organization development | Taxes | | Domestic relocation | Payroll accounting |
| Employee development | Time and attendance | | Severance administration | Benefits accounting |
| | Wage attachment | | | |

ployees. Typical of the companies of the new investment culture, the proper use of technology is bringing people closer together, not sending them further apart.

Exult signed the world's largest global outsourced HR contract when it was selected by BP. Since then it has signed on Bank of America, Unisys Prudential Financial, and International Paper, which alone represent 400,000 employees and $3.7 billion in revenue. Revenue growth in 2002 is 50%. The company has plenty of new client capacity and requires only six to nine months to get a new client up and running.

With a $290 billion market waiting, Exult will have plenty to keep it busy.

### Getting the Right Item, at the Right Time, to the Right Consumer

"Retailers have just experienced the perfect supply chain storm," says Dick Haddrill, president and CEO of Manhattan Associates (see Figure 7.6).

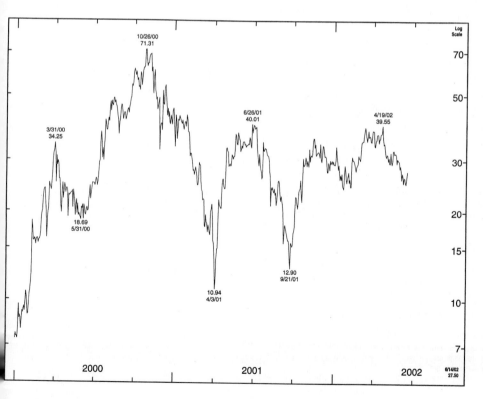

**Figure 7.6**  Manhattan Associates, Inc. (NASDAQ symbol: MANH)

A supply chain is made up of manufacturers, suppliers, carriers, distributors, retailers, and consumers, as well as the pipelines between them through which products are moved. Consumers expect that when purple tennis shoes are in vogue, they will be able to buy them. One does not think about . . .

(1) It takes weeks to make the millions of new shoes. (2) It may take weeks more to get them from the distant part of the planet where they were made to the people who want to buy them. (3) How does a smart retailer make sure that their stores have just the right amount of shoes to sell before the fad is over? To be profitable a retailer must control the intricate network linking the supply chain together.

Four elements have converged to create Haddrill's perfect storm and change retailing in the twenty-first century.

- Goods are now manufactured all over the globe. This lengthens the lead-time for delivery and increases transportation costs.

- There has been a proliferation of product lines. Where there was Coca-Cola, there is now Diet Coke, Caffeine-Free Coke, Vanilla Coke, Cherry Coke, and so on, all of which take up more shelf space and complicate the decision of how much to purchase, how much is selling, and so on.

- Where there used to be two fashion cycles per year, now there are four to six. This short product life cycle means that there is no margin for error in the timeliness and quantity of goods received by a retailer.

- Internet shopping adds a complex new link. Suppose a Polo shirt is purchased from Macy's Web site. That shirt will be sent to the customer from Polo's warehouse, but the billing will come from Macy's. If the shirt is to be personalized with someone's name, that adds another link in the chain along with the billing for the extra service. What if the customer does not like the shirt and wants to return it? Now the process must be reversed.

The new reality of retailing has created a new sort of company that is indispensable to America's consumer economy.

### Manhattan Associates

Dick Haddrill says that his company is the "plumbing" of the consumer economy. Founded in 1990 by Alan J. Dabbiere, who is now chairman of the board, Manhattan Associates has evolved from providing technical support to retailers trying to solve twentieth-century supply chain problems to being an indispensable utility, serving the complex supply chains of the twenty-first century.

This company's destiny has been shaped by two pivotal innovations. The first was the Electronic Data Interchange (EDI), which a decade ago allowed retailers to network supply chain links together, enabling them to get an update once per day on the status of orders. Then retailers began implementing quick-response initiatives with their suppliers. Manhattan Associates successfully delivered software to assist their supplier-clients in keeping pace with these new demands for efficiency. In this way Manhattan Associates became familiar with the challenges of operating a successful supply chain network.

The next evolutionary phase for Manhattan Associates was triggered by the Internet. The company was in a perfect position to understand how this new tool would create efficiencies for its clients. Macy's, for example, said that up to 40% of their buyers' time was wasted tracking orders. Because the Internet produces information in real time, errors can be spotted immediately. If an order was placed for 100 blue shirts, but 300 pink shirts are being prepared for shipment instead, the buyer can see the error and immediately stop the shipment before it reaches the stores.

One of Manhattan Associates clients, Aramark Uniform and Career Apparel, which makes uniforms for companies like McDonald's, reported that 10% of orders shipped by their suppliers were in error. The uniforms are manufactured in Latin America, and because the distance is so great, even a small number of errors can greatly increase shipping costs. Fixing them cost, on average, $50 per carton. The systems created by Manhattan Associates to access the Internet has reduced Aramark's supplier error rate to zero, producing savings that fall directly to the bottom line.

Foreign manufacturing facilities have economical Internet connections. This is all that is necessary to operate Manhattan Associates' collaboration systems. Because expensive computer networks are not necessary, any country can be connected to the supply chain network.

A fashion retailer in the United Kingdom, whose customers are in Japan and the United States, has its clothes made in Italy. Formerly, goods were transported first to a warehouse in Great Britain before being sent to their final destination. With the help of Manhattan Associates, they now ship goods directly from Italy to their Japanese and U.S. customers. The cost savings by eliminating warehouses, labor, shipping costs, and travel time are staggering.

A sampling of Manhattan Associates' clients include the following:

*Retail*
Footlocker
The Limited, Inc.

*Direct Marketing*
KB Consolidated, Inc.
Coldwater Creek

*Industrial Wholesalers*
Nissan Motor Corporation
Toyota
American Suzuki Motor Corporation

Manhattan Associates' corporate culture values the creative, entrepreneurial employee and encourages professional growth through training programs, mentoring programs, and career evaluations. Voluntary employee turnover is less than 6%, well below industry average.

As of March 31, 2002, Manhattan Associates enjoyed recurring revenue from 800 customers representing 1,100 facilities worldwide. Not only does it continue to add new customers, but in 2001 30% of new sales came from its existing customer base. Customers pay an installation charge for new services and fees when systems are upgraded.

The company was recently selected by *Forbes* magazine as one of 200 best small companies in America and by *Fortune* magazine as one of America's 100 fastest-growing companies as measured by earnings, revenues, and stock price.

## Putting Quality into Megamerchandising

That Americans are the planet's most committed consumers is supported by the fact that the company with the highest revenue in the world is Wal-Mart. But the reliability of the American consumer is a mixed blessing. The frequency with which we shop has made us picky customers, looking for bargains while expecting value. As a result, retailing has to be one of the most competitive businesses today. While answering the need for low-cost goods, the merging of general merchandise and food under one roof (megastores) has created a trend so important that a new category will be created under the NAICS to monitor its productivity.

"I can get it for you wholesale" was a concept pioneered in 1976, at the beginning of the incubation interval, by the Price Company in San Diego, California. After the Price Company created the first membership warehouse, the idea of bare-bones stores offering wholesale prices exploded in popularity. By the end of the century most everyone had heard of, if not shopped at, warehouse clubs like Costco or Sam's Club, owned by Wal-Mart.

After 30 years of growth, warehouse merchandising is entering a new phase. Customers want value as well as low prices. One step in this direction has been to give consumers the convenience of buying a wide variety of merchandise categories. Stores stock electronics, music, books, videos, hardware, tools, clothes, small appliances, kitchenware, grocery store items, furniture, and jewelry. Services include pharmacies, optical shops, and gas stations. The next step is to provide high-quality merchandise.

A company that is ready to capitalize on consumers' search for value adds a new dimension to the reckoning of how high its stock will go. *Consumer Reports* ranked Costco Wholesale (see Figure 7.7) the highest for product quality of all the warehouse megastores.[11]

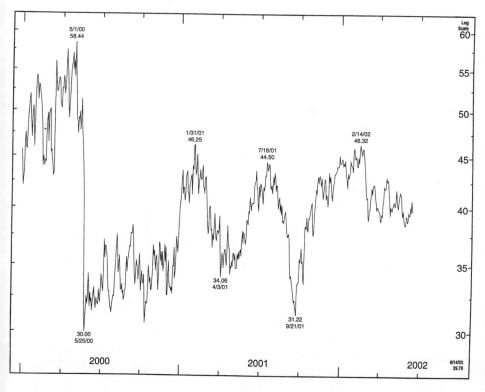

**Figure 7.7**  Costco Wholesale Corp. (NASDAQ symbol: COST)

## Costco Wholesale

"When someone walks into our stores to buy a TV set, they already have a number in mind that they want to spend. We want to give them the best product they can get with those dollars," says Jim Sinegal, president and CEO of Costco Wholesale. The *Consumer Reports* survey indicates that he is succeeding.

Costco Wholesale was founded in 1983 in Seattle, Washington, by Sinegal and Jeff Brotman, who is now chairman. In 1993 Costco merged with Price Club creating a $15 billion company. In 2002 sales exceeded $38 billion.

The company attracts new customers strictly by word of mouth. Other than a small ad in a local newspaper announcing the opening of a new store, there is no exposure on TV, radio, or any other media. After probing Sinegal for the unique retailing paradigm that allows him to avoid costly media campaigns, he finally said that he was "sorry his answer wasn't very exciting, but all it boils down to is giving the customer the highest quality products at the lowest possible prices." He said Costco's emphasis on value is much like that of Sears in the twentieth century, and it is what sets the company apart.

The focus on quality attracts not only the diehard club shoppers but also affluent customers who many may not expect to be typical warehouse-shopping club members. This means that Costco is likely to attract the growing segment of baby boomers who, facing retirement, will at last be interested in pinching pennies—especially if it means that they get the same-quality items to which they have become accustomed. Already Costco shoppers spend more, on average, than do shoppers at other discount merchandisers. The average spending for all discount stores (Sears, Target, Sam's Club, Wal-Mart, K-Mart) on everything but groceries is $474 per year.[12] Costco shoppers spend an average of $2,300 per year.

Costco Wholesale Industries is a division of Costco that operates food packaging, optical laboratories, meat processing, and jewelry distribution. It is another avenue by which Costco can save money while monitoring quality. The company is also expanding its gas station operations; over 50% of its stores were expected to have them installed by the end of 2002.

Sinegal says that the lifeblood of his company is his employees. He explained the math that proves that good wages and benefits equal higher productivity, but his conviction in this regard went past mere numbers. He said his company would be "nothing without its employees," and he puts his money where his mouth is. Costco pays the highest wages in its industry. A cashier with four years of experience will make in excess of $40,000 a year. Costco sees to its employees' health care as well: 90% receive full medical, dental, and vision benefits.

By the end of Costco's fiscal year ending in August 2002, the company had 394 locations in the United States, Canada, the United Kingdom, Taiwan, Korea, Mexico, and Japan. Another 20 stores were opened by the end of calendar year 2002 in such diverse locations as Indianapolis, Cleveland, Phoenix, Boca Raton, Boston, and a suburb of Tokyo. This expansion plan should continue to advance earnings by enhancing its volume purchase discounts and leveraging Costco's own manufacturing, packaging, and processing operations.

Sinegal makes this all sound so simple, as if he does not understand why everyone cannot grow their companies at a double-digit rate each year. Here is Costco's Mission Statement. It has only five lines:

1. Obey the law.
2. Take care of our customers.
3. Take care of our employees.
4. Respect our suppliers.
5. Reward our shareholders.

Jim Sinegal says, "By accomplishing the first four objectives, we will fulfill the last one, which is to reward our shareholders, a duty Costco takes very seriously. We intend to do our job by meeting our obligations to our customers, employees, and our shareholders."

Costco Wholesale understands that the job their customers expect of them is to provide value. As the most successful retailer of its kind, Costco obviously knows how to do all of its jobs very well.

## Reenergizing Education

The apparatus of our culture cannot function without educated people running it. Access to meaningful careers for high school graduates, retraining programs for adults, and advanced degree programs for everyone must converge with the new requirements of companies that arise out of the redesigning of corporate structures.

The notion fixed in people's minds is that the most acute need is for technical training associated with computer skills. That is an area of concern, but the demand is much broader. Health care is just one example of an area desperately in need of training programs and new employees. Every field needs those who have been trained to rethink how the new tools that are available to us can be used more productively. Professions and disciplines of all kinds are bogged down by the inability to employ successfully the innovations available to them.

Additionally, who is going to teach all the people who need to teach these necessary new skills? At every level, programs are needed for re-training and advanced degree programs for educators. The momen-tum of the changes occurring in this decade will only exacerbate the demand.

At this point, when the need has never been greater, nearly every institution of higher learning in this country is facing budget cuts. This means that these institutions must become more productive. Studies have shown that the cost of higher education is rising at a much greater rate than the consumer price index. John G. Sperling, chairman of the Apollo Group, says, "Institutions of higher education are going to have to be managed more and more as a business to stay in existence."

The solution is the incorporation of education by companies who have proved they can efficiently educate, retrain, and provide ad-vanced degrees to a variety of academic disciplines. Additionally, there is a need for these companies to teach their business skills to nonprofit educational institutions so that these schools may become more pro-ductive. The growth potential for the incorporation of education is im-mense. Currently, for-profit educational institutions account for only 4% of higher education.

### Apollo Group

In 1976 (early in the incubation interval) Sperling founded the Uni-versity of Phoenix. The Apollo Group (see Figure 7.8) was established as the holding company for the university, along with several other educational institutions, including the Institute of Professional De-velopment, the College for Financial Planning, Inc., and Western In-ternational University, Inc. The consolidated enrollment in its educa-tional programs makes Apollo the largest private institution of higher education in the United States. It offers educational programs and services at 63 campuses and 109 learning centers in 37 states, Puerto Rico, and Vancouver, British Columbia. Combined degree enrollment was 148,100 students as of May 31, 2002.

Sperling created the University of Phoenix to provide working adult students with the opportunity to return to school to fulfill their educational goals. This included developing an academic model that was built around the different learning styles and needs of the work-ing adult student. Additionally, this included creating a service model that was also geared toward this specific student population, focusing on key aspects of customer service, efficiency, quality, and availability. The university remains committed to serving the needs of this grow-ing student population.

Bear market or bull market, one thing remains certain: Our nation

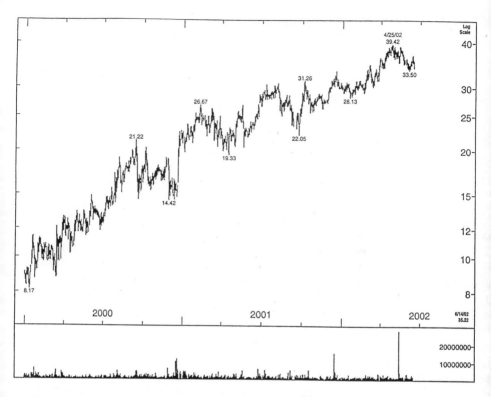

**Figure 7.8**  Apollo Group, Inc. (NASDAQ symbol: APOL)

continues to serve an ever-increasing and evolving global population. This continuous evolution occurs as our needs as a nation and a global provider continue to grow. The result is an increasing and ongoing skills gap, requiring a variety of accessible and timely education alternatives. The gap is further widened by the accelerated rate of changes in today's society. Increasing changes and complexities are slowly decreasing the half-life of an education. Skills learned 5, 10, and 20 years ago need to be updated. The University of Phoenix is positioned to assist in filling that gap.

The average age of a University of Phoenix student is 35, and the majority of students work full-time. The university provides students with both an extensive array of program offerings, ranging from associate to doctoral degrees, and a breadth of modalities. University students may attend class in a physical classroom environment, via the Internet, or in a combination of both. A comprehensive-outcomes assessment process is utilized to measure student learning outcomes in both affective and cognitive skills throughout their progression at the university. Over 160,000 students have earned degrees at the University of Phoenix.

## Dispensing the Investment Tools of the New Market Culture

Chapter 3 explained that investors must adopt a realize, capitalize, customize approach to investing, similar to the new models being adopted by businesses. For investors, this system involves "realizing" what their objectives are and then testing whether they are realistic. The testing process requires an analysis of the different styles and asset classes that compose the financial market and formulating mathematical judgments about which combinations of these are required to achieve a certain rate of return. Assessments of how much risk any of the combinations produce are necessary to ensure that the prescription for the portfolio that is proposed to the client is appropriate for the situation. As mentioned earlier, this process is called *optimization*, and it is practiced in the laboratories of financial institutions.

Optimization has been practiced for 25 years but proliferated late in the twentieth century as the pools of money needing professional advice swelled. We have delegated considerable wordage in earlier chapters to the purpose of impressing on you that in the new investment culture, an investment methodology utilizing optimization is a prerequisite for success. But the level of sophistication of the tools used to practice optimization exceeds that of the analytical tools used in any medical laboratory. Who manufactures these complex investment tools? Where do they come from?

### Barra, Inc.

Barra (see Figure 7.9) was founded in 1975 (the first years of the incubation interval) and went public in 1991. Barra is the global leader in delivering risk management systems and services to managers of portfolio and firm-wide investment risk. Since its inception, Barra's single vision—to empower its clients to make strategic investment decisions—has made Barra the industry standard in investment risk management. Headquartered in Berkeley, California, Barra has offices in all major financial centers around the world. Clients include many of the world's largest portfolio managers, plan sponsors, risk managers, and asset management firms.

Barra's core business is focused on the development and delivery of risk management technology. Its products include software and information services that are indispensable to the process of analyzing and managing portfolios of stocks, U.S. bonds, derivatives, currencies, and international bonds. In 2001, a difficult year for most of corporate America, Barra's revenue growth was 20%. Barra's perceptive decision

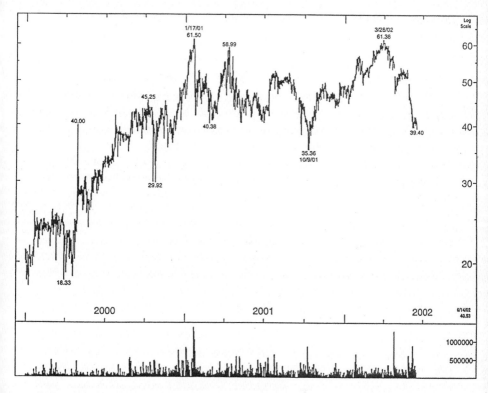

**Figure 7.9** Barra, Inc. (NASDAQ symbol: BARZ)

to sell products on evergreen contracts that renew until canceled, has contributed to its recurring revenue stream. A large portion of this revenue is used for research and development.

Barra's target market is money managers with assets under management of a half a billion dollars or more. Some of these utilize another product produced by Barra, enterprise and portfolio-level software called TotalRisk, which is used by clients like the California Public Employees' Retirement System (CalPERS), which has assets of more than $165 billion under management. CalPERS uses TotalRisk to implement a risk-budgeting strategy by aggregating and tracking its risk on a plan-wide basis. TotalRisk enables CalPERS to decompose risk into its driving factors, allocate risk optimally across assets, and communicate more effectively with its asset managers.

In the late twentieth century it was nice to have Barra's tools. In the twenty-first century, they are indispensable. Barra's investment technology is donated to 100 colleges and universities, the Wharton School and Cornell among them, so students will be able to enter the financial world with an understanding of their use and identification with the brand.

The stiff competition within the financial services industry, coupled with the need for smaller investment managers (assets under management of $500 million to $2 billion) to manage their assets using the strategies espoused in this book, has enlarged another channel for Barra's products. The mutual fund mass marketers like Schwab or Fidelity must eventually be able to provide customized optimization risk management techniques to their clients. Barra can provide solutions. Second, because Barra is such a respected industry brand, any investment management firm in competition for new business will have a leg up if it can say they use Barra products.

## DEFENDING THE DOW

A potent opportunity presents itself when the stock of certain companies, which gained such strength during the incubation internal that they enabled the construction of the framework of the new business culture, sell at a fraction of the value they attained during the discovery phase. The waves of panic that initiate the formulation phase always depress the stocks of many architects of a new investment system, but in today's new investment culture two in particular need to be singled out. These were the only two NASDAQ stocks that were part of the Dow Jones Industrial Average as it ended its term as the icon of the old dominant investment system. In fact, the growth of these two companies helped to disguise the poor performance of other Dow stocks and allowed the Dow to keep on posting stellar returns near the end of the twentieth century. We are talking about Intel and Microsoft. Because they belong to the new investment culture, they are likely to provide the Dow with returns it would not otherwise be expected to have during the formulation and acceleration phases.

### Intel

Intel (NASDAQ symbol: INTC) was founded by Gordon Moore and Robert Noye in 1968 to make silicon computer chips. Moore became famous for *Moore's law,* which predicted in 1965 that the number of transistors that can fit on a silicon chip will double every couple of years. Because silicon chips are the building blocks of the communication and computing infrastructure and because Moore's prediction was correct, Intel has been instrumental in the process of incorporating digital technology into our lives, becoming ubiquitous in ways most of us could not have foreseen even five years ago.

Some have lumped Intel into the category of a mass marketer whose strength will wane as computer chips, and their prices, can shrink no further without severely limiting the company's growth. That this view is incorrect can be explained by the fact that Intel is built around a realize, capitalize, customize philosophy that adds a dimension beyond that of a mere purveyor of product.

Right now a short list of Intel's products include central processing units (chips) that process data in computers, servers, and workstations; optical components; embedded control chips for laser printers, imaging products, and automotive systems; and hardware and software for cellular headsets and handheld computers. We can read the list of items, but as is true of many products produced by the companies of the new business culture, it does not register with us how much our lives now depend on them.

What makes Intel a twenty-first century company is its ability to customize these products to the needs of its customers. These include equipment manufacturers, individuals, and all sizes of business. It is Intel's commitment to research and development that gives it this edge. During the economic downturn of 2001 the company spent $7.3 billion, nearly as much as the previous two years combined. This has special significance now.

Intel has always believed that digital electronics will penetrate every level of human enterprise. Their new commitment to research and development proves that they are moving to a new phase, creating the building blocks for the next generation of customization.

Intel believes that in the new computing era "computers will be directly connected to the physical world and will anticipate what users want to do next—sometimes taking action on their behalf."[13] Cribs will monitor a baby's breathing, and a bracelet will monitor a diabetic's health and trigger an internal system to release insulin. "Crop conditions can be monitored down to individual plants; motors will tell you when they need maintenance."[14] Intel's wireless embedded platforms will facilitate these devices that can sense and act on the world around them.

Another set of applications stems from the merging of biology, organic chemistry, and traditional silicon technology. Minute devices will be created that can physically sense and alter organic substances. The productivity gains that this offers health care, agriculture, and the pharmaceutical industry are immense.

Just one innovation in any of these new frontiers would provide Intel with extraordinary growth prospects. But when so many innovations are underway, and so many developments that already exist still have not yet fully penetrated the economy, Intel's most rewarding years are still ahead.

## Microsoft

Bill Gates envisions companies having a "digital nervous system" so that they "can see the trend coming at you."[15] This is what the creative organization of information can do. For every new scientific advance created by a company like Intel, a wealth of software must be created to organize, monitor, and present data in an unobtrusive and natural manner. In this way it will become part of us, customized to our business and our lives, filtering out what we do not need. This is what makes Microsoft (NASDAQ symbol: MSFT) a company of the new dominant investment system

It is easy to think of Microsoft in terms of the incubation interval where the focus was on how many people would buy the next version of Windows. The structure that Microsoft helped to create has moved the software business far beyond that.

Computer software must safeguard essential services: utilities, money flow, and international trade. It must facilitate global e-commerce by solving currency and language issues. It makes the Internet functional, and it must enable every new device created by science.

The entire point of software is customization. The surge of information that digital technology generates is only going to increase. Microsoft creates the means for us to ensure that we get just what we need. This makes the company's market infinite because the evolving digital environment means that our individual responses to that environment will always be changing. The billions of dollars that Microsoft spends each year on research and development proves that it is committed to capitalizing on this permanently evolving environment.

## TRADING INFORMATION

New York Stock Exchange (NYSE) Rule 500 prohibits any company from voluntarily leaving the NYSE to trade elsewhere unless it does the following:

- Obtain approval from its board of directors.
- Issue a press release informing shareholders of its intention to delist.
- Obtain approval of its audit committee.
- Notify its 35 largest stockholders of record in writing of its intention to delist.

- Wait for a minimum of 20 business days to a maximum of 60 business days before actually switching to another market.

These restrictions on companies, by an institution that is supposed to represent the epitome of a capitalistic democracy, have some in our industry jokingly referring to the NYSE as the roach motel—once you get in, you can't get out.

Better to let a company trade its stock where it wants to. Better to have a market that is decentralized and open without the affectations of a private club. Better that it be a tool of capital formation for innovative and energetic companies and anyone in the world who wants to invest in them.

## NASDAQ

It is extraordinary that a system that developed during the incubation interval to trade upstart companies like Microsoft would evolve into an icon of an entire new business culture. What chairman and CEO Wick Simmons calls the "NASDAQ state of mind" is the atmosphere whose characteristics are reflected in the new dominant investment system and the companies that represent it.

The NASDAQ trading systems themselves are a metaphor for the accessibility and openness of the new investment system. Instead of a centralized trading floor, NASDAQ is a network of networks. It links broker-dealers, traders, electronic communications networks (ECNs), and order routing systems. The technology and market platform is accessible to any qualified market center or participant. The number of market participants it can accommodate is limitless. Already NASDAQ has the greatest capacity of any stock market in the world, and in 2001 it handled more share volume than all other major U.S. stock markets combined

Belonging to the new investment culture means seeing beyond the performing of a service for a customer, to providing the means to individualize service and making it useful at many different levels. NASDAQ has accomplished this by turning all the data generated from its trading services into a real-time information library that can be used by NASDAQ companies and their investors.

In 2002 NASDAQ took a dramatic step in facilitating our new, open investment culture when it introduced SuperMontage, the first trading platform that opens a window for investors to see what buy and sell orders have been placed for a stock. Until now, this information was privy only to specialists on the floor of an exchange.

Average investors benefit in two ways. If they invest through mutual funds, brokers, or portfolio managers, these entities will be able to find better prices when NASDAQ stocks are bought or sold on the behalf of investors. The savings accrues to the bottom line in better returns. Additionally, SuperMontage protects buy and sell orders of individual investors. That is, if a limit order is entered into SuperMontage, it will not be traded through or bypassed. By ensuring that limit orders will not be bypassed, SuperMontage helps customers manage their risk in a rapidly moving market.

SuperMontage redefines what is possible for a stock market by bringing new opportunities to investors. More buyers' and sellers' orders can be displayed, and investors will be able to see more of the orders that are available to them.

Currently, professional and individual investors see only a market participant's best buy and sell quotes in each security. In SuperMontage, market makers can input all or part of their buy or sell interest, by name or anonymously. This buy and sell interest will be available to view at five price levels, not just the best price.

Furthermore, the new open architecture has additional benefits for companies that list their stocks on NASDAQ. Corporate CEOs and CFOs need to manage relationships with investors. This includes mutual fund companies, pension and endowment funds, and money managers, to name a few. In 2002 NASDAQ threw open a window to executives who list their stocks on NASDAQ when it introduced the Market Intelligence Center. This is a telephone- and Web-based suite of services that tracks a stock's behavior in the market. Consider that Intel has 70 market makers. Before the new system, a CFO had a like number of calls to make to learn what can now be ascertained in real time on the Internet. If the executive calls the Market Intelligence Center, an analyst will be ready to discuss the aggregate of transactions and orders affecting their company's stock price.

On a typical day, NASDAQ currently disseminates more than 285 billion bytes of information, 6.5 million quotes, 2.5 million trades, 1.5 million orders, and more than 1.9 billion shares. NASDAQ's new computer architecture will allow for even greater growth.

Without NASDAQ there would be no new dominant investment system or new market culture. There would be no new business culture because there would be less of an ability to raise "capital" in the realize, capitalize, customize paradigm. There has to be a place for those companies, moving the world forward with innovations, to participate in the capital markets. Likewise, investors wishing to profit from these innovations need an efficient transaction system that stands for fairness and instills confidence.

There will be trillions of dollars entering the financial markets during the next few years. It will be attracted there by the Digital Dow² companies covered in this chapter and thousands of other NAS-DAQ companies like them that represent the new dominant investment system. Investors need to know that the markets are liquid and that the enormous number of transactions that will be generated can be absorbed without creating large price swings in any one stock. A recent study by Amivest showed that NASDAQ is prepared for the inevitable surge in volume. The analysis revealed that more stock can be bought or sold on NASDAQ with less of an impact on price than in any other U.S. market.[16]

The last two volatile decades have provided a challenging testing ground for NASDAQ. Through every crisis it has proved it can support the new market culture by posting a 99.98% market uptime. The final test was September 11, 2001. At no time were NASDAQ's systems inoperative. It closed for four days only in deference to firms and customers who were impacted by the World Trade Center attack.

## ENERGY

There is nothing unusual about a single young company discovering a new market and successfully penetrating it with a new service. But when young companies like those just described emerge from every sector of the economy, shoveling out clutter to build efficient new structures, they coalesce into a potent force. There are people waiting and deadlines to meet, or we would have described every Digital Dow² company plus the hundreds of others that are part of that force.

When it is understood that trillions of dollars of business await those corporations, whose contributions are not luxuries but necessary moving parts of our economy, it becomes clear how intrinsically meaningless discussions of five-year-old performance numbers, statistics on market averages, or comments like "What did the Dow do?" have become. All of that is behind us, and we are on a different road, widened and paved through the efforts of visionary individuals at work in the companies of the new dominant investment system. All the rest of us have to do now is put one foot in front of the other and head down it.

> One must take advantage exactly as if he were setting a ball in motion on a steep slope. The force applied is minute, but the results are enormous.
> —Sun Tzu, *The Art of War*

## NOTES

1. George Soros, *The Alchemy of Finance* (New York: Wiley, 1994).

2. Ibid.

3. *National Economic Trends* (St. Louis, MO: Federal Reserve Bank of St. Louis, August 2001).

4. "Selling the Future: Concerns about the Misuse of Mutual Fund Ratings," unpublished manuscript, Lipper Analytical Services, Inc., Summit, NJ, May 16, 1994.

5. Burton Malkiel, *Returns from Investing in Equity Mutual Funds 1971–1991* (Princeton, NJ: Princeton University, Center for Economic Policy Studies, 1992).

6. "Morning Star Power: Morningstar's Ratings Became Critical Determinant of Sales," *FRC Monitor* (1996, May): 1–7.

7. Noel Capon, Gavan J. Fitzsimons, and Russ Alan Paine, "An Individual Level Analysis of the Mutual Fund Investment Decision," *Journal of Financial Services Research* 10 (1996): 59–82.

8. Frank A. Schmid, *Monetary Trends: Gambler's Fallacy* (St. Louis, MO: Federal Reserve Bank of St. Louis, 2002).

9. George Soros, *The Alchemy of Finance* (New York: Wiley, 1994), p. 47.

10. Sun Tzu, *The Art of War,* trans. Samuel B. Griffith (New York: Oxford University Press, 1971), p. 10.

11. "Megastores Like Costco, Sears, and Wal-Mart Sell Everything from Soupbowls to Wingnuts: Which Ones Do It Best?" *Consumer Reports* 67 (2002): 13.

12. Ibid., p. 12.

13. Courtesy of Intel's Web site, "Ad Hoc Sensor Networks."

14. Ibid.

15. Bill Gates (with Collins Hemingway), *Business at the Speed of Thought: Succeeding in the Digital Economy* (New York: Warner Books, 1999), p. 5.

16. Amivest, December 2001. Pertains to companies with over $100 million value of float. The Amivest liquidity ratio measures the dollar volume of trading activity associated with a 1% change in price over a 20-day period.

# 8

# WE WILL BE ABLE TO SAY, "WE WERE THERE AT THE BEGINNING"

## Will the Last Investor to Leave the Twentieth Century Please Turn Out the Lights

*Revolution is not merely an acceleration of economic growth, but an accelera-*
*tion of growth because of and through economic and social transformation.*
—Eric Hobsbaum

"The person who tries to predict when each ocean wave will break on the shore gets nowhere, but the person who thinks about high and low tides—well, he just might come up with a theory of considerable predictive power," wrote authors William Strauss and Neil Howe in their book *Generations*.[1] Strauss and Howe were the first to define the unique personalities of four generational groups that can always be found in any given social and historic time period.

Strauss and Howe belong to the school of cyclical theorists who recognized long ago that civilizations do not advance in a linear fashion but must be explained in terms of recurring cycles. Others who could be classified as cyclical theorists include Frank Klingberg and the Arthur Schlesingers, Junior and Senior.

So we are far from being the first to study recurring historical trends, but as far as we know, other than George Soros we are the first to explain the behavior of the financial markets in terms of their cyclical historic and cultural contexts. Because we are breaking some new ground, it seemed prudent to test our conclusions about the future of investing against the body of work done by the academic cyclical theorists. What we found reaffirmed our conclusions about the present condition—and the future promise—of the financial markets.

• • •

First of all, most historians are familiar with the peculiar fact that events pivotal to the development of the United States have occurred every 80 to 90 years. The cycles begin at the roots of American history.

This remarkable pattern has inspired historians to look further into the rhythms of history, identifying other trends and events that occur with regularity. The body of work produced explains many aspects of the American experience, but Strauss and Howe have taken it a step further. They embarked on an ambitious effort to explain not only the existence of recurring cycles, but also the human behavior that creates them. What they learned offers important insights into what we can expect from the financial markets. To appreciate this, a basic understanding of the work of Strauss and Howe is necessary.

In their book, Strauss and Howe have defined the four generational types, coexisting in any given period, as follows:

- *Idealist Generation*—comes of age inspiring a spiritual awakening; fragments into narcissistic rising adults; matures into risk-taking rising adults and emerges as visionary elders during the next secular crises.

- *Reactive Generation*—grows up as underprotected and criticized youths during a spiritual awakening; matures into risk taking, alienated rising adults; mellows into pragmatic midlife

---

### Major Turning Points Affecting American History

**1590**   English navy victorious over Spanish armada

**Elapsed time 98 years**

**1688**   Glorious Revolution: overthrow of the English Catholic King James II

**Elapsed time 88 years**

**1776**   American Declaration of Independence

**Elapsed time 85 years**

**1861**   First shots fired in the Civil War

**Elapsed time 85 years**

**1946**   Japanese attack Pearl Harbor

leaders and maintains respect (but less influence) as reclusive elders.

- *Civic Generation*—grows up as increasingly protected youths; comes of age overcoming a secular crises; unites into a heroic and achieving cadre of rising adults; sustains that image while building institutions as powerful midlifers and emerges as busy elders attacked by the next spiritual awakening.

- *Adaptive Generation*—grows up as overprotected and suffocated youths during a secular crisis; matures into risk-adverse, conformist, rising adults; produces indecisive, arbitrator-leaders during a spiritual awakening; and maintains influence (but less respect) as sensitive elders.

In any given cycle these four basic types take on their own personality. In our present cycle these are described by Strauss and Howe as follows:

| Generational Type | Description in Present Cycle | Date of Birth | Age in 2003 |
|---|---|---|---|
| Idealist | Boomer | 1943–1960 | 42–59 |
| Reactive | 13er youths | 1961–1981 | 21–41 |
| Adaptive | Silent | 1925–1942 | 60–77 |
| Civic | GIs | 1901–1924 | 78+ |

A description of how these four personality types react to events is instructive in exploring the resistance we see today to the inevitable rise of a new dominant investment system. We will rely on Strauss and Howe's descriptions and insert our own analysis of how the characteristics of each will affect the unfolding of the new investment culture.

## CIVICS/GIs

These individuals fought World War II and "have left such a colossal lifelong imprint on America's political, social, and economic institutions . . . that they tend to see older and younger generations as ineffectual facsimiles of their own."[2] This group "comes of age believing that history does, or should, move in orderly straight lines." They detach themselves from new cultural trends but "retain an active role in public affairs . . . [and] they seek institutional power and economic reward."[3]

## ADAPTIVES/SILENT

These types "tend to respond ambivalently to anything they confront."[4] They might "try patching our new theory together . . . with other competing theories to yield a consensus or compromise perspective. An instinct for leadership may not be [this] generation's strong suit."[5] Later in life, "where they once took cues from Civic elders . . . now they adopt the agenda of younger idealists."[6]

## CIVICS AND ADAPTIVES: TENDING TO RESIST THE NEW MARKET CULTURE

The civics/GIs, who see history moving forward in a linear fashion, would not take to our idea that we are living through a cyclical replay of an investment pattern that occurred a century ago. Nor would they take to "Divorcing the Dow" and admitting that companies that they grew up with—and indeed a whole way of doing business—have outlived their usefulness. Some of these civics/GIs are still powerful figures, such as George Bush, Sr. Many more control vast amounts of wealth. We can expect this group to resist any effort to help the companies of the new dominant investment system prosper. It is more likely that this group would pull out the stops to support the companies of the old dominant investment system both politically and financially.

The adaptive/silent group can be expected to follow the lead of the civics/GIs until the civics age to a point where they are beyond influence. This means that at first the adaptives will join the civics in their skepticism of the new business models and the companies of the new dominant investment system. Indeed, we will be well along in the formulation phase before they will be willing to admit that it even exists. But the tide will turn. The adaptives are "flexible and culturally sensitive."[7] They can eventually be expected to accept the new investment culture that will be readily adopted by the next two generational types.

## IDEALISTS/BOOMERS

This group has no problem "recognizing how other generations have personalities very different from [their] own."[8] This group believes that they are possessed of a "unique vision, a transcendent principle, a moral acuity, more wondrous and extensive than anything ever sensed in the history of mankind."[9] This group was represented in the nineteenth century by Ralph Waldo Emerson and Henry David Thoreau. "Typically they exert their most decisive influence on history later in life."[10] Examples are Benjamin Franklin, Douglas MacArthur, and Franklin D. Roosevelt. "Producing leaders of great moral authority, idealists impose their will sternly on people of all ages. . . . From the young, they seek personal obedience and respect more than public power or reward."[11]

## REACTIVES/13ERS

Today's reactives "experienced the 'Consciousness Revolution' of the late 1960's and 1970's from a child's perspective . . . and had to grow up fast in a world of parental self-immersion or even neglect. [They are] tired of gauzy talk about Woodstock."[12] As they rise through adulthood they "engage in social and economic entrepreneurship. They accept wide gaps in personal outcomes . . . [and] their ablest peers become society's most cunning, pragmatic, and colorful public figures—military and commercial managers of great realism."[13] These include George Washington, John Hancock, George Patton, and John D. Rockefeller.

## IDEALISTS AND REACTIVES: IMPLEMENTING
## THE NEW MARKET CULTURE

To the idealist/boomer, the new market culture is a natural and obvious evolution. The new dominant investment system provides a way, at last, to reconcile the opportunities of capitalism with the cultivation of a healthy environment and a fair and vital society. For them, the ideas espoused in this book will immediately make sense, and the future will click into place. They will eagerly embrace, and want to know more about, the companies that represent the new class of dominant investments—indeed, the idealist/boomers have created and are running many of them.

The reactive/13ers will appreciate the new dominant investment system for the opportunities it presents for personal gain. These natural-born entrepreneurs will be eager to invest in Digital Dow$^2$–type companies. Additionally, this group is the work force of these companies. Reactive 13ers were educated in, and are spending their careers in, the digital age. Acclimated to the digital marketplace, they see opportunities where older generational groups may not. As the formulation phase unfolds, they can be expected to come up with ingenious ways of taking commercial advantage of scientific advances. Their practical natures will have them creating solid institutions and supporting them personally through investment in the financial markets.

The idealist/boomers and the reactive/13ers will create the success of the dominant investment system. In fact, that these two groups emerge when they do may explain the cycles of the dominant investment systems themselves. These two generational types developed the innovations of the last two incubation intervals—the reactives in the nineteenth century and the idealists in the twentieth. It is natural for the characteristics of these two groups to be reflected in the personalities of the dominant investment systems they created.

## THE REACTIVES AND THE NINETEENTH-CENTURY INCUBATION INTERVAL, 1870–1896

One of the most famous reactives to represent the nineteenth-century incubational interval was John D. Rockefeller. He was born in 1839. In 1870 he created the alliances that were to become Standard Oil. Strauss and Howe described reactives as practical, cynical, playing-to-win types. Any biography of Rockefeller will reveal that he fit that profile perfectly.

Gustavus Swift was born in 1839 and left his family farm to become a butcher. Cattle buying used to be part of a butcher's job, and Swift excelled at it. By 1875 his reactive personality had him succeeding as the owner of a cattle-buying firm in the then-ruthlessly competitive city of Chicago. He conceived the idea of shipping dressed beef in refrigerated railroad cars and the mass marketing of meat was born.

The mass marketing of general merchandise was developed and pioneered during the nineteenth-century incubation interval by Marshall Field, born in 1835.

In typical reactive fashion, many other future business leaders rose from low- and middle-class backgrounds to become industrial icons. Andrew Carnegie, Rockefeller, and Jay Gould applied their competitive, risk-taking natures to break out of any strictures imposed by social class. Cautious and cunning, they built their own institutions to protect their wealth and power. To retain control over their empires as they aged, the reactives used a militaristic business model where there was no doubt about who was in charge.

The industrialists imprinted that legacy, born of insecurity, on the companies of the twentieth-century investment system, and it remains a marker that distinguishes those companies from the new investment culture. Chains of command, pecking orders, low tolerance for individuality, and the rewarding of rank and power over competence are holdovers from the Dow's dominance. Like much useless detritus, we have lived with it so long that we have forgotten where it came from and what purpose it originally served.

## THE IDEALISTS AND THE TWENTIETH-CENTURY INCUBATION INTERVAL, 1970–1993

One of the most famous idealists to represent the twentieth-century incubation interval is Bill Gates. Born in 1955, he left Harvard and founded Microsoft in 1975. Gates is often compared to Rockefeller in terms of extraordinary business success, but Gates's style is indicative of the difference between the two dominant investment systems that these two business leaders helped to create. One cannot imagine Rockefeller describing the benefits of his products in terms like this: "A digital nervous system . . . [is] distinguished . . . by the accuracy, immediacy, and richness of the information it brings to knowledge workers and the *insight* and *collaboration* made possible by the information."[14] "Insight" and "collaboration" are not often mentioned in biographical material as being high on Rockefeller's list of business objectives.

Another idealist/boomer is Tim Berners-Lee. He graduated from Oxford University in 1976. During the incubation interval he created the first workable hyperlink system for the Internet. This innovation makes the new realize, capitalize, customize business model possible.

The idealist/boomer Steve Jobs was born in 1955. He joined Atari in 1974 to design video games in the first years of the incubation interval and then, of course, founded Apple Computer.

Strauss and Howe explain that as adults, the idealist generational types "gradually reshape institutions around new values."[15] It is easy to see that during the incubation interval, idealists created and supported the kinds of innovations that could provide the framework for these "new values." In a farsighted article published by *Good Housekeeping* in the economically bleak year of 1989, the editors had this to say about what kinds of values the idealist/boomer generation would bring to the table:

> New Traditionalists lead an unstoppable environmental juggernaut that will change and inspire corporate America, and let us all live healthier, more decent lives and make people look for what is real, what is honest, what is quality, what is valued, what is important.[16]

Mix in some less attractive traits attributable to the maturing idealist/boomer—willful, domineering, arrogant—add creativity and individualism, and you have the profile of the dominant investment system in which we will be living from now on.

It is true that we are drawing sharp distinctions where in reality there are blurry lines, but it is not hard to see that the atmosphere of the realize, capitalize, customize investment system, created by the idealists, already feels very different.

The presidents, CEOs, chairmen of the boards, and chief financial officers of the Digital Dow$^2$ companies we have spoken with do not ensconce themselves in ivory towers. They return phone calls, work alongside their employees, and put in long hours. They believe in treating their employees well, not because they have to, but because they want to. The result is a highly creative and motivated workforce. They believe in partnerships with their customers rather than adversarial relationships in which winning the upper hand is most important.

The defining characteristic of Digital Dow$^2$ companies is their insight. How did Les Muma imagine in the 1970s that Fiserv would become indispensable to twenty-first century commerce? How do Les Muma, Ed Labry, David Halbert, Richard Haddrill, Jim Sinegal, Jack London, and Jim Madden see beyond the pressure of next quarter's earnings report to find how they can enrich not only their companies but also the entire American culture? The energy that comes from vision is what sets the new investment culture apart and will make it more productive and profitable than any we have experienced so far.

We can speculate that the linear, civic generations do not have the vision, and the conforming adaptive generations are too accepting of tradition, to initiate a new investment culture. But their important contribution comes later. It is the adaptives and the civics who staunchly defend and maintain the institutions created by the idealists and the reactives. Each generational type serves a purpose during the life of a dominant investment system and lends its character to it.

Now that we know that the dominant investment system of the Dow was created by a generation of reactive types, it is easy to see why, as adults, they would strive for the security that wealth and power provide. In the words of Strauss and Howe, they had parents who "exposed their children to the real-world anxieties and dangers . . . within a self-absorbed adult society."[17] It is no surprise that this generational type's entrepreneurs built large fortress-like companies around themselves. They had parents who raised them with "little sense of mission or direction" which as adults "encouraged conformism."[18] It is no wonder that this group invented mass-marketing.

## Generational Characteristics of the Second Dominant Investment System (Dow Jones Industrial Average)

| | |
|---|---|
| Incubation interval | 1870–1896 |
| Generational type during incubation interval | Reactive |
| Characteristics of young adult reactives during incubation interval | Strong survival skills, entrepreneurial, risk-takers, desire individual success  Example: John D. Rockefeller |
| Resulting business model | Take it, make it, break it |
| Generational characteristics as adults | Play to win, cunning, pragmatic, realistic |
| Characteristics of dominant investment companies | Secretive; at war with competitors; relationships with customers often adversarial; vertical hierarchies of powerful management |

## Generational Characteristics of the Third Dominant Investment System (NASDAQ)

| | |
|---|---|
| Incubation interval | 1970–1993 |
| Generational type during incubation interval | Idealist |
| Characteristics of young adult reactives during incubational interval | Individualistic, unconventional, creative, visionary  Example: Tim Berners-Lee |
| Resulting business model | Realize, capitalize, customize |
| Generational characteristics as adults | Reshape institutions around new values, willful, creative |
| Characteristics of dominant investment companies | Accessible and open, partners with competitors to benefit all, customer is special, employees work in creative groups, management asserts less dominating power and spreads authority horizontally |

The investment system set up by the nineteenth-century reactives was followed by the adaptives who, once the ball is handed off to them, excel at carrying it. George Eastman, born in 1854, and Thomas Edison, born in 1847, were typical adaptives. They would not initiate economic or social change, but they were men of genius whose successful companies were built on the models created by the reactives before them.

The civics were there to defend and support the institutions that evolved. If the next generation of civics produces individuals of the same caliber as the last generation of civics (John Kenneth Galbraith, William Westmoreland, Joe DiMaggio, Robert McNamara), our new investment culture has a long and secure future.

Imagine building the perfect wealth-creating machine, one that would last long enough for our children's children and their children to benefit. Because such a thing has never existed before, the most creative and visionary individuals should be selected to design and engineer its architecture. Next, enterprising entrepreneurs should be found who excel in getting the most mileage possible out of a new opportunity and whose practical natures will ensure that kinks get worked out and opportunities are exploited. Its success may inflame rivals by upsetting the global balance of wealth and power so that another group of courageous individuals, inspired by the benefits they have enjoyed through the efforts of the other two, will step in to defend it. After the dust settles, a loyal group is needed to maintain and enhance its systems

When we poke our heads out of the forest long enough to see the trees, we find ourselves right now in the midst of just such a perfect wealth-creating machine. It was designed and built by the idealist/boomers during the incubation interval. Ambitious and entrepreneurial reactives are giving it momentum. Very young civics are standing in the wings to defend it from inevitable aggression—foreign and domestic—and they will be followed by adaptives who believe, as today's adaptives do about the old wealth-creating machine, that "this is the way things are supposed to be done."

There is a Chippewa saying that goes like this:

> Sometimes I go about
> Pitying myself
> And all the time
> I am being carried
> On great winds
> Across the sky

## Genealogical Map of the Dominant Investment Systems

### THE PAST

**Incubation Interval (1870–1896)**

*Young Adults:*      Reactives, born 1822–1842    entrepreneurial, individualistic

**New Dominant Investment System Begins (1897)**

*Adults:*      Reactives      cunning, realistic

*Young Adults:*      Adaptives, born 1843–1859    conform to reactives

**Discovery, Formulation and Acceleration Phases (1897–1929)**

*Adults:*      Adaptives      reinforcing standards of reactives

*Young Adults:*      Idealists, born 1860–1882    inspired by new investment system

*Youngest Adults:*      Reactives, born 1883–1900    influence muted by two World Wars and the Great Depression

**The Dow Dominates (1930–1998)**

*Dominant Generation:*    Civics, born 1901–1924    courageous in defending and expanding the companies of the dominant system

*Reinforcements:*      Adaptives, born 1925–1942    conform to and support the ideas of the civics

### THE PRESENT

**Incubation Interval (1970–1993)**

*Young Adults:*      Idealists, born 1943–1960    visionary, individualistic

**New Dominant Investment System Begins (1998)**

*Adults:*      Idealists      creative, intuitive, challenge the status quo

*Young Adults:*      Reactives, born 1961–1981    practical, independent, entrepreneurial, operate effectively in the nonhierarchal management structures of this investment system

*(continued)*

As investors we are passing through a trying incubation interval and a gut-wrenching overthrow of an old dominant investment system. All the while we have been carried along by a current of humanity to a juncture where things have finally fallen into place. Not only do we deserve to be here, but we can also point to the cycles of history

---

**THE FUTURE**

**Discovery, Formulation, and Acceleration Phases (1998–2011)**

| | | |
|---|---|---|
| *Adults:* | Idealists | medical advances and healthy lifestyles of Idealists and Reactives will extend the influence of both groups, will work well together |
| *Young Adults:* | Reactives | |
| *Youngest Adults:* | Civics, born 1982+ | |

**The Digital Dow²/NASDAQ Dominates (2012–????)**

| | | |
|---|---|---|
| *Oldest Adults:* | Idealists | crises possible, leaders of the caliber of Franklin Roosevelt could emerge |
| *Dominant Adults:* | Reactives | will achieve financial success by cleverly incorporating scientific advances into the realize, capitalize, customize business model |
| *Younger Adults:* | Civics | The oldest of this group will be 30 in 2012, will reinforce and expand the culture of the new investment system |

---

to show just how in step the new investment system is. Recall that the sequence of elapsed time between major turning points in American history looked like this:

| Pivotal Year | Elapsed Time |
|---|---|
| 1590 | |
| | 98 years |
| 1688 | |
| | 88 years |
| 1776 | |
| | 85 years |
| 1861 | |
| | 85 years |
| 1946 | |

We explained in Chapter 2 that the end of the acceleration phase for the dominant investment system of the Dow ended in 1929. We projected that the acceleration phase of our new dominant investment system represented by NASDAQ or Digital Dow² stocks would end about 2011. There are 82 years between 1929 and 2011.

To paraphrase Strauss and Howe, we may not be able to predict every rogue wave, but the historic perspective will keep us from running aground. Today the danger of grounding stems not from destruction of our assets, but rather from missing the opportunities of a lifetime while our heads are fearfully buried in the sand.

## PROGRESS REPORT: HOW THE NEW DOMINANT INVESTMENT SYSTEM IS ALREADY EVOLVING

As we completed the manuscript for this book in July 2002, the consensus was, in fact, that the financial markets have run aground—probably for keeps. Nearly everyone has the intuitive sense that something has come to an end. As is often the case, the school of public opinion is very insightful. Something has come to an end—an outdated perception of investing and the old investment culture that supported it.

But the stars are perfectly aligned to bring in a new investment culture more germane to our way of life and, consequently, with more wealth-creating power. Although the transition process is giving us some uncomfortable moments, the sooner the old system dies out, the better. In the meanwhile, the new investment culture is proceeding apace.

### Historically Significant Participation in the Financial Markets

In 1998, when the new dominant investment system was born, people 44 years old and younger owned a record amount of stock. These individuals belong predominantly to the reactive generation.

**Table 8.1**  Stock Holdings of Those under 35 as Share of Financial Assets

| 1989 | 1995 | 1998 |
| --- | --- | --- |
| 20.2% | 27.2% | 44.8% |

Stock Holdings of Those 35 to 44 as Share of Financial Assets

| 1989 | 1995 | 1998 |
| --- | --- | --- |
| 29.2% | 39.5% | 57.7% |

*Source:* infoplease.com.

The tendency has been to attribute the extraordinary high percentage of stocks owned by those under 44 to the so-called market bubble and dot-com frenzy in the last years of the decade. This explanation for the increased interest in stock by young adults is too simplistic. Now that we understand the personality of the reactive generation, it is clear that their propensity for risk taking and personal financial gain has a great deal, if not everything, to do with their enthusiastic participation in the stock market. The operative fact is that this trait will not go away. In the same way that we have come to accept the stereotypical (yet true) cliché that the huge population of baby boomers investing for retirement will keep the stock market healthy, we will adopt a new truism: that the risk-taking reactive generation, driven to accumulate personal wealth, will also continue actively to purchase stock.

And what stocks will they buy? The reactive generation in 2003 is between the ages of 21 and 41 and has absolutely no allegiance to the companies of the old dominant investment system. They could care less that Coke, DuPont, or Exxon-Mobil enabled granddad to leave a decently sized family estate. They do know that they use—and help to create—tools, products, and services that their grandparents had never conceived of and (if still alive) clearly do not understand. The reactive generation will invest in the Digital Dow$^2$ companies that they work for and that their friends and family work for. Even those employed by secondary investment system companies will become familiar with the products and services of Digital Dow$^2$ corporations as more Dow-style companies will be adopting the new tools and methodologies in order to survive.

Baby boomers will not suddenly stop investing for retirement either. With interest rates at the lowest levels in decades, the returns on money markets and bonds cannot support the lifestyle to which this group is accustomed. The growth potential for quality stocks is far more appealing, especially at the historic beginning of a new investment cycle.

The media are filled with data explaining that the baby boomers (and the older reactives) will be the beneficiaries of the biggest transfer of wealth in history as their parents either move to retirement homes or pass on. Most of this wealth is in highly appreciated real estate. Several trends are converging that are likely to result in the sale of this property and the reallocation of proceeds to the financial markets.

In the book *The Roaring 2000s* Harry Dent posits that "the typical baby-boomer family will be moving into the trade-up home-buying cycle from ages 34 to 43."[19] This means that the cycle will peak between 2000 and 2004. Additionally, many older boomers have purchased second homes in areas that are remote from their places of employment. Wireless and digital connections to their jobs allow these second-home owners to spend more time in what were formerly vacation homes. In short, the independently thinking boomers and older reactives have not waited around to inherit mom and dad's house, and it may not be their cup of tea anyway.

Another factor that will give beneficiaries second thoughts about keeping the old homestead are property taxes. Municipalities short of funds have raised taxes consistently over the last five years. Because they are already paying high taxes on their principle residence and possibly a second home, an additional tax bill could be out of the question. This will be especially true for trophy homes.

In booming towns and cities the affluent trophy home has appreciated handsomely, and its property taxes have skyrocketed as well. Living in Sarasota, Florida, it is common to see property taxes on residential homes at $25,000 to $40,000 per year. Taxes on waterfront homes can range from $80,000 to well over $100,000 per year. The 5% or so of the wealthiest boomers will keep these homes. The rest will not. Harry Dent expects that, as occurred in the early 1990s, these homes will decline in value fastest when the population boom peaks in 2009.[20]

Estate taxes will be a major factor in the liquidation of valuable real estate. If mom and dad are worth $5 million and $2 million or $3 million is in real estate, property may have to be liquidated to cover the federal estate tax bill. The nine-month deadline that must be met restricts sellers and may impact the final price.

Finally, inheritors of property will tend to sell it because it does not generate cash flow. Maintenance and repair is costly. Management and administrative issues connected with renting the property to create cash flow will not be an option for most boomers who are already occupied with careers and family.

One or two of these issues by themselves would be enough to create a wave of property sales. Taken together, it is easy to imagine billions of dollars of liquidity created from the sale of real estate and the proceeds being invested in the stock market, possibly helping to drive the acceleration phase.

## A Better System of Analyzing Mutual Funds Is Evolving

It should be clear by now that solving the problem of investment selection through an evaluation of what is past history—at least by the time one does their analysis—is a futile exercise. We have produced studies and given examples of why systems intended to rank mutual funds on past performance are not merely ineffectual but often will result in the investor's selecting the fund that in the future will be the absolute worst. Proof of this was in the study Lipper Analytical Services performed on the mutual fund research company Morningstar. This study was cited in Chapter 7.

One reason selecting a top-performing fund of the last three to five years almost guarantees that it will become the worst performer is the fact that the style sectors of the market (large cap, small cap, etc.) cycle in and out of favor. This too has been explained in great length.

In an affirmation of the kinds of fundamental changes we can expect to see during the formulation phase, Morningstar announced that it would change its rating system effective July 30, 2002. Morningstar now recognizes the cyclical nature of performance by comparing funds against those with similar emphasis. Small-cap funds will be ranked only against other small-cap funds.

Morningstar should be commended for taking such an important step. Although they will continue to use the one to five star system, it will begin to reflect the realities of the new investment culture.

## Divorcing the S&P 500 Is Finally on the Table; Separation Is Imminent

A lot of things can change in six years—a point we have been trying to make throughout. Six years ago, after developing our thesis and starting to put it on paper, it was hard to believe, even for us, that icons like the Dow and the S&P 500 would become irrelevant. Proof that major changes can occur quickly, and are in fact underway, is in an article that appeared on May 14, 2002, in *Institutional Investor Magazine:*

> The S&P 500 is not the best benchmark available. Back in the early 1960's it was but not anymore. (William F. Sharpe, Nobel prize winner in economics)
>
> The S&P 500 is a goner. (Harry Markowitz, Nobel prize winner in economics)
>
> I championed S&P 500 indexing and believe I was right in doing so. But you might find that indexing to the S&P going forward underperforms as a result of the artificial pop in the stocks that comprise the index. (Jeremy Siegel, professor at the Wharton School of Finance)[21]

William F. Sharpe developed the capital asset pricing model, a cornerstone of modern portfolio theory. He is one of the most respected financial theorists in our industry.

Harry Markowitz pioneered the theories of optimization and risk management used by every modern laboratory of finance today.

Jeremy Siegel has been on the forefront of academics seeking objectively to quantify modern market behavior.

The article further states that since 1999, one-third of the 300 major pension plans monitored by Chicago consulting firm CRA Rogers-Casey have stopped using the S&P 500 as a benchmark.

The S&P 500 will not go away anytime soon. S&P collects $80 million a year in licensing fees from the index. Billions more are collected from mutual fund companies who sell clones of the index. These are steely filaments helping to hold up the web of the old dominant investment system. Investors must avoid being caught up in it.

What is needed is for academia to produce an index along the lines of the Digital Dow[2]. It should represent the new dominant investment system with companies from every sector of the economy. Somehow, licensing it for commercial use should be made off-limits, and mutual fund companies and insurance companies should be prohibited from cloning it. Because companies would not enjoy an increase in the value of their stock by having it in the index (if the index is sold commercially, a company's inclusion in it means more investor dollars will automatically go toward purchasing the stock), there is a better chance for objectivity in the determination of which stocks ultimately comprise the new index.

## Innovations That Are Transforming Society

### *Realize, Capitalize, Customize* Comes to Air Travel

As is the case with most Americans, we live anywhere from 15 to 40 minutes away from airports we cannot fly out of. Instead, we drive 90 minutes to a large international airport. The airports that are 15 minutes from our home have been deemed too unprofitable to service by most major airlines. The ones that are 30 minutes away are too small to accommodate large jet aircraft. There are between 5,000 and 6,000 underutilized airports like this in North America.[22]

Once we have driven the 90 miles to an airport we can actually use, we spend at minimum another 30 minutes parking the car and getting to the gate, where another one to three hours will be wasted before we get on the plane. Arriving at our destination, the process repeats. Securing transportation will take at minimum 30 minutes. And once on our way, we are between 90 minutes and four hours, on average, from our intended destination. (We travel a lot and have kept track.) The fact is, Americans are still being subjected to air travel that is to the twentieth century what covered wagons were to the nineteenth.

Air transport should operate like limo services. One travels in a plane with a handful of people, all with destinations within the same general area. What is required is smaller, faster, economical jet aircraft that can take off and land at all the underutilized small airports around the country. A privately owned company called Eclipse Aviation Corporation is manufacturing such a plane.

The company was founded by Vern Raburn and Sam Williams. Raburn, now in his early 50s, spent 20 years as an executive at computer software companies like Microsoft, Lotus, and Symantec. Always interested in aviation, he bought a Lockheed Constellation from John Travolta and invested $1 million in its restoration. In the mid 1990s he met Williams, who is now 82.

A mechanical engineer, Williams has spent his life creating powerful and practical new engines. His company, Williams International, located near Detroit, Michigan, has designed products that have revolutionized weaponry. In the 1970s the military required a way to carry warheads hundreds of miles. For a missile to accomplish this task, a small, light, fuel-efficient engine is necessary. Pratt and Whitney, General Electric, and other major manufacturers said that it would not be possible to produce such an engine. Williams did not agree. He designed and manufactured thousands of the powerful and efficient little engines that power cruise missiles.

Williams turned his creative energy to the problem of commercial aviation. As he saw it, civilian transportation problems could be solved like the military's—with powerful, smaller engines. By 1997, in a joint effort with NASA, which also wanted such an engine, Williams succeeded in producing his economical and powerful aviation breakthrough. Williams met Raburn at an air show in Oshkosh, Wisconsin, where the new engine was first demonstrated, and the historic alliance was formed.

By January 2001, the third round of wind-tunnel testing on the new aircraft containing the revolutionary engine was completed. In March 2001 expansion began on the company's manufacturing and assembly plant in Albuquerque, New Mexico.

The new plane is called the Eclipse 500. "It cost less than a quarter of what the least expensive jet being delivered today costs," claims the Eclipse Aviation Web site. The operating cost is only 56 cents per mile, and the plane has a range of 1,300 nautical miles. It requires only one pilot. The Swedish company Aviace AG ordered 112 new planes in the spring of 2002.

Aviace AG is capitalizing on the new European phenomenon of flying clubs. Five different membership types are offered depending on a customer's needs. Aviace says that with the new Eclipse 500 planes, they can provide point-to-point, on-demand jet travel at reasonable prices throughout Europe. First deliveries of the aircraft are scheduled for 2004.

Because the new planes have the lowest cost of ownership ever achieved in a jet aircraft and are safer and easier to operate, it is not hard to visualize pilot-owners of small fleets of planes dotted throughout North America. Need a ride? Call or e-mail a central dispatcher with computerized tracking and scheduling systems that can calculate the cheapest and fastest way to get you where you want to go. Around all of the 5,000 underutilized airports, a new universe of businesses would spring up to service the new influx of travelers.

Flying from New York to Los Angeles would still require a large commercial airliner. But fewer people would be using the large airport hubs, and the large airlines would no longer own the skies. With more competition we could dare to expect better and better prices. The greatest benefits are likely to be those that we cannot conceive of today.

### Personalized Mobility

You stand on a small platform spread between two wheels that perform like your feet. You think about heading briskly to the store a mile and a half away—the machine takes you. You see something you want to look at and think about stopping—the machine stops. Someone bumps into you—you do not fall over. Think about going faster, slower, right, left, uphill, downhill and over any sort of terrain—it will take you. It is an extension of your feet that will do what you wish all day long for only 5 cents worth of electricity.

The machine is called a Segway and is built by the Segway Company in a 77,000-square-foot factory near Manchester, New Hampshire. During 2001, orders for the new transportation device were placed by the Postmaster General, who tested them for letter carriers, and the National Parks Service, who could use them for police and park rangers. According to an article in *Time*,[23] the Department of Defense is considering the vehicle for use by special forces. In April 2002 GE Plastics completed the first round of testing the machine and purchased 10 of them for secondary testing in three of its largest plants.

> Results of our initial test revealed potential double digit productivity gains, showed improvement in multiple worker process and have generated additional thoughts on how the SegwayHT can make a positive impact on the way we do business.[24]
> —Gary Powell, vice president of global manufacturing for GE Plastics

On June 4, 2002, Postmaster General John E. Potter announced that second-phase testing of the Segway was to begin: "The feasibility tests were conducted to determine if we could use this device to deliver the nation's mail. The results of the tests were promising. The early test results have been compelling enough to warrant expanded testing."[25]

The innovative machines were invented by Dean Kamen, who won the coveted Lemelson-MIT prize for inventors in April 2002. This is not the 50-year-old Kamen's first accolade. The college dropout, self-taught physicist, and multimillionaire holds several honorary doctorates. His vision was to "put a human being into a system where the machine acts as an extension of your body."[26]

A computer network of gyroscopes, sensors, 10 microprocessors, and diaphragms gives the users the sense that their minds are being read. In a way, they are.

The Segway is entering the marketplace first through major corporations, universities, and government agencies. Orders there could keep the company busy for years. But ultimately, Dean Kamen has his eye on capturing a portion of the $300 billion a year transportation market. John Doerr, the venture capitalist behind Netscape and Amazon.com, and one of the financiers of Segway, thinks the impact of this machine could rival that of the Internet.[27]

When the machines go on sale to the general public, the cost will be around $3,000, about the price of computers when they exploded onto the marketplace in the early 1990s. Consider the effect of this. They could replace automobiles in towns and cities. Downtown parking garages could be replaced with more productive office space, retail centers, libraries, or entertainment centers. Cars, taxis, and buses would no longer clog busy downtown streets. Noise, congestion, pollution, and energy consumption would be dramatically reduced. Just as GE is seeing a possible doubling of its corporate productivity through the use of the Segway, personal productivity could be improved as well. We would have the ability to get places faster, cheaper, and with less stress.

Ten years from now we could see a reconfiguration of communities and the businesses that serve them. Just as shopping malls and tract housing were the children of the automobile, machines like the Segway will inevitably alter where we want to live, where we want to shop, and how we choose to be entertained.

### Nanotechnology

When we build from the ground up, we put bricks and mortar together to create any sort of edifice we desire, limited only by our imagination. Nanotechnology is putting atoms and molecules together to create whatever material object we can imagine. We can create devices with extraordinary properties.

In the spring of 2002, the U.S. Army selected MIT to create lightweight molecular materials to equip foot soldiers with uniforms and gear that can heal wounds, shield them from projectiles, and protect them against chemical and biological warfare.[28]

The new clothing can have a multitude of properties. Some of these are camouflage material with a chameleon-like response to changing terrain, cloth that will become a rigid cast to support a broken limb, and paperweight chain mail made of molecular materials.

Scientists at Rand[29] explain that semiconductor manufacturing will eventually reach a ceiling where "limits to the degree that interconnections or 'wires' between transistors may be scaled could in turn limit the effective computation speed of devices because of materials' properties and compatibility, despite incremental present day advances in these areas. Thermal dissipation in chips with extremely high device densities will also pose a serious challenge."[30] In other words, in the quest for faster processing of data, computer chips as we know them today will become too packed with material to function. As long ago as 1999, Sematech, the leading consortium of semiconductor manufacturers, called for development of nanoscale semiconductors. Although implementation of organic computers for widespread use is several years off—Rand estimates 2015—discoveries are likely to be made along the way that could have ancillary benefits. For example, Rand foresees that by integrating nanotechnology with current materials technology, synergies will be uncovered that will "drive applications for drug discovery and genomics, as well as the basic understanding of many other phenomena."[31] Only a single new development, such as nanosatellites (this would recreate wireless communication), would be enough to revolutionize business. A handful of such innovations would change how we see the world.

Japan, the United States, and Europe are the major international competitors racing for dominance in the field of nanotechnology. Funding for the U.S. National Nanotechnology Initiative was $495 million in 2001. The lure of minute, disposable computers—computers that could be injected into humans to diagnose or fight disease and then self-destruct or computers that could clean up the environment, assemble consumer goods, and reinvent space travel—is behind the race for countries to dominate this new science. With the stakes so high, the intensity of the competition could bring us some of the benefits of nanotechnology sooner rather than later.

### Biotechnology

Food production was the first beneficiary of advances in biotechnology. Diverse strains of plants or animals were crossed to increase the gene pool. The hybridized offspring that were created were selected to produce the greatest number of desirable traits in future crops. This was 5000 B.C.

Although we have been practicing genetic engineering on this planet for a long time, we did not know exactly how it worked until 1953, when the American biochemist James Watson and the British biophysicist Francis Crick presented their famous double-helix DNA model. The next milestone came in 1973 when American geneticist Stanley Cohen and American biochemist Herman Boyer removed a gene from one bacterium and inserted it into another with the help of an enzyme. With this event the term *genetic engineering* officially entered our lexicon.

The Human Genome Project was the next pivotal event in the field of biotechnology. The project constructed detailed genetic and physical maps of the building blocks of DNA that Watson and Crick had uncovered in 1953. The mapping of the human genome was completed as we entered the twenty-first century. This crowns 7,000 years of evolution in the field of biotechnology.

We tend to think of biotechnology first in medical terms, possibly because the innovations are so newsworthy and personally important. An example was the manufacturing of Factor VIII in 1986. The human gene that codes for blood-clotting protein is transferred to hamster cells grown in tissue culture. The result is manmade Factor VIII, which can be given to hemophiliacs who lack this necessary blood-clotting protein. Countless lives have been saved.

Other medical advances too numerous to count are filling the pipelines of companies like Genzyme and Amgen. It is instructive to visit the Web sites of both of these companies to appreciate the array of treatments that are improving human productivity by ameliorating disabilities and keeping people healthier.

Another area benefiting from the advances in biotechnology is agriculture. The results of a study reported by the National Center for Food and Agricultural Policy (NCFAP) are stunning. The research focused on six biotech crops planted in the United States: soybeans, corn, cotton, papaya, squash, and canola. The finding was that four billion pounds of food and fiber were added to the output of the acreage utilized in the study. Farm income increased by $1.4 billion, and pesticide use declined by 46 million pounds.

### Biotechnology and Materials Engineering

That biotechnology will help us live longer has almost become a cliché. These medical advances will be fully appreciated only when we ourselves wind up on the operating table with a doctor inserting manmade cartilage into our creaking joints or a healthy section of home-grown tissue into a worn out area of our hearts.

The *agricultural* advances made by biotechnology seem to hit the news most often when people protest against them. History reveals that hostile attitudes toward improving the characteristics and the output of the food we eat eventually fade as it is discovered that the benefits outweigh any perceived threat. An example can be found in Mexico over 7000 years ago, when an agricultural experiment by the highly sophisticated civilization there created a more palatable and nourishing form of corn. For proof that this event took place, anthropologists point to the fact that as far back as 5000 B.C. no wild forms of the plant have ever been located.[32] Human nature being what it is, no doubt the first crop of sweet tender ears produced by ancient experimenters would have been thought by some to be endowed with any number of diabolical properties.

While medicine and agriculture get the biotech headlines, the applications of biotechnology to the fields of engineering, mathematics, and physics are less known. Biomimetics, for example, is the design of systems and materials that mimic nature. This work has created classes of smart materials that are already in use. One of these is the memory used in smart cards. Another is smart skis that change shape in response to stress. Smart polymers are being developed that function as muscles for robots. Biometric sensors can provide personal security systems with the ability to identify voice, fingerprints, and handwriting characteristics.

The innovations flowing from the marriage of biotechnology with physics and engineering are not futuristic speculations. They are at our fingertips. According to Rand, "The level of development and integration of these technologies into everyday life will probably depend more on consumer attitude than on technical developments."[33] Consider how these developments will change the way we view the world: clothes that respond to weather, interface with information systems, monitor vital signs, deliver medicines, and automatically protect wounds; airfoils that respond to air flow; buildings that adjust to weather; bridges and roads that sense and repair cracks; kitchens that cook with wireless instructions; virtual reality telephones and entertainment centers; and personal medical diagnosis possibly interfaced with medical centers.

The convergence of biotechnology with nanotechnology, according to Rand, is the "most promising near-term event. Over the next 5 to 10 years, chemical, fluidic, optical, mechanical, and biological components will be integrated with computational logic in commercial chip designs."[34] Large-scale systems such as satellites, laboratory equipment, communication equipment, and computer networks can be integrated with micro-scale components and built at a fraction of today's cost.

• • •

Who is paying attention? Who takes down the fact that air travel and personal transportation are being revolutionized and that sensors can fit on the head of a pin? Besides the people who are creating these things, airplane, science, and engineering buffs do—people like Nathan Myhrvold, who was Microsoft's chief technology officer and who Bill Gates "put in charge of the future" and who formed a new company dedicated to generating and growing innovations.[35] He pays attention, and so do the people at Rand and at corporate laboratories across the nation. Companies like Microsoft and Intel already have plans in place and structures set up to capitalize on new science. Economists at the Federal Reserve pay attention because it explains high productivity growth and low inflation. And Hollywood pays attention. Steven Spielberg consults at length with scientists and engineers about the effect of innovations on our daily lives. But the movie version makes it seem futuristic; it is not. A single development sends waves of new business opportunities fanning out across the economic pond. But when an extraordinary number converge, as they have early in our twenty-first century, they bring the deluge of wealth-creating potency that is at our fingertips right now.

It is investors who should be paying attention. It is the companies of the Digital Dow[2] index and the other companies of the new investment culture that are capitalizing on the long list of innovations, including those explained earlier. If we pay attention, we will not get left behind like so many did a century ago when they ignored those new-fangled Dow Jones companies—like Edison General Electric.

## THE PEOPLES' MARKET

A certain alertness is required now. The investment culture is under new management. It is led by visionaries who favor creativity over conformity. They are supported by can-do, entrepreneurial individualists. We can expect things to move very fast. At the same time, barriers have come down. The new business culture needs everyone with a new idea and the skills to make it useful. It is okay to be a dreamer, or a nut, as long as you just do something.

The engine of the new market culture is information. Access the Web site of any Digital Dow[2] company, and the doors will open to everything from the lunchroom to the executive suite—although often there is not much of an executive suite. Even the way most of these companies trade their stock provides transaction visibility that had not existed before the birth of the new dominant investment system.

Barriers between companies have fallen. Corporations share information and form alliances across geographic, cultural, and economic sectors. Lines have blurred between the disciplines of engineering, biotechnology, and computer science as new discoveries are made that can benefit all concerned.

By joining these collaborations, the school of investment analysis could discover ways to quantify the value of the companies of the new dominant investment system. In her book, *Market Magic,*[36] Louise Yamada explained how the laws of physics should be applied to measurements of economic output. Her convincing arguments lead one naturally to ponder how the principles of physics, microtechnology, and engineering can be applied to individual stock analysis as well.

Barriers between investors and their advisors have fallen as new forms of compensation put investment professionals and their clients on the same side of the table. Financial professionals can give each investor access to information that the financial laboratories had previously reserved for only the largest pools of money. In this way each person can find the zone where he or she can best capitalize on the new investment culture that we are fortunate to have the chance to be a part of.

There is a lot to do. The market has been handed over to us by a noble old guard, who—though weary at the end—had created a mighty thing. Now it is our turn . . . and we are open for business.

## NOTES

1. William Strauss and Neil Howe, *Generations* (New York: Quill, 1991), p. 105.
2. Ibid., p. 9.
3. Ibid., p. 362.
4. Ibid., p. 10.
5. Ibid.
6. Ibid.
7. Ibid., p. 364.
8. Ibid., p. 8.
9. Ibid., p. 11.
10. Ibid.
11. Ibid., p. 359.
12. Ibid., p. 356.
13. Ibid.
14. Bill Gates (with Collins Hemingway), *Business at the Speed of Thought* (New York: Warner Books, 2000), p. xviii.
15. William Strauss and Neil Howe, *Generations* (New York: Quill, 1991), p. 358.

16. *New York Times,* December 2, 1989, as it appears in *Generations.*

17. William Strauss and Neil Howe, *Generations* (New York: Quill, 1991), p. 360.

18. Ibid.

19. Harry Dent, *The Roaring 2000s* (New York: Simon & Schuster, 1998), p. 256.

20. Ibid.

21. Rich Blake, "Is Time Running Out for the S&P 500?" *Institutional Investor Magazine* (American Edition), May 14, 2002, p. 2.

22. James Fallows, "Freedom of the Skies," *Atlantic Monthly* (June 2001): 37–49.

23. John Heilemann, "Reinventing the Wheel," *Time* (December 10, 2001): 81.

24. Segway Press Release, April 30, 2002.

25. John Heilemann, "Reinventing the Wheel," *Time* (December 10, 2001): 81.

26. Ibid.

27. Ibid.

28. "Army selects MIT for $50 million institute to use nanomaterials to clothe, equip soldiers," *MIT News.* Retrieved June 11, 2002, from web.mit.edu/newsoffice.

29. Rand is an independent nonprofit organization dedicated to promoting scientific inquiry. It was created in 1948. Today Rand stands for bringing empirical, nonpartisan, independent analysis to the study of economic and scientific problems.

30. "Global Technology Revolution." Retrieved June 12, 2002 from www.rand.org/publications.

31. "Global Technology Revolution." Retrieved June 12, 2002, from www.rand.org/publications.

32. Encarta, "History of Biotechnology." Retrieved July 15, 2002, from encarta.msn.com/encnet/refpages.

33. "Global Technology Revolution." Retrieved June 30, 2002, from www.rand.org/publications.

34. Ibid.

35. Evan I. Schwartz, "The Invention Factory," May 2002. Retrieved June 12, 2002, from www.technologyreview.com.

36. Louise Yamada, *Market Magic* (New York: Wiley, 1998).

# Appendix A

# BONDS

## The Misunderstood and Underutilized Securities of the First Dominant Investment System

We see very few investors with bond portfolios or bond mutual funds who are properly diversified over the broad spectrum of what our industry defines as *fixed income securities*. This is particularly unsettling because most bond investors tend to see themselves as conservative, or at least that part of their portfolio allocated to bonds will be thought to be subjected to less risk.

Additionally, few 401(k) plans offer employees more than one or two bond funds. Either the vendor or the plan sponsor suffers, like most people, from a dangerous lack of knowledge about the diversity of the bond market.

Listed next is a sampling of different fixed-income securities and their performance in 1997 and 1998—peak stock market years—and 2001, when the bear stock market had set in. The returns vary widely from year to year and across different sectors of the fixed-income markets.

| Bond Classification | 1997 | 1998 | 2001 |
|---|---|---|---|
| Convertibles | 16.92% | 6.55% | –6.42% |
| Global government | 10.86% | 11.41% | 16.15% |
| International | –3.78% | 18.29% | –3.61% |
| Short-term U.S. government | 6.65% | 6.98% | 8.53% |
| 15-year GNMA | 8.61% | 6.84% | 8.29% |
| 20-year tax free | 10.85% | 6.83% | 4.85% |
| 30-year GNMA | 9.59% | 6.98% | 8.22% |
| High yield | 12.66% | 1.87% | 5.28% |
| Intermediate agency | 7.93% | 7.77% | 8.85% |
| Intermediate treasury | 7.69% | 8.62% | 8.16% |
| 10-year tax free | 9.92% | 6.67% | 5.09% |

The variety of fixed income securities and their rates of return means opportunity for investors to decrease a portfolio's risk while improving performance. At least a basic knowledge of some of the major classifications is necessary.

**U.S. Treasuries** (several types are issued by the government)
- *Bills:* Usually called T-Bills; mature in 3 months to a year; sold at a discount (the interest accrues during the holding period to the bond's face value)
- *Notes:* Pay interest semiannually and are issued in two, five- and ten-year maturities
- *Bonds:* 30-year maturities, issuance has been discontinued by the U.S. government
- *TIPS:* Stands for U.S. Treasury Inflation-Indexed Bonds; provide a hedge against inflation because their interest payments are periodically adjusted against the Consumer Price Index
- *STRIPS:* Stands for Separate Trading of Registered Interest and Principal of Securities; like bills they are sold at a discount, and the interest accrues to the face value; many different maturities are available

**Agencies** (issued by government sponsored enterprises [GSEs; examples are Fannie Mae and Freddie Mac] and fully owned U.S. government agencies)
- Sold in denominations of $1,000 to $100,000
- Pay semiannual interest
- Wide variety of maturities
- Interest payment may be exempt from state and local taxes
- Discount notes are also available and work like bills or STRIPS

**Mortgages** (sold from mortgages originated by financial institutions that pool and sell them to mortgage-backed security issuers)
- Sold in multiples of $1,000
- Pass-throughs collect mortgage payments from homeowners and pass it on to bond holder
- Collateralized mortgage obligations (CMOs) attempt to provide a more predictable payment stream by grouping mortgages into tranches that will meet certain investment objectives
- Investors will have principle returned along with each interest payment instead of receiving it in a lump sum at maturity

**Corporates** (issued by public and private companies; there are more corporate bonds than stocks listed on the New York Stock Exchange)

- Issued in multiples of $1,000
- Pay semiannual interest
- Wide range of maturities

Credit ratings are assigned by Moody's and Standard and Poor's (S&P) as an indication of an issuer's ability to make all interest payments and return the investors principle at maturity.

**Municipals** (issued by states, cities, counties, and towns)

- General obligation bonds (GOs) are backed by the full taxing authority of the issuer
- Revenue bonds are backed by the income from the project being financed
- Credit ratings are the same as for corporates
- Many municipalities have insured the interest payments of the bonds, getting them an immediate AAA/Aaa rating
- Municipal bonds are not taxed by the federal government; interest rates are considerably lower than for other types of bonds

**Convertibles** (corporate bonds that can be converted into stock of the issuing company)

- Usually available in denominations of $1,000
- Pay semiannual interest until converted into stock
- Conversion dates, conversion stock price, and number of common stock shares that investor will receive are predetermined by the issuer and set out in the prospectus

**Preferred Stock** (issued by public corporations; name derives from the fact that in case of bankruptcy, the owners of these securities receive payment preference over common stock holders)

- Secondary to bond holders
- Issued at $25 per share
- Usually callable within 5 to 10 years of issuance
- Trade on New York Stock Exchange
- Rated similarly to corporate bonds

All types of bonds are available to be purchased individually, through mutual funds, or individual, professionally managed accounts.

The $4 trillion corporate bond market can be particularly intriguing. Good corporate bond managers do their own research and do not rely on Moody's or

S&P. The market is far too big for these agencies to thoroughly research every corporate bond. Talented bond managers, just like stock managers, have their methods of knowing when a bond is a good value. If the analysis of the bond is accurate, the manager can generate handsome returns. We will use the example of a Ford Motor Company corporate to explain how this can work.

Let us say that the bond was issued in 1997 to mature in 10 years. Its interest rate, sometimes called the *coupon*, is 7.00%. The bond's face value is $10,000. In our example, someone purchased that bond when it was issued in 1997 and paid $10,000, which they will get back if they hold the bond until maturity in 2007. Two things have happened. First, the person who bought the bond needs to sell it now, and second, some bad news on Ford's financial condition causes the bond to slump in value from $10,000 to $9,400. A smart money manager who concludes that the bad news about Ford is overblown will buy that bond for $9,400. One year later the bad news on Ford is forgotten, and the bond is trading at $10,000 again. The manager received a 7% interest payment plus a growth in value from $9,400 to $10,000, a 6.38% increase. 7% plus 6.38% equals a one-year total return of 13.38%. The manager may sell the bond to lock in the profit.

This example is simplistic. Millions of dollars of bonds would be bought and sold like this, not $10,000, but the principle is the same. Professional investors do not usually buy bonds to hold them until maturity.

Similar opportunities exist in the municipal market as well when talented municipal bond managers do their own research. Here is an example of another way a professional can create value for his or her client. Let us say that the city of Chicago wants to issue a revenue bond to improve its water and sewer systems. The portfolio manager researches the revenue that the system creates as well as demographics and any circumstances that could prevent the city of Chicago from paying interest on the bonds. The portfolio manager concludes that the bonds are very low risk. The probability that interest and principle can be easily paid is very high.

The city of Chicago was planning to issue the bonds to yield 3.75%. They had intended to pay an investment banking firm to help them underwrite and sell the bonds. They had intended to pay Moody and S&P to rate the bonds so that they would be more attractive in the marketplace. Both of these things cost a lot of money.

Instead, the portfolio manager who had carefully researched the bond issue offered to buy all the bonds if he could get a tax-free interest rate of 4.25%. The city of Chicago agreed because they would have spent the difference between 3.75%, the interest rate they were originally going to pay, and the 4.25% on underwriter and rating agencies. The money managers got to add a high-quality security to their client's portfolios at an above-average yield.

This is just one example of why every investor needs to have a pipeline to the fixed-income markets—through either a skilled fixed-income portfolio manager or an investment advisor with access to a research and trading desk.

# Appendix B

# APPRECIATING THE POTENTIAL OF THE EMERGING MARKETS

We hear people misunderstanding the term *emerging markets*. Some mutual funds are called *emerging growth funds,* which means that they invest in younger U.S. companies beginning to realize their moneymaking potential. This is not the same as an emerging market mutual fund or stock. The emerging markets represent the countries outside of the United States whose economies and businesses are not as entrenched as are those of the developed countries such as Japan, the United States, or many of the countries of Europe. Some of the countries that are categorized as emerging are:

| | |
|---|---|
| Bermuda | Malaysia |
| Brazil | Mexico |
| Cayman Islands | Peru |
| Chile | Poland |
| China | Russia |
| Czech Republic | Singapore |
| Hong Kong | South Africa |
| Hungary | South Korea |
| India | Taiwan |
| Indonesia | Thailand |
| Israel | Turkey |

Where we refer to businesses or economies of these countries as being less entrenched, more fluid, and entrepreneurial, others call them underdeveloped countries or third-world countries—appellations that sound vaguely, if not blatantly, condescending. This negative spin uses the same backward logic that lumps a visionary company like Exult with fly-by-night.com.

Just as Digital Dow[2] companies do not have to battle internal bureaucracies or suffer the expenditure of cost and time related to destroying old infrastructures, the emerging economies of the world can more easily incorporate the new business strategies enabled by the tools of the digital age.

China's productive economy has created an enormous need for office supplies. The country is dotted with plants manufacturing pencils, staples, staplers, and all the other sorts of equipment used to operate any office. What was needed was a way to connect all the manufacturers with wholesalers, retailers, and eventually the buying public.

Asia.com was able to fill the gap by creating a comprehensive catalog of office supplies and facilitating the opening up of channels to get the products to a wider market. Stories like these are the stories of emerging markets. It is instructive to note that wireless technology has proliferated in Southeast Asia and Latin America. There are more cell phones in use in these countries than in the United States. These areas never had a network of lines and poles crisscrossing their continents to impede the spread of the new communication systems.

Because profit follows productivity, it is instructive to look at the economic growth of emerging-market countries compared to the United States.

## Average Annual Percentage Increase in Gross Domestic Product, 1990–1999

| Country | Value | Country | Value |
|---|---|---|---|
| Bosnia | 35.2 | Jordan | 5.3 |
| China | 10.7 | Sri Lanka | 5.3 |
| Sudan | 8.2 | Israel | 5.2 |
| Vietnam | 8.1 | Costa Rica | 5.1 |
| Singapore | 8.0 | Mauritius | 5.1 |
| Lebanon | 7.7 | El Salvador | 5.0 |
| Malaysia | 7.3 | Eritrea | 5.0 |
| Chile | 7.2 | Peru | 5.0 |
| Uganda | 7.2 | Argentina | 4.9 |
| Ireland | 6.9 | Nepal | 4.9 |
| Laos | 6.6 | Cambodia | 5.8 |
| Myanmar | 6.3 | Bangladesh | 4.7 |
| Mozambique | 6.2 | Benin | 4.7 |
| Taiwan | 6.2 | Indonesia | 5.7 |
| India | 6.0 | Papua New Guinea | 4.7 |
| Oman | 5.9 | Thailand | 4.7 |
| Dominican Republic | 5.8 | Ethiopia | 4.6 |
| South Korea | 5.7 | Tunisia | 4.6 |
| Syria | 5.7 | Poland | 4.5 |
| United States | 5.7 | Egypt | 4.4 |
| Syria | 5.7 | Lesotho | 4.4 |

| Botswana | 4.3 | Australia | 4.1 |
|----------|-----|-----------|-----|
| Ghana | 4.3 | Hong Kong | 3.9 |
| Bolivia | 4.2 | Norway | 3.8 |
| Guatemala | 4.2 | Pakistan | 3.8 |
| Guinea | 4.2 | Turkey | 3.8 |
| Mauritania | 4.2 | Uruguay | 3.8 |
| Panama | 4.2 | | |

It is important to view this growth during the global economic slowdown at the start of the twenty-first century. During this period, economic uncertainty was created by the World Trade Center attack and increasing tensions between Israel and the Arab nations.

**Percent Increase in Gross Domestic Product over Previous Year Period Ending April 2002 (from *Economist,* May 11, 2002)**

| China | 7.6 |
|-------|-----|
| India | 6.3 |
| Indonesia | 4.1 |
| Philippines | 3.8 |
| South Korea | 3.7 |
| Thailand | 2.1 |
| Venezuela | 2.8 |
| Egypt | 4.9 |
| Czech Republic | 3.3 |
| Russia | 4.3 |
| United States | 1.6 |

You can only imagine the resistance we faced from clients when, during the perceived soaring of growth stocks in late 1999 and during 2000, we advised that a small percentage of their portfolios be allocated to emerging markets stocks. By the end of 2000 the emerging markets index had fallen 30.61%.

As global economies slowed in 2001, as turmoil set in over fears of terrorists and financial disasters, imagine the reaction of these same clients when we recommended *increasing* their allocations to emerging markets. The result is that as of June 12, 2002, the emerging markets were the best place to have had money amid the difficult period since December 31, 2001.

**Table B.1**　Performance of Major Styles and Asset Classes from
January 1, 2002, to June 12, 2002

| Lipper Category | Lipper Index |
| --- | --- |
| Large-cap growth | (14.76) |
| Large-cap value | (6.94) |
| Small-cap growth | (13.09) |
| Small-cap value | 3.25 |
| International fund | 1.02 |
| Emerging markets | 10.28 |
| S&P 500 funds | (10.06) |
| Balanced fund | (4.42) |
| Intermediate Investment Grade | 2.86 |
| Corporate Debt BBB Rated Funds | 1.78 |
| High current yield | (1.34) |
| International income | 5.39 |
| GNMA | 3.80 |
| General Municipal Debt | 3.74 |

*Source:* Lipper Analytical Services.

The story reinforces two lessons from earlier chapters: (1) Successful investors must ignore preconceived notions from the old dominant investment system, and (2) investors must work with investment advisors who have access to the laboratories of finance we discussed in Chapter 3. It was from one of these laboratories that we received the information that led us to the decision to invest appropriate clients in the emerging markets.

The ability for billions of dollars to be moved instantly from one market to another, without control or regulation, can create enormous volatility in the financial markets of emerging countries. It is appalling that this has not yet been corrected, but avoiding this asset class means missing out on important opportunities. The right financial advisor is your best source of information as to how much money should be allocated to this overlooked and underappreciated set of securities.

# Appendix C

# AN ALTERNATIVE TO INDEX FUNDS

An efficient way to achieve diversification in portfolios used to be to invest in index mutual funds. Index funds attempt to duplicate the exact holdings of an index that represents some part of the financial markets. Index funds theoretically provide a passive investment alternative. That is to say, the investor does not need to be concerned with issues like capital gains or whether a money manager is adding value. The index investor would hold the entire portfolio of stocks mirroring the index until they themselves decided to sell.

Many index funds no longer provide the advantages for which they were intended. Frequently, it is their popularity that has created the problem. We will use the example of the most popular index funds, those claiming to duplicate that S&P 500, as an example:

- Lipper analytical services monitors 176 S&P 500 index funds. This does not include the hundreds more S&P 500 index funds held within universal life insurance or annuity products. It does not include smaller or newer funds. The Fidelity Spartan 500 Index fund alone holds $8.5 billion of assets. Investors are permitted to buy and sell fund shares daily. Typically, when markets are rising, there is a greater flow of money into the funds, and more shares of stock are immediately purchased. When the market is down, many people panic and sell their index funds, necessitating the sale of stocks within the index. Unfortunately this creates wide swings in the value of the indexes for the patient investors who were holding on for long-term growth.

- The constant flow of money in and out of the index mutual funds and the high level of buying and selling that this generates increases transaction costs of the fund. A mutual fund must pay transaction costs or commissions to buy and sell securities like everyone else. Although the cost per share is minimal, the volume of trades can make the overall transaction expenses enormous. You will not know what the transaction expenses are because there is no requirement that they be reported. It is a hidden cost impacting the performance of every retail mutual fund. In his book *Bogle on Mutual Funds,* John Bogle calculates this cost by doubling the annual turnover of a funds portfolio and multiplying it by 16% (a figure that comes from a 1993 study in *Financial Analysts Journal*). This means that some funds have additional unreported expenses as high as 3–4% per year. Trading expenses of 1.5–2% are common.

- Because of the issues just described, performance of S&P 500 index funds seldom duplicates performance of the index itself. Lipper Analytics ranks S&P 500 index funds just as it does any other fund type, affirming the variety of performance results between index funds

For investors who require passive portfolios that represent a variety of market sectors, the solution is to use a tool called structured portfolios. Formerly known as unit trusts, these are predefined portfolios of securities that are designed to remain fixed during the predetermined life of the portfolio. Because these are unmanaged portfolios, only a nominal supervisory fee in the range of .15% to .30% is charged each year. There are no hidden transaction costs to eat into the performance. There is usually a nominal charge to purchase the entire portfolio that is less than it would cost to purchase the individual shares themselves at even a deeply discounted rate.

The following lists are a sampling of the different types of structured portfolios available to investors.

## Stock Portfolios

Energy

Communications

Financials

Global telecommunications

Health care

Media

Real estate investment trusts (REITs)

S&P Industrial

Technology

## Fixed Income Portfolios (these portfolios are usually structured to provide monthly income)

Corporate bonds

GNMAs

Insured tax-free bonds

Tax-free bonds

State-specific tax-free bonds

U.S. government bonds

# Appendix D

# PROFESSIONALLY MANAGED PORTFOLIOS
## When and How to Use Them

The original intent of mutual funds was to provide diversification to investors with smaller amounts of money. In the 1980s mutual funds were not as popular as they are today. It used to be difficult to convince people with smaller amounts of money that they should diversify by using a mutual fund rather than buying individual stocks.

By the late twentieth century the pendulum had swung the other way. Now it is always surprising to see investors making mutual fund investments that go well into six figures and beyond. We can only conclude that most people do not understand that there is an alternative.

The alternative is a professionally managed portfolio of individual stocks managed according to the objectives set out by the owner of the portfolio. If you do not want your money sent into a pool where the value of the portfolio can be subject to the whims of other investors, a professionally managed portfolio may be appropriate. Because your money and securities are not commingled with others, you realize several advantages:

- The prices of your holdings will not be subject to the high amount of volatility that occurs in mutual funds when investors bail out when the market is low and pour money in when the market is high.

- Tax advantages accrue to the investor because the portfolio manager can generate capital gains or capital losses according to the needs of the account owner.

- In most cases it can be significantly cheaper than using a mutual fund. The fee structure is completely different. No matter how much money you invest in a mutual fund, you will never get a discount. All investors, no matter how big, pay the same. Money managers charge on a sliding scale, and there are no hidden transaction costs.

Here is how it works:

1. Cash or securities are deposited into an account at a financial institution. (In most cases, reputable money mangers do not take receipt of your money or existing securities.)
2. The manager you have selected executes transactions through your financial institution on your behalf.
3. You receive monthly statements from your financial institution and performance reports from your money manager.

## SELECTING THE RIGHT MANAGER

A manager should not be selected until the process outlined in Chapter 3 to determine your optimal portfolio is completed. Professional managers specialize in different styles and asset classes of securities. This makes the selection process easier. Obviously, only a manager with a long and successful record of managing small-cap value stocks should be selected to fill the small-cap value slot in your investment program.

Most of our clients are always surprised to find that even within a certain style of investing (e.g., small-cap value), there is a wide range of methods that professionals use to manage portfolios. Many small-cap managers will buy up to 75 or even 100 different stocks in a portfolio to achieve the necessary diversity to decrease risk. Some managers visit each company whose stock they buy, keeping in regular contact with executives to stay updated on management philosophies and current projects. Other managers never want to talk to the company whose stock they are buying. They say it clouds their objectivity. They prefer to rely on results only and monitor factors like sales or increasing revenue.

Understanding a portfolio manager's system for making money is important from two perspectives. First, the investor can decide whether the process makes sense to them and whether they are comfortable with it. Money management firms tell us that they will often lose an account that has had wonderful performance only because the client could not understand or appreciate the philosophy behind the investment decisions. Either their financial advisor had not taken the time to explain it, or the client had not taken time to listen.

The second reason to understand a money manager's methodology is more intriguing. It takes us back to the issue of real diversification. Within a single equity style—we will use small-cap value again as an example—the different methodologies will perform differently at any given point in time.

Here is why it is important to understand the rotational performance of different managers. Consider a 20-month period when small-cap value stocks are outperforming all other stock styles. A client has two small-cap value managers, Manager A and Manager B. For the first nine months Manager A significantly outperforms Manager B. Invariably, the client will decide that all of the small-cap value money should be allocated to Manager A. We discourage the client from changing managers because just as soon as all the money is moved to Manager A, Manager B begins to outperform by wide margins.

We have not seen any studies on this phenomenon, but our empirical experience is extensive. Assuming that there has been no change in the management firm's process or operation—this is the job of your financial advisor to monitor—a manager's performance will come in waves. The account should not be interrupted without very good reason.

This knowledge helps the manager selection process. If possible, more than one manager should be selected for each style of stock. The investment methodologies of the managers should be very different. Risk will be decreased and the possibility of better returns increased. Incidentally, these same truths hold for mutual funds; it should shed more light on the foolishness of using past performance as the primary criteria in making investment decisions.

We have observed another phenomenon once the money manager is selected and the account is set up: The level of performance tends to increase the longer the account is in place. The portfolios are less affected by declining markets and tend to do better in rising markets. Our industry could benefit by a thorough study of how frequently this occurs and why. We can only conclude that it takes time for the portfolio, the manager's technique, and the market to synchronize.

## WHEN TO USE A PROFESSIONALLY MANAGED PORTFOLIO

The total amount you have to invest determines whether you employ a professional manager, use a mutual fund, or some combination of both. Professional managers can have minimums as low as $100,000–$250,000. If your investable assets are $250,000, you can employ only one or two managers. This is inconsistent with the optimization principles that will be so important to twenty-first century investing. Mutual funds will allow a $250,000 account to diversify across as many styles and asset classes as necessary because their minimums are usually as low as $1,000. A mutual fund can accommodate an investor with a $250,000 portfolio who needs to take a 5% position ($12,500) in emerging-markets stocks.

An investor with $800,000 probably needs a combination of money managers and mutual funds. If the prescription calls for 30% large-cap value stocks ($240,000), two large-cap value managers could be hired. If a 5% position ($40,000) were required in high-yield bonds, a mutual fund would work. A 25% position ($200,000) in small-cap growth could accommodate two professional small-cap growth portfolios, and so on.

Although there are always exceptions, at the $5,000,000 level and up, individually managed portfolios should be used almost exclusively. It is far more cost effective than mutual funds, and this efficiency alone can improve performance.

## Appendix E

# THE IMPENDING PENSION PLAN CRISES

The necessity of adapting the management of pension plan assets to the new dominant investment system is acute. To emphasize and expand on the critical nature of this problem, which we introduced in Chapter 5, we offer the complete text of a 2002 publication by Ryan Labs, the leading authority in the field of asset/liability management. The following is reprinted with permission.

# Pension Alert !

The fall in equity markets combined with the decline in interest rates across the term structure of interest rates has ravaged defined benefit pension plan finances in the last two calendar years (2000 and 2001). Applying the average pension fund asset allocation (courtesy of Pension & Investment) to appropriate index benchmarks show that *on average pension fund assets underperformed pension liabilities by about 37%* during this period. If the funding ratio for most plans decreases by 37%, several undesirable financial accounting measurements will occur : reduced earnings, higher contributions, higher PBGC insurance premiums, lower credit rating valuations, all of which impact the financial health of pension America.

Ryan Labs invented the first Liability Index in 1991 and we trademarked it in 1992. This research is dedicated to support pension plans in their battle against a most difficult and misunderstood opponent, the pension liability. The following pages highlight the client objective, accounting, hedging problems, myths and solutions to asset/liability management for defined benefit pension plans.

## The Objective

The objective of a Pension Fund is (1) to fully fund the pension liability, (2) at the lowest cost to the Plan Sponsor, (3) subject to sensible risk. This should be the function of the pension assets rather than pension contributions (added costs) coming from the employer/employees, or in the case of Public Funds, current or future taxpayers.

In "best case scenarios," pension holidays may be achieved by growing the asset portfolio in excess of the liability portfolio (pension surplus). *Plan sponsors' run the risk of higher contributions if the asset portfolio is not constructed to both match the present value of liabilities (cash flows) and the volatile interest rate behavior of liabilities..* Fluctuations in the present value of assets vs. liabilities (funding ratios) represent high financial risk for most plan sponsors. Yet, because of actuarial and accounting smoothing of financial statements, most plan sponsors are unaware of this danger !

## The Problem

Using the Ryan Labs generic Liability Index to serve as a proxy for liabilities (average duration of 15.5 years) and using a static asset allocation (based upon the annual P&I survey), pension assets have underperformed pension liabilities by about 37% for the period 12/31/99 to 12/31/01 (see Asset/Liability Watch Table). *Ryan Labs reported that the calendar year 2000 was the worst pension year in history* with assets underperforming liabilities by more than twice the previous worst year of 1995 (-28.46 vs. -12.49%). Calendar year 2001 fared no better, losing to liabilities by about 8.48%.

Moreover, since December 1988 the cumulative total return difference of pension assets minus liabilities is -7.32 % ... no value added. It is hard to believe that an asset allocation heavily skewed to equities (which enjoyed the greatest bull market in American history) could not significantly outperform a low yielding, high quality liability portfolio over 13 years. Perhaps, traditional asset allocation models and asset management strategies need rethinking !

# Asset / Liability Watch
## (December 31, 2001)

| Index | Weight | 1989 | 1990 | 1991 | 1992 | 1993 | 1994 | 1995 | 1996 | 1997 | 1998 | 1999 | 2000 | 2001 |
|---|---|---|---|---|---|---|---|---|---|---|---|---|---|---|
| RL CASH | 5% | 9.34 | 8.73 | 7.42 | 4.12 | 3.51 | 3.94 | 7.11 | 5.59 | 5.72 | 5.48 | 4.24 | 6.49 | 4.97 |
| LB AGGREGATE | 30% | 14.53 | 8.96 | 16.00 | 7.40 | 9.75 | -2.92 | 18.47 | 3.63 | 9.65 | 8.69 | -0.82 | 11.63 | 8.44 |
| S&P 500 | 60% | 31.68 | -3.15 | 30.45 | 7.64 | 10.07 | 1.29 | 37.57 | 22.93 | 33.34 | 28.55 | 21.03 | -9.09 | -11.86 |
| MS EAFE | 5% | 10.80 | -23.32 | 12.48 | -11.85 | 32.95 | 8.06 | 11.56 | 6.37 | 2.08 | 20.24 | 27.32 | -13.87 | -21.11 |
| ASSET PORTFOLIO | 100% | 24.31 | 0.16 | 24.13 | 6.44 | 10.79 | 0.55 | 28.67 | 15.21 | 22.98 | 21.37 | 13.69 | -2.50 | -5.40 |
| RL LIABILITIES | 100% | 25.40 | 3.23 | 19.26 | 7.87 | 22.46 | -12.60 | 41.16 | -3.70 | 19.63 | 16.23 | -12.70 | 25.96 | 3.08 |
| ASSETS - LIABILITIES | | -1.09 | -3.07 | 4.87 | -1.43 | -11.67 | 13.15 | -12.49 | 18.91 | 3.35 | 5.14 | 26.39 | -28.46 | -8.48 |

**Given the poor performance from 12/99 to 12/01, several unfavorable results follow:**

1. **Loss of Transition Amortization of Surplus**
2. **Extra PBGC premium if underfunded**
3. **Higher Contributions**
4. **Earnings Drag for Corporations**

**Ryan Labs Indexes used are:**

    **RL Cash = Treasury Bill Curve (Equity weighted)**
    **RL Liabilities = Treasury Strip Curve (Equally weighted)**

**RYAN RESEARCH**

## FASB

The Financial Accounting Standards Board (FASB) governs the financial accounting reports of corporations, while GASB governs Public Funds. GASB tends to accept and model itself around FASB. FASB is quite clear on how pension liabilities are to be priced and hence behave. FAS 87, paragraphs 44 and 199 supported by FAS 106 paragraph 186 require that each liability be priced as a high quality zero-coupon bond whose par value matches the liability payment amount and whose maturity matches the liability payment date.

This should not be anything new to institutional investors since defeasance, dedication and immunization strategies have always considered liabilities equal to a bond portfolio such that the best liability matching asset is a bond portfolio with the same or very similar cash flows. Investors used defeasance, dedication and immunization strategies for decades to construct bond portfolios that offset their liability exposure. The portfolios were constructed to match the projected liabilities by cash flow, term structure and duration.

The economic *present value of pension liabilities is extremely interest rate sensitive* especially for long duration (younger) plans. Since recent interest rates have rallied to some of the lowest yields in modern history, the growth in present value of liabilities has been enormous. According to FASB and all asset/liability calculations, it is the present value of assets versus the present value of liabilities that is being measured, compared and amortized in the financial statements.

# FAS-87, FAS-106 and SEC Citations

A.    FAS-87

**Paragraph 199:** *"Interest rates vary depending on the duration of the investments; for example, US Treasury bill, 7-year bonds, and 30-year bonds have different interest rates...The disclosures required by this Statement regarding components of pension benefit obligation will be more representationally **faithful if individual discount rates** to various benefit deferral periods are selected."*

**Paragraph 44:**
*"In making those estimates, employers may also look to rates of return on **high-quality fixed income investments** currently available and expected to be available **during the period to maturity of the pension benefits.**"*

B.    FAS-106        (Discount rates defined 12/15/90)
**Paragraph 186:**

*"The objective of selecting assumed discount rates is to measure the single amount that, if invested at the measurement date in a portfolio of high-quality debt instruments, would provide the necessary future cash flows to pay the accumulated benefits when due. Notionally, that single amount, the accumulated post-retirement benefit obligation, would equal the current market value of a portfolio of **high-quality zero coupon bonds** whose maturity dates and amounts would be the same as the timing and amount of the expected future benefit payments."*

C.    SEC Guidelines on FAS 87 (June '93 letter to all corporations).

*"The SEC staff believes that the guidance that is provided in paragraph 186 of FASB 106, for selecting discount rates to measure the post-retirement benefit obligation also is appropriate guidance for measuring the pension benefit obligation."*

*"Rates that cannot be justified or are just too high will be passed on to the SEC's enforcement division for further action. The enforcement division could require restatement of the company's financial statements, as well as seek to impose civil or criminal penalties."*

## FAS 87 Transition Amortization

When FAS 87 was enacted, corporate pension funds were allowed to amortize (straight line) their current surplus or deficit over the remaining service period of employees, or 15 years whichever was greater, starting between 1/1/85 and 1/1/87. Most companies, had a pension surplus in the middle 80's since liabilities had higher discount rates and equities had performed well. This surplus amortization has boosted earnings for the last 15 years. The year 2000 financials saw the end of this amortization for many companies suggesting 2001 earnings and beyond would suffer accordingly due to the loss of this earnings support.

---

**FAS 87 Amortization**
**Transition Amount**

Represents the amortization of the Pension Surplus or Deficit as of Transition Date

| Sample Calculation : | Underfunded Plan | Overfunded Plan |
|---|---|---|
| Benefit Obligation | 1,000,000,000 | 1,000,000,000 |
| Fair Value of the Assets | 800,000,000 | 1,200,000,000 |
| Transition (Liability) or Asset | ( 200,000,000) | 2,000,000,000 |
| Divided by 15 years | ( 13,333,333) | 13,333,333 |

Amortization of transition liability (Deficit) increases pension cost
Amortization of transition asset (Surplus) decreases pension cost (increases pension income)

FAS 87, pgh. 76 (Pension) :
Straight-line amortization over remaining service period of employees, or 15 years
if the service period was expected to be less starting between 1/1/85 and 1/1/87

FAS 106 (Medical) :
Required 20-year, straight-line amortization unless the liability was expensed immediately
starting between 1/1/90 and 1/1/93

*Source: FASB*

---

## Extra PBGC Premiums

The Pension Benefit Guaranty Corp. (PBGC) was established in 1974 as a quasi-governmental insurance agency to provide pension benefits in case the corporation could not (bankruptcy). The PBGC charges a flat rate insurance premium per employee to provide this insurance coverage. These premiums have risen significantly over the years and then stabilized since 1991. In addition, the PBGC charges a variable premium for underfunded plans. [A plan is underfunded when the actuarially smoothed value of the assets falls below the present value of the current liability discounted at 85% of the 30-year Treasury rate.] Since the 30 year Treasury is at a historically low rate and since pension equity assets have performed so poorly, many pension plans would be labeled underfunded by the PBGC. This extra premium is 9/10 of 1% (90 basis points) on the underfunded pension benefit amount. For every $100 million of underfunded liabilities an annual charge of $900,000 will be applied. This charge represents an additional annual cost to the plan sponsor that is not recoverable or amortizable.

---

### Pension Benefit Guaranty Corporation

#### Insurance Premium Rates

| Plan Year | Flat Rate for Fully Funded Plan | Variable Premium For Underfunded Plan* |
|---|---|---|
| 9/2/74 to 12/31/77 | $ 1.00 | -0- |
| 1/1/78 to 12/31/85 | 2.60 | -0- |
| 1/1/86 to 12/31/87 | 8.50 | -0- |
| 1/1/88 to 12/31/90 | 16.00 | $6 per $1,000 of unfunded benefits (Maximum of $34 per participant) |
| 1/1/91 to 6/30/94 | 19.00 | $9 per $1,000 of unfunded vested benefits (Maximum of $53 per participant) |
| 7/1/94 to 6/30/95 | 19.00 | $9 per $1,000 of unfunded vested benefits (Maximum of $53 per participant plus 20% of uncapped variable premium in excess of $53 per participant) |
| 7/1/95 to 6/30/96 | 19.00 | $9 per $1,000 of unfunded vested benefits (Maximum of $53 per participant plus 60% of uncapped variable premium in excess of $53 per participant) |
| On or After 7/1/96 | 19.00 | $9 per $1,000 of unfunded vested benefits (no maximum) |

\* A plan is underfunded when the actuarially smoothed value of the assets falls below the present value of the current liability discounted at 85% of the 30-year Treasury rate.

## Higher Contributions

IRS Rule 404(a) governs pension contributions. Rules here are tedious but are focused on the calculation of the Current Liability (i.e. the present value of all accumulated plan benefits using Current Service, Current Salary). This calculation uses the 30-year Treasury as its discount rate on a moving average basis. Under the Retirement Protection Act of 1994 (RPA '94), the calculation is based on a *weighted average of the last four years of 30-year Treasury rates* using a corridor range of 90% to 105% of this weighted rate.

If current assets are below 90% of this current liability calculation, then a higher contribution must be paid to bring it in line. This discount rate is slightly lower so far this year than last year (5.63% vs. 5.74%). With pension asset growth lagging liability growth by about 8.48% for 2001, a higher contribution is more likely for 2002. Many pension holidays (no contribution) should also be ending resulting from two years of lower discount rates and lower asset values. Interest rates have to go above a 5.65% by 12/31/01 on the 30-year Treasury for the Current Liability discount rate to go up.

### Current Liability

Under RPA '94 the present value of all accumulated plan benefits is determined by using a discount rate within a range of 90% to 105% of the weighted average rate on 30-year Treasury bonds during the previous four years.

| Year | 30-Year Treasury | IRS Discount Rate(s) Rate | @90% | @105% |
|---|---|---|---|---|
| 12/31/01 | 5.47 | 5.63 | 5.08 | 5.92 |
| 12/31/00 | 5.46 | 5.74 | 5.17 | 6.03 |
| 12/31/99 | 6.48 | 5.97 | 5.37 | 6.27 |
| 12/31/98 | 5.09 | 5.75 | 5.18 | 6.04 |
| 12/31/97 | 5.93 | 6.33 | 5.70 | 6.65 |

IRS Weighted Average Discount Rate Calculation :

      40%   of  Last year end
      30 %  of  1 year ago
      20 %  of  2 years ago
      10 %  of  3 years ago

*Source: FASB, RPA '94*

## Earnings Drag

The average company in the S&P 500 has enjoyed a 7-10% increase in earnings due to pension income (lower pension expense) for the last several years with the Aerospace industry receiving as much as 35%. *According to the latest study by Bear Stearns this will now shift to pension expense and become a drag on earnings.* How much is difficult to estimate and is certainly unique to each company. Ryan Labs believes that it may be a significant and recurring annual expense going forward.

Pensions affect corporate earnings as a cost factor or expense item. A reduction in this expense boosts earnings and vice-versa. Several items comprise the pension cost and expense calculation :

1. **Interest**           **The interest cost of PBO liabilities based upon discount rate used times the beginning present value of liabilities.**

2. **Service Cost**           **The present value of benefits earned (accrued) during the year.**

3. **Benefit Payments**      **Benefit payments made during the year.**

4. **Plan Amendments**      **Changes to benefits from new plan amendments.**

5. **Prior Service Cost**     **Present value of unrecognized benefits assigned to employees for their service before a given date (usually due to mergers).**

---

**FAS 87 Amortization**
**Prior Service Cost**

Represents the systematic recognition over several periods of an increase (decrease) in the benefit obligation resulting from a change in the amount of the retirement benefit expected to be paid to employees based on services they have already performed.

Source: FASB

---

**6. Actuarial Gain/Loss** — Actuaries forecast a year in advance the growth in pension assets and liabilities. The actual growth is then compared to this forecast. The difference, to the extent that it exceeds curtain specified limits, is amortized over the average life of the pension (@ 15 years).

### Sample Pension Fund
### Calculation of Actuarial Gain/(Loss)

|  | 12/99 | 12/00 | | 12/01 | |
|---|---|---|---|---|---|
| 1. Asset / Liability Ratio | 130% | | 100.6% | | 92.3% |
| | | | | | |
| 2. Assets ($ 000) | 1,300,000 | | 1,267,500 | | 1,199,055 |
| 3. Actual Growth Rate | | - 2.5% | (32,500) | -5.4% | (68,445) |
| 4. Assumed ROR | | 9.0% | 117,000 | 9.0% | 114,075 |
| 5. Difference | | -11.5% | (149,500) | -14.4% | (182,520) |
| | | | | | |
| 6. Liabilities ($ 000) | 1,000,000 | | 1,259,600 | | 1,298,396 |
| 7. Actual Growth Rate | | 25.96% | 259,600 | 3.08% | 38,796 |
| 8. Discount Rate | | 7.00% | 70,000 | 7.00% | 88,172 |
| 9. Difference | | 18.96% | 189,600 | -3.92% | (49,376) |
| | | | | | |
| *Actuarial Gain/Loss ($ 000)* | | | | | |
| 10. Asset - Liability Difference | | -30.46% | (339,100) | -10.48% | (133,144) |
| 11. Divided by 15 years | | | (22,607) | | (8,876) |
| 12. Cumulative Amortization (2000+2001) | | | | | (31,483) |

The above exhibit tries to depict what may have happened throughout pension America. Lines 2 and 6 show assets of $1.3 billion and liabilities of $1.0 billion as of 12/31/99. The actuarial estimated growth rates are shown on lines 4 and 8 (9% = assets and 7% = liabilities). If the actual growth rate of assets was line 3 and liabilities on line 7, there would be an actuarial loss amortization of ($22,607,000) for 12/31/00 (line 11) and an additional ($8,876,000) for 12/31/01 creating a cumulative amortization and earnings drag of ($31,483,000) for 2001 (line 12) and the next 14 years.

This is modified by each year's change to this amortization. *Notice that the Asset/Liability ratio started at 130% and ended at 92.3%. Notice that the amortization is an extra cost of $31.5 million per year for the next 14 years.* Unfortunately, this may be typical of most traditional defined benefit plans in America.

## Solution(s)

Corporations and Public Funds do not want volatility or added cost on their financial statements and budgets. Since FASB, IRS and PBGC all require the pricing of liabilities as a high-quality bond portfolio it is fitting that a *bond portfolio matched to liabilities provides the least volatile solution.* The question then is cost. Many practitioners fail to appreciate that the pension game is an annual calculation. Although smoothing techniques are used, such amortizations are still part of the annual analysis. Investments that severely underperform liability growth usually result in higher cost. A prudent strategy is to avoid serious underperformance of assets vs. liabilities *annually.* Accordingly, the following solutions are highly recommended :

### 1. Custom Liability Index
Hard to believe that the asset side can function without clear, frequent information of how liabilities are shaped and behave on a risk/reward basis. Asset Allocation, asset management and performance measurement are all dependent on the true objective (i.e. funding liabilities) to function properly. *A Custom Index based on the actuarial benefit schedule is critical for the asset side to perform.* This Index should be decomposed to measure liability growth (return) by term structure (short, intermediate, long) as well as total liabilities. A proper strategy should include a Liability Index for Retired Lives, Active Lives and Total Liabilities

### 2. Retired Lives
These liabilities are rather certain and fixed. Because they are the shortest and most imminent liabilities they become the most critical to fund. *As a result, a bond portfolio properly matched by term structure (Liability Index Fund) would provide the least volatility and risk to the financial statement and budget.* This should produce a predictable contribution budget with no added costs due to underperformance.

### 3. Active Lives
These liabilities are less certain and more volatile due to inflation and labor sensitivity (future values) as well as high interest rate sensitivity (present values) since these are the longest pension liabilities. More dynamic asset classes are needed here that can match or outperform long liabilities. Long zero-coupon bonds, TIPS, Structured Notes and equity are likely candidates but so too are alternative investments and unconventional assets (i.e. timber, real estate, etc.). A *pro-active asset allocation strategy* is recommended here. Active Lives are the most volatile area of pensions requiring consistent monitoring. If there is a significant deficit or surplus, it first has to be known (vs. Custom Liability Index) and then corrected or rebalanced.

### 4. Surplus Optimization
Surplus should be the reward of effective asset/liability management. Retired Lives will produce limited value added since its objective is a matching strategy to reduce volatility and costs (Liability Index Fund as the anchor or core portfolio). Active Lives are the expected area of value added. Dynamic asset allocation strategy is the methodology to achieve such surplus growth. If the fund has a surplus, it should be isolated and treated as a separate portfolio with a distinct objective and policy constraints. Liabilities will not be funded here, hopefully. Time horizons could be of any duration. Investment restrictions could be the most relaxed. New and exciting investment ideas could be tried here rather than on an asset/liability frontier where failure could be costly. Asset allocation could be the most adventuresome depending on the plan's style and culture. Indeed, *surplus optimization may best come from the surplus portfolio* as the asset/liability portfolios are structured to perform annually such as not to cause any drain on the surplus portfolio; not to cause volatility and added cost on the financials.

# Examples

The following tables summarize the financial impacts we have been discussing. In reviewing them, the reader should recall that changes in assets and liabilities are treated as deviations from expected returns (growth) ... typically about 9% for assets and 7.5% for liabilities. These deviations are amortized into earnings over the average life of the pension plan (@15 years). Hence, in addition to 2001 earnings, the legacy of the last 21 months (12/31/99-9/30/01) will dampen earnings for the next 14 years !

**Example 1 :** shows that per one million dollars of pension liability and a beginning funding ratio of 130%, how the double indemnity of lower market rates and falling equity prices combined to create a 13% deficit (87% funding ratio). Even the one year amortization of 3.6875% ($36,875 per million) of pension liabilities can loom large for companies with high ratios of pension liabilities to earnings.

**Example 2 :** shows that the total growth in liabilities using the Moody's Aa bond rate starting at 7.90% on 12/31/99 and moving to a 7.49% (12/31/00) and 7.23% (9/30/01). This rate is popular with many plan sponsors since it is a higher rate than the Treasury yield curve although it is only a spot rate for long corporates. Over the 21 month period under review, using the Moody's Aa rate would have produced a growth in liabilities of 27.04% (absent new service costs), well above the -13.95% estimated growth of pension assets.

## Example 1:
### Impact of Pension Fund Asset/Liability Performance on Earnings
### Corporate Return on Asset Assumption = 9%
(Per $1 Million of Pension Liabilities, Duration at 15 years)

| | Asset/Liability Actual versus Assumed Performance | | | | $ Surplus | % Funding | Change in Actuarial Amortization | 15-Year Amortization | |
| | Assets | | Liabilities | | | | | Current Impact | Deferred Impact |
|---|---|---|---|---|---|---|---|---|---|
| 12/31/99 | 1,300,000 | | 1,000,000 | | 300,000 | 130% | | | |
| Actual | -32,500 | -2.5% | 259,600 | 25.96% | -292,100 | | | | |
| Assumed | 117,000 | 9.0% | 70,000 | 7.00% | 47,000 | | | | |
| Difference | -149,500 | -11.5% | 189,600 | 18.96% | -339,100 | | -339,100 | -22,607 | -316,493 |
| | | | | | | | | | |
| 12/31/00 | 1,267,500 | | 1,259,600 | | 7,900 | 101% | | | |
| Actual | -68,445 | -5.4% | 38,796 | 3.08% | -107,241 | -793% | | | |
| Assumed | 114,075 | 9.0% | 88,172 | 7.00% | 38,499 | 124% | | -22,607 | |
| Difference | -182,520 | -14.4% | -49,376 | -3.92% | -145,740 | -917% | -133,144 | -8,876 | -124,267 |
| | | | | | | | | | |
| 12/31/01 | 1,199,055 | | 1,298,396 | | -99,341 | 92% | | | |
| Total Period | -100,945 | -7.8% | 298,396 | 29.8% | -399,341 | | As a % of Liability | -31,483 2.4% | -418,154 32.2% |

## Example 2:
### Impact of Pension Fund Asset/Liability Performance on Earnings
### Assuming Liabilities Discounted at Moody's AA Long Maturity Rate
(Assume duration at 15 years)

| Date | Moody's AA | Change | Duration | Liability %Change | Interest | Total Return | 1,000,000 |
|---|---|---|---|---|---|---|---|
| 12/99 | 7.90% | | | | | | |
| 12/00 | 7.49% | 0.41% | 15 | 6.15% | 7.90% | 14.05% | 1,140,500 |
| 12/01 | 7.23% | 0.26% | 15 | 3.90% | 7.49% | 11.39% | 1,270,403 |

# Appendix F

# ESTIMATING THE LENGTH OF THE TWENTY-FIRST CENTURY FORMULATION AND ACCELERATION PHASES

The NASDAQ's discovery phase took 27% less time than the Dow Jones Industrial Average's discovery phase.

Dow Jones discovery phase    8/8/1896–9/7/1899   = **37 months**

NASDAQ discovery phase     1/9/1998–3/10/2000 = **27 months**

27 months is 27% less than 37 months

The Dow's formulation phase took 21 years, or 252 months.

If NASDAQ's formulation phase relates to the Dow's like the discovery phase did, we could apply a 27% reduction to the Dow's 21-year (252-month) formulation phase.

252 months less 27% = **184 months**

*Insert these numbers into the equation*    $\dfrac{A \times B}{A + B}$

$$\frac{252 \text{ months} \times 184 \text{ months}}{252 \text{ months} + 184 \text{ months}} = \frac{46368}{436} = 106.35 \text{ months}$$

106 months = 8.8 years

Therefore, the formulation phase that began in March 2000 could end between 2008 and 2009.

The acceleration phase is measured thus:

252 months (Dow's Formulation Phase)

+96 months (Dow's Acceleration Phase)
___

**348 months** total

348 months minus 27% = 254 total months for NASDAQ formulation and acceleration phases

Insert 348 and 254 into the equation $\dfrac{A \times B}{A + B}$

$$\frac{348 \times 254 = 88392}{348 + 254 = 602} = \frac{88392}{602} = 146.83 \text{ months}$$

146.83 months = 12.2 years

**12.20 years**   **NASDAQ formulation and acceleration phase**

**–8.80 years**   **NASDAQ formulation phase**
___

**3.40 years**   **NASDAQ acceleration phase**

Therefore, if the acceleration phase begins between 2008 and 2009, it will end between 2011 and 2012.

# Appendix G

# READING LIST

Countless sources provided the foundation and inspiration for this project. The following lists contain must-read editions for those wanting a complete understanding of the birth of the third dominant investment system. Those with stars are our personal favorites.

## General References

*Atack, Jeremy, and Peter Passell. *A New Economic View of American History from Colonial Times to 1940* (2nd edition). New York: W.W. Norton, 1994.

Barzun, Jacques. *From Dawn to Decadence: 1500 to the Present—500 Years of Western Cultural Life*. New York: HarperCollins, 2000.

Cohen, Jerome B., Edward Zimbarg, Arthur Zeikel, and Richard D. Irwin. *Investment Analysis and Portfolio Management* (5th edition). Homewood, IL: Irwin, 1987.

Curruth, Gordon. *Encyclopedia of American Facts and Dates* (7th edition). New York: Harper & Row, 1979.

Dent, Harry S., Jr. *The Roaring 2000s*. New York: Simon & Schuster, 1998.

*Downes, Larry, and Chunka Mui. *Unleashing the Killer App: Digital Strategies for Market Dominance*. Boston: Harvard Business School Press, 1998.

Ettenberg, Elliott. *The Next Economy: Will You Know Where Your Customers Are?* New York: McGraw Hill, 2002.

*Fischer, David Hackett. *The Great Wave: Price Revolutions and the Rhythm of History*. New York: Oxford University Press, 1996.

Fogel, Robert William. *The Fourth Great Awakening and the Future of Egalitarianism*. Chicago: University of Chicago Press, 2000.

Friedman, Milton, and Anna Jacobson Schwartz. *A Monetary History of the United States, 1857–1960*. Princeton, NJ: Princeton University Press.

Galbraith, John Kenneth. *Economics in Perspective*. Boston: Houghton Mifflin, 1987.

Garraty, John A., editor, and Jerome Sternstein, associate editor. *Encyclopedia of American Biography*. New York: Harper & Row, 1974.

Gates, Bill (with Collins Hemingway). *Business at the Speed of Thought*. New York: Warner Books, 2000.

*Heilbroner, Robert. *The Worldly Philosophers*. New York: Simon & Schuster, 1986.

Hobsbawm, E.J. *Industry and Empire* (revised and updated by Chris Wrigley). New York: New Press, 1999.

*Homer, Sidney. *A History of Interest Rates* (2nd edition). New Brunswick, NJ: Rutgers University Press, 1963.

Houghton, Walter. *The Victorian Frame of Mind, 1830–1870*. New Haven, CT: Yale University Press, 1985.

Johnson, Paul. *A History of the American People*. New York: HarperCollins, 1998.

Korn, Jerry, editor. *This Fabulous Century* (Vols. 1 and 2). New York: Time-Life Books, 1970.

Lewis, Michael. *The New New Thing*. New York: W.W. Norton, 2000.

Morison, Samuel Eliot. *The Oxford History of the American People*. New York: Oxford University Press, 1965.

*The National Data Book: Statistical Abstract of the United States, 1997* (117th edition). Washington, DC: U.S. Department of Commerce, Economics, and Statistics Administration, Bureau of the Census, 1997.

Reilly, Frank, and Keith Brown. *Investment Analysis and Portfolio Management* (6th edition). Fort Worth, TX: Harcourt College, 2000.

Schwert, G. William, and Clifford W. Smith Jr. *Empirical Research in Capital Markets*. New York: McGraw Hill, 1992.

Shiller, Robert J. *Irrational Exuberance*. Princeton, NJ: Princeton University Press, 2000.

*Siegel, Jeremy J. *Stocks for the Long Run: A Guide to Selecting Markets for Long-Term Growth*. Chicago: Irwin Professional, 1994.

*Soros, George. *The Alchemy of Finance: Reading the Mind of the Market*. New York: Wiley, 1987.

*Sun Tzu. *The Art of War*. Translated by Samuel B. Griffith. New York: Oxford University Press, 1963.

*Strauss, William, and Neil Howe. *Generations: The History of America's Future, 1584–2064*. New York: Quill, William Morrow, 1991.

Traxel, David. *1898, The Birth of the American Century*. New York: Random House, 1999.

*Yamada, Louise. *Market Magic: Riding the Greatest Bull Market of the Century*. New York: Wiley, 1998.

## Biotechnology

Dennis, Carina, Richard Gallagher, and Philip Campbell, editors. *The Human Genome* (special issue). *Nature* 409, no. 6822 (2002).

## Materials Technology

Good, Mary. "Designer Materials." *R&D Magazine* 41, no. 7 (1999): 76–77.

Gupta, T.N. "Materials for the Human Habitat." *MRS Bulletin* 25, no. 4 (1999): 60–63.

Kazmaier, P., and N. Chopra, "Bridging Size Scales with Self-Assembling Supramolecular Materials." *MRS Bulletin* 25, no. 4 (2000): 30–35.

*Manufacturing a la Carte: Agile Assembly Lines, Faster Development Cycles* (special issue). *IEEE Spectrum* 30, no. 9 (1993).

*Smart Structures and Materials: Industrial and Commercial Applications of Smart Structures Technologies, Proceedings of SPIE* 3044 (1997), 3326 (1998), and 3674 (1999). Bellingham, WA: International Society for Optical Engineering.

## Nanotechnology

"National Nanotechnology Initiative: Leading to the Next Industrial Revolution." Executive Office of the President of the United States. Retrieved June 13, 2002, from http://www.nano.gov/

"Nanostructure Science and Technology: A Worldwide Study." National Science and Technology Council, Committee on Technology and the Interagency Working Group on Nanoscience, Engineering, and Technology. Retrieved July 4, 2002, from http://www.nano.gov/

Smalley, R.E.. "Nanotechnology and the Next 50 Years." Paper presented at the University of Dallas, Board of Councilors, December 7, 1995. Retrieved July 4, 2002, from http://cnst.rice.edu/

# INDEX